Robot Learning

edited by

Dr. Suraiya Jabin

Robot Learning

Edited by Dr. Suraiya Jabin

Republished by InTech

Janeza Trdine 9, 51000 Rijeka, Croatia

Publishing Process Manager Iva Lipovic

Technical Editor Goran Bajac

Cover Designer Martina Sirotic

Additional hard copies can be obtained from orders@intechopen.com

Robot Learning, Edited by Dr. Suraiya Jabin
p. cm.
ISBN 978-953-307-104-6

For EU product safety concerns:
IN TECH d.o.o., Prolaz Marije Krucifikse Kozulić 3, 51000 Rijeka, Croatia,
info@intechopen.com or visit our website at intechopen.com.

Meet the editor

Suraiya Jabin currently works as Associate Professor at the Department of Computer Science, Jamia Millia Islamia. Her research interests include Artificial Intelligence, Pattern Recognition, Soft Computing, Biometrics. She has more than 15 years of teaching experience at both undergraduate and postgraduate levels. She has contributed over 30 research articles in refereed international journals, conference proceedings and as book chapters. Her current project is 'Online Social Network Data Crawler.'

Contents

Preface

Robot Learning is now a well-developed research area. This book explores the full scope of the field which encompasses Evolutionary Techniques, Reinforcement Learning, Hidden Markov Models, Uncertainty, Action Models, Navigation and Biped Locomotion, etc. Robot Learning in realistic environments requires novel algorithms for learning to identify important events in the stream of sensory inputs and to temporarily memorize them in adaptive, dynamic, internal states, until the memories can help to compute proper control actions. The book covers many of such algorithms in its 8 chapters.

This book is primarily intended for the use in a postgraduate course. To use it effectively, students should have some background knowledge in both Computer Science and Mathematics. Because of its comprehensive coverage and algorithms, it is useful as a primary reference for the graduate students and professionals wishing to branch out beyond their subfield. Given the interdisciplinary nature of the robot learning problem, the book may be of interest to wide variety of readers, including computer scientists, roboticists, mechanical engineers, psychologists, ethologists, mathematicians, etc.

The editor wishes to thank the authors of all chapters, whose combined efforts made this book possible, for sharing their current research work on Robot Learning.

Editor

Dr. Suraiya Jabin,
Department of Computer Science,
Jamia Millia Islamia (Central University),
New Delhi - 110025,
India

1

Robot Learning using Learning Classifier Systems Approach

Suraiya Jabin
Jamia Millia Islamia, Central University
(Department of Computer Science)
India

1. Introduction

Efforts to develop highly complex and adaptable machines that meet the ideal of mechanical human equivalents are now reaching the proof-of concept stage. Enabling a human to efficiently transfer knowledge and skills to a machine has inspired decades of research. I present a learning mechanism in which a robot learns new tasks using genetic-based machine learning technique, learning classifier system (LCS). LCSs are rule-based systems that automatically build their ruleset. At the origin of Holland's work, LCSs were seen as a model of the emergence of cognitive abilities thanks to adaptive mechanisms, particularly evolutionary processes. After a renewal of the field more focused on learning, LCSs are now considered as sequential decision problem-solving systems endowed with a generalization property. Indeed, from a Reinforcement Learning point of view, LCSs can be seen as learning systems building a compact representation of their problem. More recently, LCSs have proved efficient at solving automatic classification tasks (Sigaud et al., 2007). The aim of the present contribution is to describe the state-of the-art of LCSs, emphasizing recent developments, and focusing more on the application of LCS for Robotics domain.

In previous robot learning studies, optimization of parameters has been applied to acquire suitable behaviors in a real environment. Also in most of such studies, a model of human evaluation has been used for validation of learned behaviors. However, since it is very difficult to build human evaluation function and adjust parameters, a system hardly learns behavior intended by a human operator.

In order to reach that goal, I first present the two mechanisms on which they rely, namely GAs and Reinforcement Learning (RL). Then I provide a brief history of LCS research intended to highlight the emergence of three families of systems: strength-based LCSs, accuracy-based LCSs, and anticipatory LCSs (ALCSs) but mainly XCS as XCS, is the most studied LCS at this time. Afterward, in section 5, I present some examples of existing LCSs which have LCS applied for robotics. The next sections are dedicated to the particular aspects of theoretical and applied extensions of Intelligent Robotics. Finally, I try to highlight what seem to be the most promising lines of research given the current state of the art, and I conclude with the available resources that can be consulted in order to get a more detailed knowledge of these systems.

2. Basic formalism of LCS

A learning classifier system (LCS) is an adaptive system that learns to perform the best action given its input. By "best" is generally meant the action that will receive the most reward or reinforcement from the system's environment. By "input" is meant the environment as sensed by the system, usually a vector of numerical values. The set of available actions depends on the system context: if the system is a mobile robot, the available actions may be physical: "turn left", "turn right", etc. In a classification context, the available actions may be "yes", "no", or "benign", "malignant", etc. In a decision context, for instance a financial one, the actions might be "buy", "sell", etc. In general, an LCS is a simple model of an intelligent agent interacting with an environment.

A schematic depicting the rule and message system, the apportionment of credit system, and the genetic algorithm is shown in Figure 1. Information flows from the environment through the detectors-the classifier system's eyes and ears-where it is decoded to one or more finite length messages. These environmental messages are posted to a finite-length message list where the messages may then activate string rules called classifiers. When activated, a classifier posts a message to the message list. These messages may then invoke other classifiers or they may cause an action to be taken through the system's action triggers called effectors.

An LCS is "adaptive" in the sense that its ability to choose the best action improves with experience. The source of the improvement is reinforcement—technically, payoff provided by the environment. In many cases, the payoff is arranged by the experimenter or trainer of the LCS. For instance, in a classification context, the payoff may be 1.0 for "correct" and 0.0 for "incorrect". In a robotic context, the payoff could be a number representing the change in distance to a recharging source, with more desirable changes (getting closer) represented by larger positive numbers, etc. Often, systems can be set up so that effective reinforcement is provided automatically, for instance via a distance sensor. Payoff received for a given action

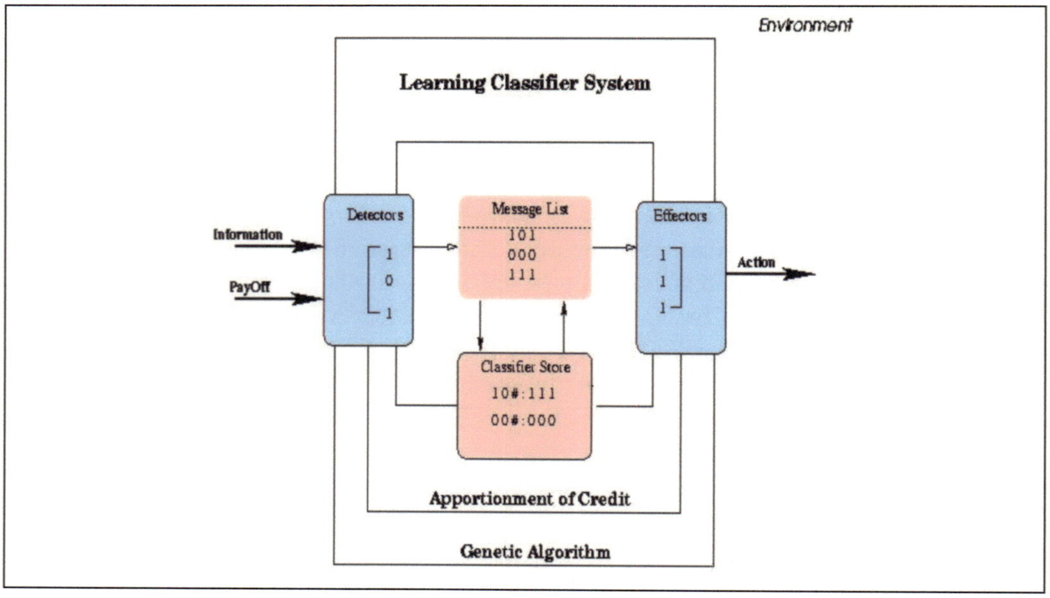

Fig. 1. A general Learning Classifier System

is used by the LCS to alter the likelihood of taking that action, in those circumstances, in the future. To understand how this works, it is necessary to describe some of the LCS mechanics.

Inside the LCS is a set technically, a population—of "condition-action rules" called classifiers. There may be hundreds of classifiers in the population. When a particular input occurs, the LCS forms a so-called match set of classifiers whose conditions are satisfied by that input. Technically, a condition is a truth function t(x) which is satisfied for certain input vectors x. For instance, in a certain classifier, it may be that t(x) = 1 (true) for 43 < x3 < 54, where x3 is a component of x, and represents, say, the age of a medical patient. In general, a classifier's condition will refer to more than one of the input components, usually all of them. If a classifier's condition is satisfied, i.e. its t(x) = 1, then that classifier joins the match set and influences the system's action decision. In a sense, the match set consists of classifiers in the population that recognize the current input.

Among the classifiers—the condition-action rules—of the match set will be some that advocate one of the possible actions, some that advocate another of the actions, and so forth. Besides advocating an action, a classifier will also contain a prediction of the amount of payoff which, speaking loosely, "it thinks" will be received if the system takes that action. How can the LCS decide which action to take? Clearly, it should pick the action that is likely to receive the highest payoff, but with all the classifiers making (in general) different predictions, how can it decide? The technique adopted is to compute, for each action, an average of the predictions of the classifiers advocating that action—and then choose the action with the largest average. The prediction average is in fact weighted by another classifier quantity, its fitness, which will be described later but is intended to reflect the reliability of the classifier's prediction.

The LCS takes the action with the largest average prediction, and in response the environment returns some amount of payoff. If it is in a learning mode, the LCS will use this payoff, P, to alter the predictions of the responsible classifiers, namely those advocating the chosen action; they form what is called the action set. In this adjustment, each action set classifier's prediction p is changed mathematically to bring it slightly closer to P, with the aim of increasing its accuracy. Besides its prediction, each classifier maintains an estimate q of the error of its predictions. Like p, q is adjusted on each learning encounter with the environment by moving q slightly closer to the current absolute error $|p - P|$. Finally, a quantity called the classifier's fitness is adjusted by moving it closer to an inverse function of q, which can be regarded as measuring the accuracy of the classifier. The result of these adjustments will hopefully be to improve the classifier's prediction and to derive a measure—the fitness—that indicates its accuracy.

The adaptivity of the LCS is not, however, limited to adjusting classifier predictions. At a deeper level, the system treats the classifiers as an evolving population in which accurate i.e. high fitness—classifiers are reproduced over less accurate ones and the "offspring" are modified by genetic operators such as mutation and crossover. In this way, the population of classifiers gradually changes over time, that is, it adapts structurally. Evolution of the population is the key to high performance since the accuracy of predictions depends closely on the classifier conditions, which are changed by evolution.

Evolution takes place in the background as the system is interacting with its environment. Each time an action set is formed, there is finite chance that a genetic algorithm will occur in the set. Specifically, two classifiers are selected from the set with probabilities proportional to their fitnesses. The two are copied and the copies (offspring) may, with certain probabilities, be mutated and recombined ("crossed"). Mutation means changing, slightly, some quantity or aspect of the classifier condition; the action may also be changed to one of the other actions. Crossover means exchanging parts of the two classifiers. Then the offspring are inserted into the population and two classifiers are deleted to keep the population at a constant size. The new classifiers, in effect, compete with their parents, which are still (with high probability) in the population.

The effect of classifier evolution is to modify their conditions so as to increase the overall prediction accuracy of the population. This occurs because fitness is based on accuracy. In addition, however, the evolution leads to an increase in what can be called the "accurate generality" of the population. That is, classifier conditions evolve to be as general as possible without sacrificing accuracy. Here, general means maximizing the number of input vectors that the condition matches. The increase in generality results in the population needing fewer distinct classifiers to cover all inputs, which means (if identical classifiers are merged) that populations are smaller and also that the knowledge contained in the population is more visible to humans—which is important in many applications. The specific mechanism by which generality increases is a major, if subtle, side-effect of the overall evolution.

3. Brief history of learning classifier systems

The first important evolution in the history of LCS research is correlated to the parallel progress in RL research, particularly with the publication of the Q-LEARNING algorithm (Watkins, 1989).

Classical RL algorithms such as Q-LEARNING rely on an explicit enumeration of all the states of the system. But, since they represent the state as a collection of a set of sensations called "attributes", LCSs do not need this explicit enumeration thanks to a generalization property that is described later. This generalization property has been recognized as the distinguishing feature of LCSs with respect to the classical RL framework. Indeed, it led Lanzi to define LCSs as RL systems endowed with a generalization capability (Lanzi, 2002).

An important step in this change of perspective was the analysis by Dorigo and Bersini of the similarity between the BUCKET BRIGADE algorithm (Holland, 1986) used so far in LCSs and the Q-LEARNING algorithm (Dorigo & Bersini, 1994). At the same time, Wilson published a radically simplified version of the initial LCS architecture, called Zeroth-level Classifier System ZCS (Wilson, 1994), in which the list of internal messages was removed.

ZCS defines the fitness or strength of a classifier as the accumulated reward that the agent can get from firing the classifier, giving rise to the "strength-based" family of LCSs. As a result, the GA eliminates classifiers providing less reward than others from the population.

After ZCS, Wilson invented a more subtle system called XCS (Wilson, 1995), in which the fitness is bound to the capacity of the classifier to accurately predict the reward received when firing it, while action selection still relies on the expected reward itself. XCS appeared very efficient and is the starting point of a new family of "accuracy-based" LCSs. Finally, two years later, Stolzmann proposed an anticipatory LCS called ACS (Stolzmann, 1998; Butz et al., 2000) giving rise to the "anticipation-based" LCS family.

This third family is quite distinct from the other two. Its scientific roots come from research in experimental psychology about latent learning (Tolman, 1932; Seward, 1949). More precisely, Stolzmann was a student of Hoffmann (Hoffmann, 1993) who built a

psychological theory of learning called "Anticipatory Behavioral Control" inspired from Herbart's work (Herbart, 1825).
The extension of these three families is at the heart of modern LCS research. Before closing this historical overview, after a second survey of the field (Lanzi and Riolo, 2000), a further important evolution is taking place. Even if the initial impulse in modern LCS research was based on the solution of sequential decision problems, the excellent results of XCS on data mining problems (Bernado et al., 2001) have given rise to an important extension of researches towards automatic classification problems, as exemplified by Booker (2000) or Holmes (2002).

4. Mechanisms of learning classifier systems

4.1 Genetic algorithm

First, I briefly present GAs (Holland, 1975; Booker et al., 1989; Goldberg, 1989), which are freely inspired from the neo-darwinist theory of natural selection. These algorithms manipulate a population of individuals representing possible solutions to a given problem. GAs rely on four analogies with their biological counterpart: they use a code, the genotype or genome, simple transformations operating on that code, the genetic operators, the expression of a solution from the code, the genotype-to-phenotype mapping, and a solution selection process, the survival of the fittest. The genetic operators are used to introduce some variations in the genotypes. There are two classes of operators: crossover operators, which create new genotypes by recombining sub-parts of the genotypes of two or more individuals, and mutation operators, which randomly modify the genotype of an individual. The selection process extracts the genotypes that deserve to be reproduced, upon which genetic operators will be applied. A GA manipulates a set of arbitrarily initialized genotypes which are selected and modified generation after generation. Those which are not selected are eliminated. A utility function, or fitness function, evaluates the interest of a phenotype with regard to a given problem. The survival of the corresponding solution or its number of offspring in the next generation depends on this evaluation. The offspring of an individual are built from copies of its genotype to which genetic operators are applied. As a result, the overall process consists in the iteration of the following loop:

1. select n_e genotypes according to the fitness of corresponding phenotypes,
2. apply genetic operators to these genotypes to generate offspring,
3. build phenotypes from these new genotypes and evaluate them,
4. go to 1.

If some empirical conditions that we will not detail here are fulfilled, such a process gives rise to an improvement of the fitnesses of the individuals over the generations.
Though GAs are at their root, LCSs have made limited use of the important extensions of this field. As a consequence, in order to introduce the GAs used in LCSs, it is only necessary to describe the following aspects:

a. One must classically distinguish between the one-point crossover operator, which cuts two genotypes into two parts at a randomly selected place and builds a new genotype by inverting the sub-parts from distinct parents, and the multi-point crossover operator, which does the same after cutting the parent genotypes into several pieces. Historically, most early LCSs were using the one-point crossover operator. Recently, a surge of interest on the discovery of complex 'building blocks' in the structure of input data led to a more frequent use of multi-point crossover.

b. One must also distinguish between generational GAs, where all or an important part of the population is renewed from one generation to the next, and steady state GAs, where individuals are changed in the population one by one without notion of generation. Most LCSs use a steady-state GA, since this less disruptive mechanism results in a better interplay between the evolutionary process and the learning process, as explained below.

4.2 Markov Decision Processes and reinforcement learning

The second fundamental mechanism in LCSs is Reinforcement Learning. In order to describe this mechanism, it is necessary to briefly present the Markov Decision Process (MDP) framework and the Q-LEARNING algorithm, which is now the learning algorithm most used in LCSs. This presentation is as succinct as possible; the reader who wants to get a deeper view is referred to Sutton and Barto (1998).

4.2.1 Markov Decision Processes

A MDP is defined as the collection of the following elements:

- a finite set S of discrete states s of an agent;
- a finite set A of discrete actions a;
- a transition function $P : S \times A \rightarrow \prod(S)$ where $\prod(S)$ is the set of probability distributions over S. A particular probability distribution $Pr(s_{t+1} \mid st, a_t)$ indicates the probabilities that the agent reaches the different s_{t+1} possible states when he performs action a_t in state s_t;
- a reward function $R : S \times A \rightarrow IR$ which gives for each (st, at) pair the scalar reward signal that the agent receives when he performs action a_t in state s_t .

The MDP formalism describes the stochastic structure of a problem faced by an agent, and does not tell anything about the behavior of this agent in its environment. It only tells what, depending on its current state and action, will be its future situation and reward.

The above definition of the transition function implies a specific assumption about the nature of the state of the agent. This assumption, known as the Markov property, stipulates that the probability distribution specifying the s_{t+1} state only depends on s_t and a_t, but not on the past of the agent. Thus $P(s_{t+1} \mid s_t, a_t) = P(s_{t+1} \mid s_t, a_t, s_{t-1}, a_{t-1}, \ldots, s_0, a_0)$. This means that, when the Markov property holds, a knowledge of the past of the agent does not bring any further information on its next state.

The behavior of the agent is described by a policy $\prod$ giving for each state the probability distribution of the choice of all possible actions.

When the transition and reward functions are known in advance, Dynamic Programming (DP) methods such as policy iteration (Bellman, 1961; Puterman & Shin, 1978) and value iteration (Bellman, 1957) efficiently find a policy maximizing the accumulated reward that the agent can get out of its behavior.

In order to define the accumulated reward, we introduce the discount factor $\gamma \in [0, 1]$. This factor defines how much the future rewards are taken into account in the computation of the accumulated reward at time *t* as follows:

$$Rc_{\pi}(t)=\sum_{k=t}^{T_{\max}} \gamma^{(k-t)} r_{\pi}(k)$$

where T_{max} can be finite or infinite and $r_\pi(k)$ represents the immediate reward received at time k if the agent follows policy π.
DP methods introduce a value function V^π where $V^\pi(s)$ represents for each state s the accumulated reward that the agent can expect if it follows policy π from state s. If the Markov property holds, V^π is solution of the Bellman equation (Bertsekas, 1995):

$$\forall s \in S, V^{\pi}(s) = \sum_{a} \pi(s_t, a_t)[R(s_t, a_t) + \gamma \sum_{s_{t+1}} P(s_{t+1} \mid s_t, a_t) V^{\pi}(s_{t+1})] \tag{1}$$

Rather than the value function V^π, it is often useful to introduce an action value function Q^π where $Q^\pi(s, a)$ represents the accumulated reward that the agent can expect if it follows policy π after having done action a in state s. Everything that was said of V^π directly applies to Q^π, given that $V^\pi(s) = maxa\ Q^\pi(s, a)$.
The corresponding optimal functions are independent of the policy of the agent; they are denoted V* and Q*.
(a) The manuscript must be written in English, (b) use common technical terms, (c) avoid

4.2.2 Reinforcement learning

Learning becomes necessary when the transition and reward functions are not known in advance. In such a case, the agent must explore the outcome of each action in each situation, looking for the (s_t, a_t) pairs that bring it a high reward.
The main RL methods consist in trying to estimate V* or Q* iteratively from the trials of the agent in its environment. All these methods rely on a general approximation technique in order to estimate the average of a stochastic signal received at each time step without storing any information from the past of the agent. Let us consider the case of the average immediate reward. Its exact value after k iterations is

$E_k(s) = (r_1 + r_2 + \cdots + r_k)/k$

Furthermore,

$E_{k+1}(s) = (r_1 + r_2 + \cdots + r_k + r_{k+1})/(k + 1)$

thus

$E_{k+1}(s) = k/(k + 1)\, E_k(s) + r_{k+1}/(k + 1)$

which can be rewritten:

$E_{k+1}(s) = (k + 1)/(k + 1)\, E_k(s) - E_k(s)/(k + 1) + r_{k+1}/(k + 1)$

or

$E_{k+1}(s) = E_k(s) + 1/(k + 1)[r_{k+1} - E_k(s)]$

Formulated that way, we can compute the exact average by merely storing k. If we do not want to store even k, we can approximate $1/(k + 1)$ with α, which results in equation (2) whose general form is found everywhere in RL:

$$E_{k+1}(s) = E_k(s) + \alpha[r_{k+1} - E_k(s)] \tag{2}$$

The parameter α, called learning rate, must be tuned adequately because it influences the speed of convergence towards the exact average.
The update equation of the Q-LEARNING algorithm, which is the following:

$$Q(s_t, a_t) \leftarrow Q(s_t, a_t) + \alpha[r_{t+1} + \gamma \max Q(s_{t+1}, a) - Q(s_t, a_t)] \quad (3)$$

5. Some existing LCSs for robotics

LCSs were invented by Holland (Holland, 1975) in order to model the emergence of cognition based on adaptive mechanisms. They consist of a set of rules called classifiers combined with adaptive mechanisms in charge of evolving the population of rules. The initial goal was to solve problems of interaction with an environment such as the one presented in figure 2, as was described by Wilson as the "Animat problem" (Wilson, 1985).
In the context of the initial research on LCSs, the emphasis was put on parallelism in the architecture and evolutionary processes that let it adapt at any time to the variations of the environment (Golberg & Holland, 1988). This approach was seen as a way of "escaping brittleness" (Holland, 1986) in reference to the lack of robustness of traditional artificial intelligence systems faced with problems more complex than toy or closed-world problems.

5.1 Pittsburgh versus Michigan

This period of research on LCSs was structured by the controversy between the so-called "Pittsburgh" and "Michigan" approaches. In Smith's approach (Smith, 1980), from the University of Pittsburgh, the only adaptive process was a GA applied to a population of LCSs in order to choose from among this population the fittest LCS for a given problem.
By contrast, in the systems from Holland and his PhD students, at the University of Michigan, the GA was combined since the very beginning with an RL mechanism and was applied more subtly within a single LCS, the population being represented by the set of classifiers in this system.
Though the Pittsburgh approach is becoming more popular again currently, (Llora & Garrell, 2002; Bacardit & Garrell, 2003; Landau et al., 2005), the Michigan approach quickly became the standard LCS framework, the Pittsburgh approach becoming absorbed into the wider evolutionary computation research domain.

5.2 The ANIMAT classifier system

Inspired by Booker's two-dimensional critter, Wilson developed a roaming classifier system that searched a two-dimensional jungle, seeking food and avoiding trees. Laid out on an 18 by 58 rectangular grid, each woods contained clusters of trees (T's) and food (F's) placed in regular clusters about the space. A typical woods is shown in figure 2. The ANIMAT (represented by a *) in a woods has knowledge concerning his immediate surroundings. For example, ANIMAT is surrounded by two trees (T), one food parcel (F), and blank spaces (B) as shown below:

B T T

B * F

B B B

This pattern generates an environmental message by unwrapping a string starting at compass north and moving clockwise:

T T F B B B B B

Under the mapping T→01, F→11, B→00 (the first position may be thought of as a binary smell detector and the second position as a binary opacity detector) the following message is generated:

0101110000000000

ANIMAT responds to environmental messages using simple classifiers with 16-position condition (corresponding to the 16-position message) and eight actions (actions 0-7). Each action corresponds to a one-step move in one of the eight directions (north, north east, east and so on).

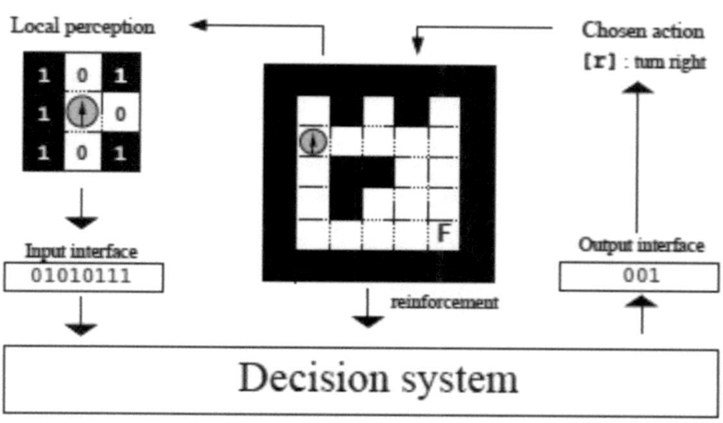

Fig. 2. Representation of an interaction problem. The agent senses a situation as a set of attributes. In this example, it is situated in a maze and senses either the presence (symbol 1) or the absence (symbol 0) of walls in the eight surrounding cells, considered clockwise starting from the north. Thus, in the above example it senses [01010111]. This information is sent to its input interface. At each time step, the agent must choose between going forward [f], turning right [r] or left [l]. The chosen action is sent through the output interface.

It is remarkable that ANIMAT learned the task as well as it did considering how little knowledge it actually possessed. For it to do much better, it would have to construct a mental map of the woods so it could know where to go when it was surrounded by blanks. This kind of internal modelling can be developed within a classifier system framework; however work in this direction has been largely theoretical.

5.3 Interactive classifier system for real robot learning

Reinforcement learning has been applied to robot learning in a real environment (Uchibe et al., 1996). In contrast with modeling human evaluation analytically, another approach is introduced in which a system learns suitable behavior using human direct evaluation without its modeling. Such an interactive method with *Evolutionary Computation (EC)* as a search algorithm is called *Interactive* EC (Dawkins, 1989), and a lot of studies on it have been done thus far (Nakanishi; Oshaki et al.; Unemi). The most significant issue of *Interactive EC* is how it reduces human teaching load. The human operator needs to evaluate a lot of individuals at every generation, and this evaluation makes him/her so tired. Specially in the *interactive EC* applied to robotics, the execution of behaviors by a robot significantly costs and a human operator can not endure such a boring task. Additionally reinforcement learning has been applied to robot learning in a real environment (Uchibe et al., 1996). Unfortunately the learning takes pretty much time to converge. Furthermore, when a robot hardly gets the first reward because of no priori knowledge, the learning convergence becomes far slower. Since most of the time that are necessary for one time of action moreover is spent in processing time of sense system and action system of a robot, the reduction of learning trials is necessary to speedup the learning.

In the Interactive Classifier System (D. Katagami et al., 2000), a human operator instructs a mobile robot while watching the information that a robot can acquire as sensor information and camera information of a robot shown on the screen top. In other words, the operator acquires information from a viewpoint of a robot instead of a viewpoint of a designer. In this example, an *interactive **EC*** framework is build which quickly learns rules with operation signal of a robot by a human operator as teacher signal. Its objective is to make initial learning more efficient and learn the behaviors that a human operator intended through interaction with him/her. To the purpose, a classifier system is utilized as a learner because it is able to learn suitable behaviors by the small number of trials, and also extend the classifier system to be adaptive to a dynamic environment.

In this system, a human operator instructs a mobile robot while watching the information that a robot can acquire as sensor information and camera information of a robot shown on the screen top. In other words, the operator acquires information from a viewpoint of a robot instead of a viewpoint of a designer. Operator performs teaching with joystick by direct operating a physical robot. The ICS inform operator about robot's state by a robot send a vibration signal of joystick to the ICS according to inside state. This system is a fast learning method based on ICS for mobile robots which acquire autonomous behaviors from experience of interaction between a human and a robot.

6. Intelligent robotics: past, present and future

Robotics began in the 1960s as a field studying a new type of universal machine implemented with a computer-controlled mechanism. This period represented an age of over expectation, which inevitably led to frustration and discontent with what could realistically be achieved given the technological capabilities at that time. In the 1980s, the field entered an era of realism as engineers grappled with these limitations and reconciled them with earlier expectations. Only in the past few years have we achieved a state in which we can feasibly implement many of those early expectations. As we do so, we enter the 'age of exploitation (Hall, 2001).

For more than 25 years, progress in concepts and applications of robots have been described, discussed, and debated. Most recently we saw the development of 'intelligent' robots, or robots designed and programmed to perform intricate, complex tasks that require the use of adaptive sensors. Before we describe some of these adaptations, we ought to admit that some confusion exists about what intelligent robots are and what they can do. This uncertainty traces back to those early over expectations, when our ideas about robots were fostered by science fiction or by our reflections in the mirror. We owe much to their influence on the field of robotics. After all, it is no coincidence that the submarines or airplanes described by Jules Verne and Leonardo da Vinci now exist. Our ideas have origins, and the imaginations of fiction writers always ignite the minds of scientists young and old, continually inspiring invention. This, in turn, inspires exploitation.

We use this term in a positive manner, referring to the act of maximizing the number of applications for, and usefulness of inventions.

Years of patient and realistic development have tempered our definition of intelligent robots. We now view them as mechanisms that may or may not look like us but can perform tasks as well as or better than humans, in that they sense and adapt to changing requirements in their environments or related to their tasks, or both. Robotics as a science has advanced from building robots that solve relatively simple problems, such as those presented by games, to machines that can solve sophisticated problems, like navigating dangerous or unexplored territory, or assisting surgeons. One such intelligent robot is the autonomous vehicle. This type of modern, sensor-guided, mobile robot is a remarkable combination of mechanisms, sensors, computer controls, and power sources, as represented by the conceptual framework in Figure 3. Each component, as well as the proper interfaces between them, is essential to building an intelligent robot that can successfully perform assigned tasks.

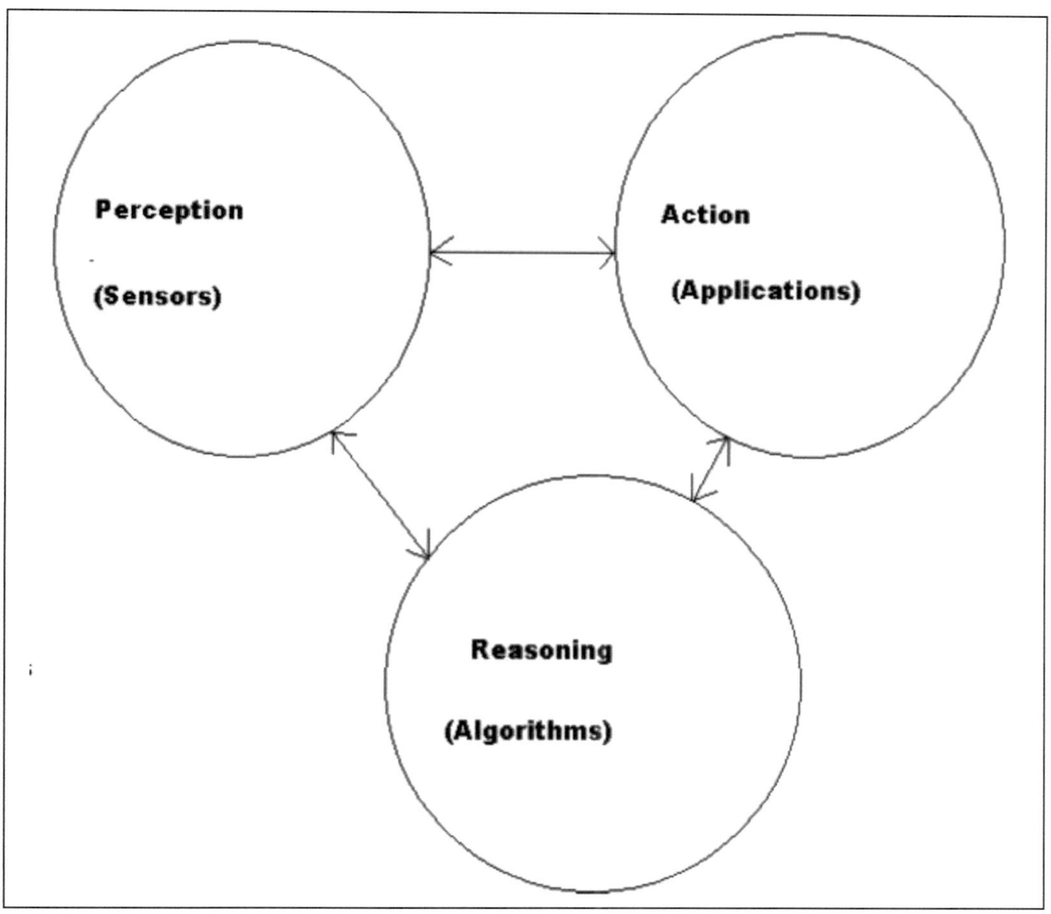

Fig. 3. Conceptual framework of components for intelligent robot design.

An example of an autonomous-vehicle effort is the work of the University of Cincinnati Robot Team. They exploit the lessons learned from several successive years of autonomous ground-vehicle research to design and build a variety of smart vehicles for unmanned operation. They have demonstrated their robots for the past few years (see Figure 2) at the Intelligent Ground Vehicle Contest and the Defense Advanced Research Project Agency's (DARPA) Urban Challenge.

Fig. 4. 'Bearcat Cub' intelligent vehicle designed for the Intelligent Ground Vehicle Contest

These and other intelligent robots developed in recent years can look deceptively ordinary and simple. Their appearances belie the incredible array of new technologies and methodologies that simply were not available more than a few years ago. For example, the vehicle shown in Figure 4 incorporates some of these emergent capabilities. Its operation is based on the theory of dynamic programming and optimal control defined by Bertsekas,5 and it uses a problem-solving approach called backwards induction. Dynamic programming permits sequential optimization. This optimization is applicable to mechanisms operating in nonlinear, stochastic environments, which exist naturally.

It requires efficient approximation methods to overcome the high-dimensionality demands. Only since the invention of artificial neural networks and backpropagation has this powerful and universal approach become realizable. Another concept that was incorporated into the robot is an eclectic controller (Hall et al., 2007). The robot uses a real-time controller to orchestrate the information gathered from sensors in a dynamic environment to perform tasks as required. This eclectic controller is one of the latest attempts to simplify the operation of intelligent machines in general, and of intelligent robots in particular. The idea is to use a task-control center and dynamic programming approach with learning to optimize performance against multiple criteria.

Universities and other research laboratories have long been dedicated to building autonomous mobile robots and showcasing their results at conferences. Alternative forums for exhibiting advances in mobile robots are the various industry or government sponsored competitions. Robot contests showcase the achievements of current and future roboticists and often result in lasting friendships among the contestants. The contests range from those for students at the highest educational level, such as the DARPA Urban Challenge, to K-12 pupils, such as the First Lego League and Junior Lego League Robotics competitions. These contests encourage students to engage with science, technology, engineering, and mathematics, foster critical thinking, promote creative problem solving, and build professionalism and teamwork. They also offer an alternative to physical sports and reward scholastic achievement.

Why are these contests important, and why do we mention them here? Such competitions have a simple requirement, which the entry either works or does not work. This type of proof-of concept pervades many creative fields. Whether inventors showcase their work at conferences or contests, most hope to eventually capitalize on and exploit their inventions, or at least appeal to those who are looking for new ideas, products, and applications.

As we enter the age of exploitation for robotics, we can expect to see many more proofs-of-concept following the advances that have been made in optics, sensors, mechanics, and computing. We will see new systems designed and existing systems redesigned. The challenges for tomorrow are to implement and exploit the new capabilities offered by emergent technologies—such as petacomputing and neural networks—to solve real problems in real time and in cost-effective ways. As scientists and engineers master the component technologies, many more solutions to practical problems will emerge. This is an exciting time for roboticists. We are approaching the ability to control a robot that is becoming as complicated in some ways as the human body. What could be accomplished by such machines? Will the design of intelligent robots be biologically inspired or will it continue to follow a completely different framework? Can we achieve the realization of a mathematical theory that gives us a functional model of the human brain, or can we develop the mathematics needed to model and predict behavior in large scale, distributed systems? These are our personal challenges, but all efforts in robotics—from K-12 students to established research laboratories—show the spirit of research to achieve the ultimate in intelligent machines. For now, it is clear that roboticists have laid the foundation to develop practical, realizable, intelligent robots. We only need the confidence and capital to take them to the next level for the benefit of humanity.

7. Conclusion

In this chapter, I have presented Learning Classifier Systems, which add to the classical Reinforcement Learning framework the possibility of representing the state as a vector of attributes and finding a compact expression of the representation so induced. Their formalism conveys a nice interaction between learning and evolution, which makes them a class of particularly rich systems, at the intersection of several research domains. As a result, they profit from the accumulated extensions of these domains.

I hope that this presentation has given to the interested reader an appropriate starting point to investigate the different streams of research that underlie the rapid evolution of LCS. In particular, a key starting point is the website dedicated to the LCS community, which can be found at the following URL: http://lcsweb.cs.bath.ac.uk/.

8. References

Bacardit, J. and Garrell, J. M. (2003). Evolving multiple discretizations with adaptive intervals for a Pittsburgh rule-based learning classifier system. In Cantú Paz, E., Foster, J. A., Deb, K., Davis, D., Roy, R., O'Reilly, U.-M., Beyer, H.-G., Standish, R., Kendall, G., Wilson, S., Harman, M., Wegener, J., Dasgupta, D., Potter, M. A.,

Schultz, A. C., Dowsland, K., Jonoska, N., and Miller, J., (Eds.), Genetic and Evolutionary Computation - GECCO-2003, pages 1818–1831, Berlin. Springer-Verlag.

Bellman, R. E. (1957). Dynamic Programming. Princeton University Press, Princeton, NJ.

Bellman, R. E. (1961). Adaptive Control Processes: A Guided Tour. Princeton University Press.

Bernado, E., Llorá, X., and Garrel, J. M. (2001). XCS and GALE : a comparative study of two Learning Classifer Systems with six other learning algorithms on classification tasks. In Lanzi, P.-L., Stolzmann, W., and Wilson, S. W., (Eds.), Proceedings of the fourth international workshop on Learning Classifer Systems.

Booker, L., Goldberg, D. E., and Holland, J. H. (1989). Classifier Systems and Genetic Algorithms. Artificial Intelligence, 40(1-3):235–282.

Booker, L. B. (2000). Do we really need to estimate rule utilities in classifier systems? In Lanzi, P.-L., Stolzmann, W., and Wilson, S. W., (Eds.), Learning Classifier Systems. From Foundations to Applications, volume 1813 of Lecture Notes in Artificial Intelligence, pages 125–142, Berlin. Springer-Verlag.

Dorigo, M. and Bersini, H. (1994). A comparison of Q-Learning and Classifier Systems. In Cliff, D., Husbands, P., Meyer, J.-A., and Wilson, S. W., (Eds.), From Animals to Animats 3, pages 248–255, Cambridge, MA. MIT Press.

Golberg, D. E. and Holland, J. H. (1988). Guest Editorial: Genetic Algorithms and Machine Learning. Machine Learning, 3:95–99.

Goldberg, D. E. (1989). Genetic Algorithms in Search, Optimization, and Machine Learning. Addison Wesley, Reading, MA.

Hall, E. L. (2001), Intelligent robot trends and predictions for the .net future, Proc. SPIE 4572, pp. 70–80, 2001. doi:10.1117/12.444228

Hall, E. L., Ghaffari M., Liao X., Ali S. M. Alhaj, Sarkar S., Reynolds S., and Mathur K., (2007).*Eclectic theory of intelligent robots*, Proc. SPIE 6764, p. 676403, 2007. doi:10.1117/12.730799

Herbart, J. F. (1825). Psychologie als Wissenschaft neu gegr¨undet auf Erfahrung, Metaphysik und Mathematik. Zweiter, analytischer Teil. AugustWilhem Unzer, Koenigsberg, Germany.

Holland, J. H. (1975). Adaptation in Natural and Artificial Systems: An Introductory Analysis with Applications to Biology, Control, and Artificial Intelligence. University of Michigan Press, Ann Arbor, MI.

Holland, J. H. (1986). Escaping brittleness: The possibilities of general-purpose learning algorithms applied to parallel rule-based systems. In Machine Learning, An Artificial Intelligence Approach (volume II). Morgan Kaufmann.

Holmes, J. H. (2002). A new representation for assessing classifier performance in mining large databases. In Stolzmann, W., Lanzi, P.-L., and Wilson, S. W., (Eds.), IWLCS-02. Proceedings of the International Workshop on Learning Classifier Systems, LNAI, Granada. Springer-Verlag.

Katagami, D.; Yamada, S. (2000). Interactive Classifier System for Real Robot Learning, *Proceedings of the 2000 IEEE International Workshop on Robot and Human Interactive Communication,* pp. 258-264, ISBN 0-7803-6273, Osaka, Japan, September 27-29 2000

Landau, S., Sigaud, O., and Schoenauer, M. (2005). ATNoSFERES revisited. In Beyer, H.-G., O'Reilly, U.-M., Arnold, D., Banzhaf, W., Blum, C., Bonabeau, E., Cant Paz, E., Dasgupta, D., Deb, K., Foste r, J., de Jong, E., Lipson, H., Llora, X., Mancoridis, S., Pelikan, M., Raidl, G., Soule, T., Tyrrell, A., Watson, J.-P., and Zitzler, E., (Eds.), Proceedings of the Genetic and Evolutionary Computation Conference, GECCO-2005, pages 1867–1874, Washington DC. ACM Press.

Lanzi, P.-L. (2002). Learning Classifier Systems from a Reinforcement Learning Perspective. Journal of Soft Computing, 6(3-4):162–170.

Ohsaki, M., Takagi H. and T. Ingu. Methods to Reduce the Human Burden of Interactive Evolutionary Computation. Asian Fuzzy System Symposium (AFSS'98), pages 4955500, 1998.

Puterman, M. L. and Shin, M. C. (1978). Modified Policy Iteration Algorithms for Discounted Markov Decision Problems. Management Science, 24:1127–1137.

R. Dawkins. *TlLe Blind Watchmaker.* Longman, Essex, 1986.

R. Dawkins. The Evolution of Evolvability. In Langton, C. G., editor, Artificial Life, pages 201-220. Addison-Wesley, 1989.

Seward, J. P. (1949). An Experimental Analysis of Latent Learning. Journal of Experimental Psychology, 39:177–186.

Sigaud, O. and Wilson, S.W. (2007). Learning Classifier Systems: A Survey, Journal of Soft Computing, Springer-Verlag (2007)

Smith, S. F. (1980). A Learning System Based on Genetic Algorithms. PhD thesis, Department of Computer Science, University of Pittsburg, Pittsburg, MA.

Stolzmann, W. (1998). Anticipatory Classifier Systems. In Koza, J., Banzhaf, W., Chellapilla, K., Deb, K., Dorigo, M., Fogel, D. B., Garzon, M. H., Goldberg, D. E., Iba, H., and Riolo, R., (Eds.), Genetic Programming, pages 658–664. Morgan Kaufmann Publishers, Inc., San Francisco, CA.

Sutton, R. S. and Barto, A. G. (1998). Reinforcement Learning: An Introduction. MIT Press.

Tolman, E. C. (1932). Purposive behavior in animals and men. Appletown, New York.

Uchibe, E., Asad M. and Hosoda, K. Behavior coordination for a mobile robot using modular reinforcement learning. In IEEE/RSJ International Conference on Intelligent Robots and Systems 1996 (IROS96), pages 1329-1336, 1996.

Wilson, S. W. (1985). Knowledge Growth in an Artificial Animat. In Grefenstette, J. J., (Ed.), Proceedings of the 1st international Conference on Genetic Algorithms and their applications (ICGA85), pages 16–23. L. E. Associates.

Wilson, S. W. (1994). ZCS, a Zeroth level Classifier System. Evolutionary Computation, 2(1):1–18.

Wilson, S. W. (1995). Classifier Fitness Based on Accuracy. Evolutionary Computation, 3(2):149–175.

Y. Nakanishi. Capturing Preference into a Function Using Interactions with a Manual Evolutionary Design Aid System. Genetic Programming, pages 133-140, 1996.

University of Cincinnati robot team. http://www.robotics.uc.edu
Intelligent Ground Vehicle Contest. http://www.igvc.org
Defense Advanced Research Project Agency's Urban Challenge. http: //www. darpa. mil / grandchallenge

2

Combining and Comparing Multiple Algorithms for Better Learning and Classification: A Case Study of MARF

Serguei A. Mokhov
Concordia University, Montreal, QC, Canada

1. Introduction

This case study of MARF, an open-source Java-based Modular Audio Recognition Framework, is intended to show the general pattern recognition pipeline design methodology and, more specifically, the supporting interfaces, classes and data structures for machine learning in order to test and compare multiple algorithms and their combinations at the pipeline's stages, including supervised and unsupervised, statistical, etc. learning and classification. This approach is used for a spectrum of recognition tasks, not only applicable to audio, but rather to general pattern recognition for various applications, such as in digital forensic analysis, writer identification, natural language processing (NLP), and others.

2. Chapter overview

First, we present the research problem at hand in Section 3. This is to serve as an example of what researchers can do and choose for their machine learning applications – the types of data structures and the best combinations of available algorithm implementations to suit their needs (or to highlight the need to implement better algorithms if the ones available are not adequate). In MARF, acting as a testbed, the researchers can also test the performance of their own, external algorithms against the ones available. Thus, the overview of the related software engineering aspects and practical considerations are discussed with respect to the machine learning using MARF as a case study with appropriate references to our own and others' related work in Section 4 and Section 5. We discuss to some extent the design and implementation of the data structures and the corresponding interfaces to support learning and comparison of multiple algorithms and approaches in a single framework, and the corresponding implementing system in a consistent environment in Section 6. There we also provide the references to the actual practical implementation of the said data structures within the current framework. We then illustrate some of the concrete results of various MARF applications and discuss them in that perspective in Section 7. We conclude afterwards in Section 8 by outlining some of the advantages and disadvantages of the framework approach and some of the design decisions in Section 8.1 and lay out future research plans in Section 8.2.

3. Problem

The main problem we are addressing is to provide researchers with a tool to test a variety of pattern recognition and NLP algorithms and their combinations for whatever task at hand there is, and then select the best available combination(s) for that final task. The testing should be in a uniform environment to compare and contrast all kinds of algorithms, their parameters, at all stages, and gather metrics such as the precision, run-time, memory usage, recall, f-measure, and others. At the same time, the framework should allow for adding external plug-ins for algorithms written elsewhere as wrappers implementing the framework's API for the same comparative studies.

The system built upon the framework has to have the data structures and interfaces that support such types of experiments in a common, uniform way for comprehensive comparative studies and should allow for scripting of the recognition tasks (for potential batch, distributed, and parallel processing).

These are very broad and general requirements we outlined, and further we describe our approach to them to a various degree using what we call the *Modular Audio Recognition Framework* (MARF). Over the course of years and efforts put into the project, the term *Audio* in the name became a lot less descriptive as the tool grew to be a lot more general and applicable to the other domains than just audio and signal processing, so we will refer to the framework as just *MARF* (while reserving the right to rename it later).

Our philosophy also includes the concept that the tool should be publicly available as an open-source project such that any valuable input and feedback from the community can help everyone involved and make it for the better experimentation platform widely available to all who needs it. Relative simplicity is another aspect that we require the tool to be to be usable by many.

To enable all this, we need to answer the question of "How do we represent what we learn and how do we store it for future use?" What follows is the summary of our take on answering it and the relevant background information.

4. Related work

There are a number of items in the related work; most of them were used as a source to gather the algorithms from to implement within MARF. This includes a variety of classical distance classifiers, such as Euclidean, Chebyshev (a.k.a city-block), Hamming, Mahalanobis, Minkowski, and others, as well as artificial neural networks (ANNs) and all the supporting general mathematics modules found in Abdi (2007); Hamming (1950); Mahalanobis (1936); Russell & Norvig (1995). This also includes the cosine similarity measure as one of the classifiers described in Garcia (2006); Khalifé (2004). Other related work is of course in digital signal processing, digital filters, study of acoustics, digital communication and speech, and the corresponding statistical processing; again for the purpose of gathering of the algorithms for the implementation in a uniform manner in the framework including the ideas presented in Bernsee (1999–2005); Haridas (2006); Haykin (1988); Ifeachor & Jervis (2002); Jurafsky & Martin (2000); O'Shaughnessy (2000); Press (1993); Zwicker & Fastl (1990). These primarily include the design and implementation of the Fast Fourier Transform (FFT) (used for both preprocessing as in low-pass, high-pass, band-pass, etc. filters as well as in feature extraction), Linear Predictive Coding (LPC), Continuous Fraction Expansion (CFE) filters and the corresponding testing applications

implemented by Clement, Mokhov, Nicolacopoulos, Fan & the MARF Research & Development Group (2002–2010); Clement, Mokhov & the MARF Research & Development Group (2002–2010); Mokhov, Fan & the MARF Research & Development Group (2002–2010b; 2005–2010a); Sinclair et al. (2002–2010).
Combining algorithms, an specifically, classifiers is not new, e.g. see Cavalin et al. (2010); Khalifé (2004). We, however, get to combine and chain not only classifiers but algorithms at every stage of the pattern recognition pipeline.
Some of the spectral techniques and statistical techniques are also applicable to the natural language processing that we also implement in some form Jurafsky & Martin (2000); Vaillant et al. (2006); Zipf (1935) where the text is treated as a signal.
Finally, there are open-source speech recognition frameworks, such as CMU Sphinx (see The Sphinx Group at Carnegie Mellon (2007–2010)) that implement a number of algorithms for speech-to-text translation that MARF does not currently implement, but they are quite complex to work with. The advantages of Sphinx is that it is also implemented in Java and is under the same open-source license as MARF, so the latter can integrate the algorithms from Sphinx as external plug-ins. Its disadvantages for the kind of work we are doing are its size and complexity.

5. Our approach and accomplishments

MARF's approach is to define a common set of integrated APIs for the pattern recognition pipeline to allow flexible comparative environment for diverse algorithm implementations for sample loading, preprocessing, feature extraction, and classification. On top of that, the algorithms within each stage can be composed and chained. The conceptual pipeline is shown in Figure 1 and the corresponding UML sequence diagram, shown in Figure 2, details the API invocation and message passing between the core modules, as per Mokhov (2008d); Mokhov et al. (2002–2003); The MARF Research and Development Group (2002–2010).

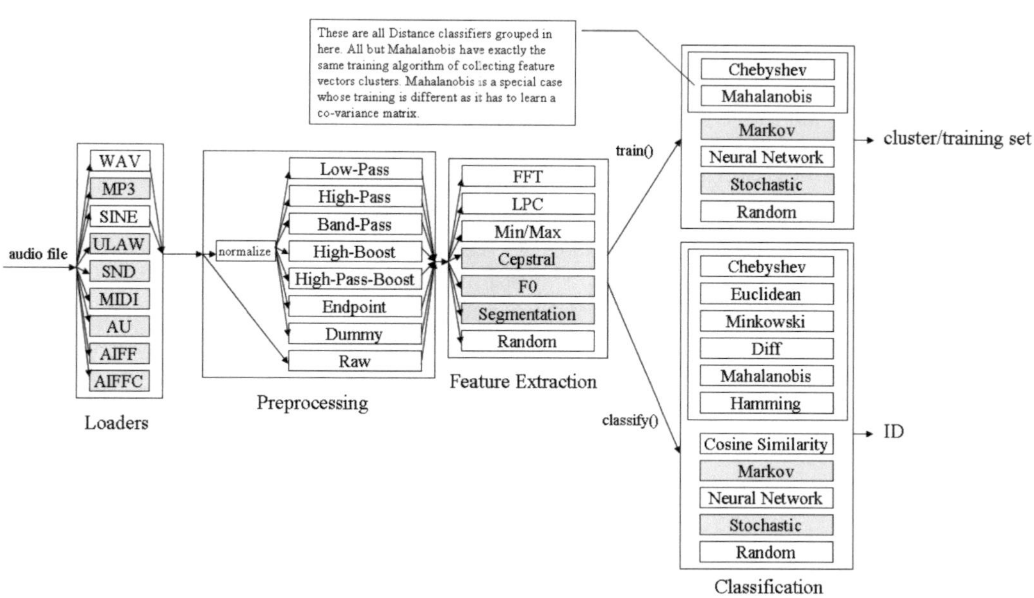

Fig. 1. Classical Pattern Recognition Pipeline of MARF

MARF has been published or is under review and publication with a variety of experimental pattern recognition and software engineering results in multiple venues. The core founding works for this chapter are found in Mokhov (2008a;d; 2010b); Mokhov & Debbabi (2008); Mokhov et al. (2002–2003); The MARF Research and Development Group (2002–2010).

At the beginning, the framework evolved for stand-alone, mostly sequential, applications with limited support for multithreading. Then, the next natural step in its evolution was to make it distributed. Having a distributed MARF (DMARF) still required a lot of manual management, and a proposal was put forward to make it into an autonomic system. A brief overview of the distributed autonomic MARF (DMARF and ADMARF) is given in terms of how the design and practical implementation are accomplished for local and distributed learning and self-management in Mokhov (2006); Mokhov, Huynh & Li (2007); Mokhov et al. (2008); Mokhov & Jayakumar (2008); Mokhov & Vassev (2009a); Vassev & Mokhov (2009; 2010) primarily relying on distributed technologies provided by Java as described in Jini Community (2007); Sun Microsystems, Inc. (2004; 2006); Wollrath & Waldo (1995–2005).

Some scripting aspects of MARF applications are also formally proposed in Mokhov (2008f). Additionally, another frontier of the MARF's use in security is explored in Mokhov (2008e); Mokhov, Huynh, Li & Rassai (2007) as well as the digital forensics aspects that are discussed for various needs of forensic file type analysis, conversion of the MARF's internal data structures as MARFL expressions into the Forensic Lucid language for follow up forensic analysis, self-forensic analysis of MARF, and writer identification of hand-written digitized documents described in Mokhov (2008b); Mokhov & Debbabi (2008); Mokhov et al. (2009); Mokhov & Vassev (2009c).

Furthermore, we have a use case and applicability of MARF's algorithms for various multimedia tasks, e.g. as described in Mokhov (2007b) combined with PureData (see Puckette & PD Community (2007–2010)) as well as in simulation of a solution to the intelligent systems challenge problem Mokhov & Vassev (2009b) and simply various aspects of software engineering associated with the requirements, design, and implementation of the framework outlined in Mokhov (2007a); Mokhov, Miladinova, Ormandjieva, Fang & Amirghahari (2008–2010).

Some MARF example applications, such as text-independent speaker-identification, natural and programming language identification, natural language probabilistic parsing, etc. are released along with MARF as open-source and are discussed in several publications mentioned earlier, specifically in Mokhov (2008–2010c); Mokhov, Sinclair, Clement, Nicolacopoulos & the MARF Research & Development Group (2002–2010); Mokhov & the MARF Research & Development Group (2003–2010a;-), as well as voice-based authentication application of MARF as an utterance engine is in a proprietary VocalVeritas system. The most recent advancements in MARF's applications include the results on identification of the decades and place of origin in the francophone press in the DEFT2010 challenge presented in Forest et al. (2010) with the results described in Mokhov (2010a;b).

6. Methods and tools

To keep the framework flexible and open for comparative uniform studies of algorithms and their external plug-ins we need to define a number of interfaces that the main modules would implement with the corresponding well-documented API as well as what kind of data structures they exchange and populate while using that API. We have to provide the data structures to encapsulate the incoming data for processing as well as the data

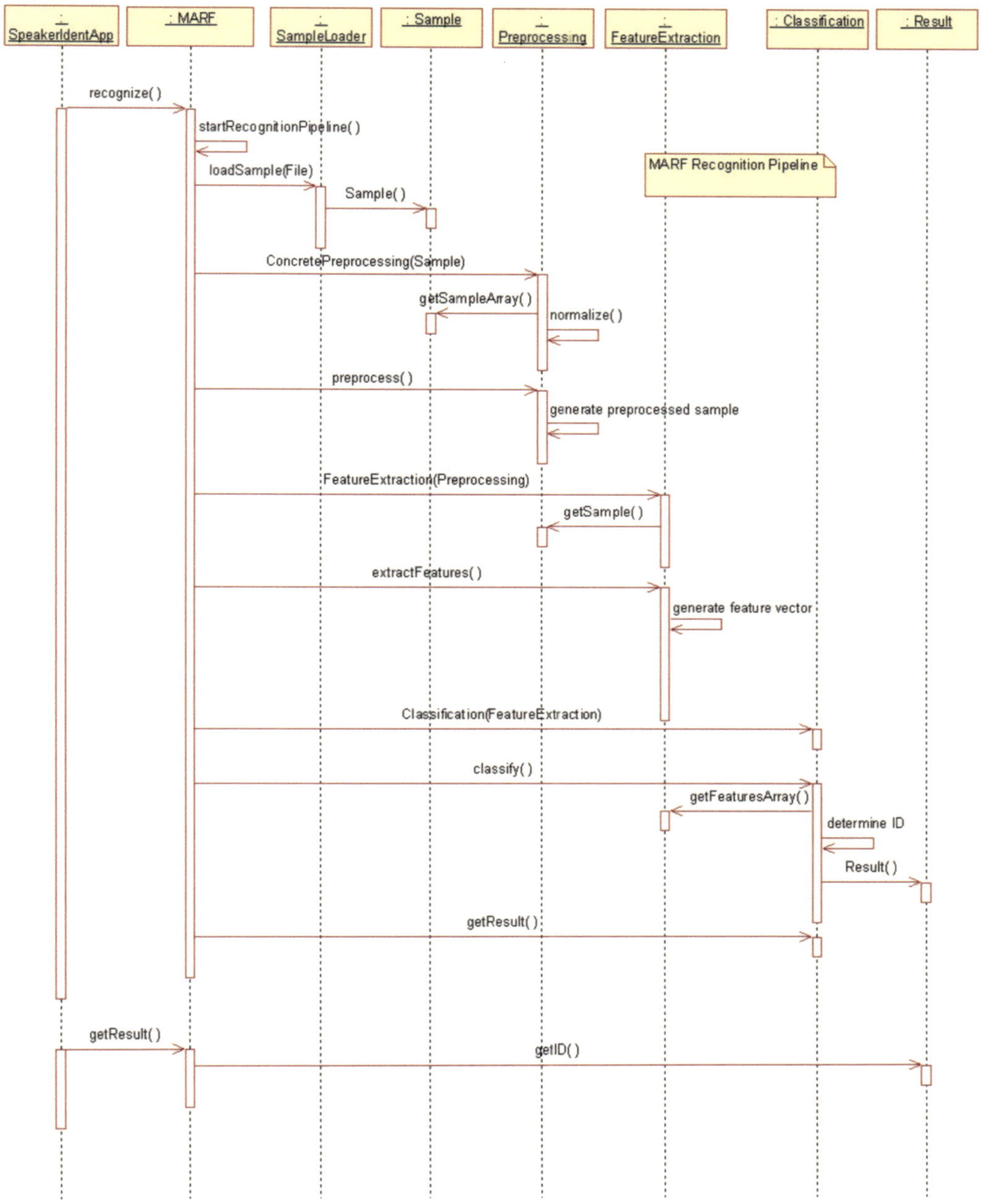

Fig. 2. UML Sequence Diagram of the Classical Pattern Recognition Pipeline of MARF

structures to store the processed data for later retrieval and comparison. In the case of classification, it is necessary also to be able to store more than one classification result, a result set, ordered according to the classification criteria (e.g. sorted in ascending manner for minimal distance or in descending manner for higher probability or similarity). The external applications should be able to pass configuration settings from their own options to the MARF's configuration state as well as collect back the results and aggregate statistics.

While algorithm modules are made fit into the same framework, they all may have arbitrary number of reconfigurable parameters for experiments (e.g. compare the behavior of the same algorithm under different settings) that take some defaults if not explicitly specified. There has to be a generic way of setting those parameters by the applications that are built upon the framework, whose Javadoc's API is detailed here: http://marf.sourceforge.net/api-dev/.
In the rest of the section we describe what we used to achieve the above requirements.

1. We use the Java programming language and the associated set of tools from Sun Microsystems, Inc. (1994–2009) and others as our primary development and run-time environment. This is primarily because it is dynamic, supports reflection (see Green (2001– 2005)), various design patterns and OO programming (Flanagan (1997); Merx & Norman (2007)), exception handling, multithreading, distributed technologies, collections, and other convenient built-in features. We employ Java interfaces for the most major modules to allow for plug-ins.
2. All objects involved in storage are `Serializable`, such that they can be safely stored on disk or transmitted over the network.
3. Many of the data structures are also `Cloneable` to aid copying of the data structure the Java standard way.
4. All major modules in the classical MARF pipeline implement the `IStorageManager` interface, such that they know how to save and reload their state. The default API of `IStorageManager` provides for modules to implement their serialization in a variety of binary and textual formats. Its latest open-source version is at:
http://marf.cvs.sf.net/viewvc/marf/marf/src/marf/Storage/IStorageManager.java?view=markup
5. The `Configuration` object instance is designed to encapsulate the global state of a MARF instance. It can be set by the applications, saved and reloaded or propagated to the distributed nodes. Details:
http://marf.cvs.sf.net/viewvc/marf/marf/src/marf/Configuration.java?view=markup
6. The module parameters class, represented as `ModuleParams`, allows more fine-grained settings for individual algorithms and modules – there can be arbitrary number of the settings in there. Combined with `Configuration` it's the way for applications to pass the specific parameters to the internals of the implementation for diverse experiments. Details:
http://marf.cvs.sf.net/viewvc/marf/marf/src/marf/Storage/ModuleParams.java?view=markup
7. The `Sample` class represents the values either just loaded from an external source (e.g. a file) for preprocessing, or a "massaged" version thereof that was preprocessed already (e.g. had its noise and silence removed, filtered otherwise, and normalized) and is ready for feature extraction. The `Sample` class has a buffer of `Double` values (an array) representing the amplitudes of the sample values being processed at various frequencies and other parameters. It is not important that the input data may be an audio signal, a text, an image, or any kind of binary data – they all can be treated similarly in the spectral approach, so only one way to represent them such that all the modules can understand them. The `Sample` instances are usually of arbitrary length. Details:
http://marf.cvs.sf.net/viewvc/marf/marf/src/marf/Storage/Sample.java?view=markup
8. The `ITrainingSample` interface is very crucial to specify the core storage models for all training samples and training sets. The latter are updated during the training mode of the classifiers and used in read-only manner during the classification stage. The interface also defines what and how to store of the data and how to accumulate the feature vectors that come from the feature extraction modules. Details:
http://marf.cvs.sf.net/viewvc/marf/marf/src/marf/Storage/ITrainingSample.java?view=markup

9. The `TrainingSample` class is the first implementation of the `ITrainingSample` interface. It maintains the ID of the subject that training sample data corresponds to, the training data vector itself (usually either a mean or median cluster or a single feature vector), and a list of files (or entries alike) the training was performed on (this list is optionally used by the classification modules to avoid double-training on the same sample). Details:
http://marf.cvs.sf.net/viewvc/marf/marf/src/marf/Storage/TrainingSample.java?view=markup
10. The `Cluster` is a `TrainingSample` with a mean cluster data embedded and counted how many feature vectors were particularly trained on. Details:
http://marf.cvs.sf.net/viewvc/marf/marf/src/marf/Storage/Cluster.java?view=markup
11. The `TrainingSet` class encapsulates a collection of object instances implementing the `ITrainingSample` interface and whether they are simply `TrainingSamples`, `Clusters`, or `FeatureSets`. It also caries the information about which preprocessing and feature extraction methods were used to disambiguate the sets. Most commonly, the serialized instances of this class are preserved during the training sessions and used during the classification sessions. Details:
http://marf.cvs.sf.net/viewvc/marf/marf/src/marf/Storage/TrainingSet.java?view=markup
12. The `FeatureSet` class instance is a `Cluster` that allows maintaining individual feature vectors instead of just a compressed (mean or median) clusters thereof. It allows for the most flexibility and retains the most training information available at the cost of extra storage and look up requirements. The flexibility allows to compute the mean and median vectors and cache them dynamically if the feature set was not altered increasing performance. Details:
http://marf.cvs.sf.net/viewvc/marf/marf/src/marf/Storage/FeatureSet.java?view=markup
13. An instance of the `Result` data structure encapsulates the classification ID (usually supplied during training), the outcome for that result, and a particular optional description if required (e.g. human-readable interpretation of the ID). The outcome may mean a number of things depending on the classifier used: it is a scalar `Double` value that can represent the distance from the subject, the similarity to the subject, or probability of this result. These meanings are employed by the particular classifiers when returning the "best" and "second best", etc. results or sort them from the "best" to the "worst" whatever these qualifiers mean. Details:
http://marf.cvs.sf.net/viewvc/marf/marf/src/marf/Storage/Result.java?view=markup
14. The `ResultSet` class corresponds to the collection of `Results`, that can be sorted according to each classifier's requirements. It provides the basic API to get minima, maxima (both first, and second), as well as average and random and the entire collection of the results. Details:
http://marf.cvs.sf.net/viewvc/marf/marf/src/marf/Storage/ResultSet.java?view=markup
15. The `IDatabase` interface is there to be used by applications to maintain their instances of database abstractions to maintain statistics they need, such as precision of recognition, etc. generally following the Builder design pattern (see Freeman et al. (2004); Gamma et al. (1995); Larman (2006)). Details:
http://marf.cvs.sf.net/viewvc/marf/marf/src/marf/Storage/IDatabase.java?view=markup
16. The `Database` class instance is the most generic implementation of the `IDatabase` interface in case applications decide to use it. The applications such as `SpeakerIdentApp`, `WriterIdentApp`, `FileTypeIdentApp`, `DEFT2010App` and others have their corresponding subclasses of this class. Details:
http://marf.cvs.sf.net/viewvc/marf/marf/src/marf/Storage/Database.java?view=markup

17. The `StatisticalObject` class is a generic record about frequency of occurrences and potentially a rank of any statistical value. In MARF, typically it is the basis for various NLP-related observations. Details:
http://marf.cvs.sf.net/viewvc/marf/marf/src/marf/Stats/StatisticalObject.java?view=markup
18. The `WordStats` class is a `StatisticalObject` that is more suitable for text analysis and extends it with the lexeme being observed. Details:
http://marf.cvs.sf.net/viewvc/marf/marf/src/marf/Stats/WordStats.java?view=markup
19. The `Observation` class is a refinement of `WordStats` to augment it with prior and posterior probabilities as well as the fact it has been "seen" or not yet. Details:
http://marf.cvs.sf.net/viewvc/marf/marf/src/marf/Stats/Observation.java?view=markup
20. The `Ngram` instance is an `Observation` of an occurrence of an n-ngram usually in the natural language text with $n = 1, 2, 3, \ldots$ characters or lexeme elements that follow each other. Details:
http://marf.cvs.sf.net/viewvc/marf/marf/src/marf/Stats/Ngram.java?view=markup
21. The `ProbabilityTable` class instance builds matrices of n-grams and their computed or counted probabilities for training and classification (e.g. in `LangIdentApp`). Details:
http://marf.cvs.sf.net/viewvc/marf/marf/src/marf/Stats/ProbabilityTable.java?view=markup

7. Results

We applied the MARF approach to a variety experiments, that gave us equally a variety of results. The approaches tried refer to text independent-speaker identification using median and mean clusters, gender identification, age group, spoken accent, and biometrics alike. On the other hand, other experiments involved writer identification from scanned hand-written documents, forensic file type analysis of file systems, an intelligent systems challenge, natural language identification, identification of decades in French corpora as well as place of origin of publication (such as Quebec vs. France or the particular journal).

All these experiments yielded top, intermediate, and worst configurations for each task given the set of available algorithms implemented at the time. Here we recite some of the results with their configurations. This is a small fraction of the experiments conducted and results recorded as a normal session is about ≈ 1500+ configurations.

1. Text-independent speaker (Mokhov (2008a;c); Mokhov et al. (2002–2003)), including gender, and spoken accent identification using mean vs. median clustering experimental (Mokhov (2008a;d)) results are illustrated in Table 1, Table 2, Table 3, Table 4, Table 5, and Table 6. These are primarily results with the top precision. The point these serve to illustrate is that the top configurations of algorithms are distinct depending on (a) the recognition task ("who" vs. "spoken accent" vs. "gender") and (b) type of clustering performed. For instance, by using the mean clustering the configuration that removes silence gaps from the sample, uses the band-stop FFT filter, and uses the aggregation of the FFT and LPC features in one feature vector and the cosine similarity measure as the classifier yielded the top result in Table 1. However, an equivalent experiment in Table 2 with median clusters yielded band-stop FFT filter with FFT feature extractor and cosine similarity classifier as a top configuration; and the configuration that was the top for the mean was no longer that accurate. The individual modules used in the pipeline were all at their default settings (see Mokhov (2008d)). The meanings of the options are also described in Mokhov (2008d; 2010b); The MARF

Rank #	Configuration	$GOOD_{1st}$	BAD_{1st}	$Precision_{1st}$,%	$GOOD_{2nd}$	BAD_{2nd}	$Precision_{2nd}$,%
1	-silence -bandstop -aggr -cos	29	3	90.62	30	2	93.75
1	-silence -bandstop -fft -cos	29	3	90.62	30	2	93.75
1	-bandstop -fft -cos	28	4	87.50	29	3	90.62
2	-silence -noise -bandstop -fft -cos	28	4	87.50	30	2	93.75
2	-silence -low -aggr -cos	28	4	87.50	30	2	93.75
2	-silence -noise -norm -aggr -cos	28	4	87.50	30	2	93.75
2	-silence -low -fft -cos	28	4	87.50	30	2	93.75
2	-silence -noise -norm -fft -cos	28	4	87.50	30	2	93.75
2	-silence -noise -low -aggr -cos	28	4	87.50	30	2	93.75
2	-silence -noise -low -fft -cos	28	4	87.50	30	2	93.75
2	-bandstop -aggr -cos	28	4	87.50	29	3	90.62
2	-norm -fft -cos	28	4	87.50	29	3	90.62
2	-silence -raw -aggr -cos	28	4	87.50	30	2	93.75
2	-silence -noise -raw -aggr -cos	28	4	87.50	30	2	93.75
2	-norm -aggr -cos	28	4	87.50	30	2	93.75
2	-silence -noise -bandstop -aggr -cos	28	4	87.50	30	2	93.75
3	-silence -norm -fft -cos	27	5	84.38	30	2	93.75
3	-silence -norm -aggr -cos	27	5	84.38	30	2	93.75
3	-low -fft -cos	27	5	84.38	28	4	87.50
3	-noise -bandstop -aggr -cos	27	5	84.38	29	3	90.62
3	-silence -raw -fft -cos	27	5	84.38	29	3	90.62
3	-noise -raw -aggr -cos	27	5	84.38	30	2	93.75
3	-silence -noise -raw -fft -cos	27	5	84.38	29	3	90.62
3	-noise -low -fft -cos	27	5	84.38	28	4	87.50
3	-raw -fft -cos	27	5	84.38	29	3	90.62
3	-noise -bandstop -fft -cos	27	5	84.38	29	3	90.62
3	-low -aggr -cos	27	5	84.38	28	4	87.50
3	-noise -raw -fft -cos	27	5	84.38	29	3	90.62
3	-noise -norm -fft -cos	27	5	84.38	28	4	87.50
3	-noise -norm -aggr -cos	27	5	84.38	28	4	87.50
3	-noise -low -aggr -cos	27	5	84.38	28	4	87.50
4	-noise -raw -lpc -cos	26	6	81.25	28	4	87.50
4	-silence -raw -lpc -cos	26	6	81.25	28	4	87.50
4	-silence -noise -raw -lpc -cos	26	6	81.25	28	4	87.50
4	-raw -lpc -cos	26	6	81.25	28	4	87.50
4	-norm -lpc -cos	26	6	81.25	28	4	87.50
5	-endp -lpc -cheb	25	7	78.12	26	6	81.25
6	-silence -bandstop -fft -eucl	24	8	75.00	26	6	81.25
6	-bandstop -lpc -eucl	24	8	75.00	28	4	87.50
6	-silence -norm -fft -eucl	24	8	75.00	26	6	81.25
6	-silence -bandstop -fft -diff	24	8	75.00	26	6	81.25
6	-silence -norm -aggr -eucl	24	8	75.00	26	6	81.25
6	-raw -fft -eucl	24	8	75.00	26	6	81.25
6	-noise -raw -aggr -eucl	24	8	75.00	26	6	81.25
6	-silence -bandstop -aggr -eucl	24	8	75.00	26	6	81.25
6	-bandstop -aggr -cheb	24	8	75.00	26	6	81.25
6	-noise -raw -fft -eucl	24	8	75.00	26	6	81.25
6	-silence -raw -fft -eucl	24	8	75.00	26	6	81.25
6	-silence -bandstop -aggr -diff	24	8	75.00	26	6	81.25
6	-silence -noise -raw -aggr -eucl	24	8	75.00	26	6	81.25

Table 1. Top Most Accurate Configurations for Speaker Identification, 1st and 2nd Guesses, Mean Clustering (Mokhov (2008d))

Research and Development Group (2002–2010). We also illustrate the "2nd guess" statistics - often what happens is that if we are mistaken in our first guess, the second one is usually the right one. It may not be obvious how to exploit it, but we provide the statistics to show if the hypothesis is true or not.

While the options listed of the MARF application (`SpeakerIdentApp`, see Mokhov, Sinclair, Clement, Nicolacopoulos & the MARF Research & Development Group (2002–2010)) are described at length in the cited works, here we briefly summarize their meaning for the unaware reader: `-silence` and `-noise` tell to remove the silence and noise components of a sample; `-band`, `-bandstop`, `-high` and `-low` correspond to the band-pass, band-stop, high-pass and low-pass FFT filters; `-norm` means normalization; `-endp` corresponds to endpointing; `-raw` does a pass-through (no-op) preprocessing;

Rank #	Configuration	$GOOD_{1st}$	BAD_{1st}	$Precision_{1st}$,%	$GOOD_{2nd}$	BAD_{2nd}	$Precision_{2nd}$,%
1	-bandstop -fft -cos	29	3	90.62	30	2	93.75
1	-bandstop -aggr -cos	29	3	90.62	30	2	93.75
2	-silence -bandstop -aggr -cos	28	4	87.5	30	2	93.75
2	-silence -bandstop -fft -cos	28	4	87.5	30	2	93.75
2	-low -fft -cos	28	4	87.5	29	3	90.62
2	-noise -bandstop -aggr -cos	28	4	87.5	29	3	90.62
2	-silence -raw -fft -cos	28	4	87.5	30	2	93.75
2	-noise -raw -aggr -cos	28	4	87.5	30	2	93.75
2	-silence -noise -raw -fft -cos	28	4	87.5	30	2	93.75
2	-noise -low -fft -cos	28	4	87.5	29	3	90.62
2	-raw -fft -cos	28	4	87.5	30	2	93.75
2	-noise -bandstop -fft -cos	28	4	87.5	29	3	90.62
2	-norm -fft -cos	28	4	87.5	30	2	93.75
2	-noise -raw -fft -cos	28	4	87.5	30	2	93.75
2	-noise -norm -fft -cos	28	4	87.5	29	3	90.62
2	-noise -low -aggr -cos	28	4	87.5	29	3	90.62
2	-norm -aggr -cos	28	4	87.5	30	2	93.75
3	-silence -norm -fft -cos	27	5	84.38	29	3	90.62
3	-silence -low -aggr -cos	27	5	84.38	30	2	93.75
3	-silence -noise -norm -aggr -cos	27	5	84.38	30	2	93.75
3	-silence -norm -aggr -cos	27	5	84.38	29	3	90.62
3	-silence -low -fft -cos	27	5	84.38	30	2	93.75
3	-silence -noise -norm -fft -cos	27	5	84.38	30	2	93.75
3	-silence -noise -low -aggr -cos	27	5	84.38	30	2	93.75
3	-silence -noise -low -fft -cos	27	5	84.38	30	2	93.75
3	-raw -aggr -cos	27	5	84.38	30	2	93.75
3	-low -aggr -cos	27	5	84.38	29	3	90.62
3	-silence -raw -aggr -cos	27	5	84.38	30	2	93.75
3	-silence -noise -raw -aggr -cos	27	5	84.38	30	2	93.75
3	-noise -norm -aggr -cos	27	5	84.38	29	3	90.62
4	-silence -noise -bandstop -fft -cos	26	6	81.25	30	2	93.75
4	-bandstop -lpc -diff	26	6	81.25	31	1	96.88
4	-bandstop -lpc -cheb	26	6	81.25	31	1	96.88
4	-silence -noise -bandstop -aggr -cos	26	6	81.25	30	2	93.75
5	-bandstop -lpc -eucl	25	7	78.12	31	1	96.88
5	-noise -raw -lpc -cos	25	7	78.12	26	6	81.25
5	-bandstop -lpc -cos	25	7	78.12	29	3	90.62
5	-silence -raw -lpc -cos	25	7	78.12	26	6	81.25
5	-silence -noise -raw -lpc -cos	25	7	78.12	26	6	81.25
5	-raw -lpc -cos	25	7	78.12	26	6	81.25
5	-norm -lpc -cos	25	7	78.12	26	6	81.25
6	-silence -norm -fft -eucl	24	8	75	26	6	81.25
6	-bandstop -fft -cheb	24	8	75	26	6	81.25
6	-silence -norm -aggr -eucl	24	8	75	26	6	81.25
6	-endp -lpc -cheb	24	8	75	27	5	84.38
6	-bandstop -aggr -cheb	24	8	75	26	6	81.25
6	-bandstop -fft -diff	24	8	75	26	6	81.25
6	-bandstop -aggr -diff	24	8	75	26	6	81.25
6	-bandstop -lpc -mink	24	8	75	30	2	93.75
7	-silence -bandstop -fft -eucl	23	9	71.88	26	6	81.25
7	-silence -bandstop -aggr -cheb	23	9	71.88	26	6	81.25
7	-bandstop -fft -eucl	23	9	71.88	26	6	81.25
7	-silence -bandstop -aggr -eucl	23	9	71.88	26	6	81.25
7	-silence -endp -lpc -cheb	23	9	71.88	25	7	78.12
7	-endp -lpc -eucl	23	9	71.88	26	6	81.25

Table 2. Top Most Accurate Configurations for Speaker Identification, 1st and 2nd Guesses, Median Clustering (Mokhov (2008d))

`-fft`, `-lpc`, and `-aggr` correspond to the FFT-based, LPC-based, or aggregation of the two feature extractors; `-cos`, `-eucl`, `-cheb`, `-hamming`, `-mink`, and `-diff` correspond to the classifiers, such as cosine similarity measure, Euclidean, Chebyshev, Hamming, Minkowski, and diff distances respectively.

2. In Mokhov & Debbabi (2008), an experiment was conducted to use a MARF-based `FileTypeIdentApp` for bulk forensic analysis of file types using signal processing techniques as opposed to the Unix `file` utility (see Darwin et al. (1973–2007;-)). That experiment was a "cross product" of:

Rank #	Configuration	$GOOD_{1st}$	BAD_{1st}	$Precision_{1st}$, %	$GOOD_{2nd}$	BAD_{2nd}	$Precision_{2nd}$, %
1	-silence -endp -lpc -cheb	24	8	75	26	6	81.25
2	-bandstop -fft -cos	23	9	71.88	27	5	84.38
2	-low -aggr -cos	23	9	71.88	26	6	81.25
2	-noise -norm -aggr -cos	23	9	71.88	26	6	81.25
2	-noise -low -aggr -cos	23	9	71.88	26	6	81.25
3	-noise -bandstop -aggr -cos	22	10	68.75	27	5	84.38
3	-noise -low -fft -cos	22	10	68.75	26	6	81.25
3	-noise -bandstop -fft -cos	22	10	68.75	27	5	84.38
3	-norm -aggr -cos	22	10	68.75	26	6	81.25
4	-endp -lpc -cheb	21	11	65.62	24	8	75
4	-silence -noise -low -aggr -cos	21	11	65.62	25	7	78.12
4	-low -fft -cos	21	11	65.62	27	5	84.38
4	-noise -norm -fft -cos	21	11	65.62	27	5	84.38
5	-silence -bandstop -aggr -cos	20	12	62.5	25	7	78.12
5	-silence -low -aggr -cos	20	12	62.5	25	7	78.12
5	-silence -noise -norm -aggr -cos	20	12	62.5	25	7	78.12
5	-silence -bandstop -fft -cos	20	12	62.5	25	7	78.12
5	-silence -low -fft -cos	20	12	62.5	25	7	78.12
5	-silence -noise -norm -fft -cos	20	12	62.5	25	7	78.12
5	-silence -noise -low -fft -cos	20	12	62.5	25	7	78.12
5	-endp -lpc -diff	20	12	62.5	24	8	75
5	-norm -fft -cos	20	12	62.5	26	6	81.25
5	-silence -endp -lpc -eucl	20	12	62.5	23	9	71.88
5	-noise -band -lpc -cos	20	12	62.5	26	6	81.25
5	-silence -endp -lpc -diff	20	12	62.5	26	6	81.25
6	-silence -noise -bandstop -fft -cos	19	13	59.38	25	7	78.12
6	-noise -band -fft -eucl	19	13	59.38	23	9	71.88
6	-silence -norm -fft -cos	19	13	59.38	27	5	84.38
6	-silence -norm -aggr -cos	19	13	59.38	27	5	84.38
6	-silence -raw -fft -cos	19	13	59.38	27	5	84.38
6	-silence -noise -band -aggr -mink	19	13	59.38	25	7	78.12
6	-silence -noise -band -fft -mink	19	13	59.38	25	7	78.12
6	-silence -noise -raw -fft -cos	19	13	59.38	27	5	84.38
6	-raw -fft -cos	19	13	59.38	27	5	84.38
6	-silence -noise -bandstop -fft -cheb	19	13	59.38	24	8	75
6	-noise -raw -fft -cos	19	13	59.38	27	5	84.38
6	-noise -endp -lpc -cos	19	13	59.38	25	7	78.12
6	-silence -noise -bandstop -aggr -cos	19	13	59.38	25	7	78.12
7	-silence -noise -bandstop -aggr -cheb	16	12	57.14	20	8	71.43
8	-silence -noise -bandstop -fft -diff	18	14	56.25	25	7	78.12
8	-noise -high -aggr -cos	18	14	56.25	20	12	62.5
8	-silence -endp -lpc -cos	18	14	56.25	23	9	71.88
8	-silence -noise -low -lpc -hamming	18	14	56.25	25	7	78.12
8	-silence -noise -low -aggr -cheb	18	14	56.25	23	9	71.88
8	-silence -noise -endp -lpc -cos	18	14	56.25	25	7	78.12
8	-silence -noise -low -fft -diff	18	14	56.25	22	10	68.75
8	-raw -aggr -cos	18	14	56.25	28	4	87.5
8	-noise -bandstop -fft -diff	18	14	56.25	24	8	75
8	-noise -band -lpc -cheb	18	14	56.25	27	5	84.38
8	-silence -endp -lpc -hamming	18	14	56.25	24	8	75
8	-low -aggr -diff	18	14	56.25	24	8	75
8	-noise -band -fft -cos	18	14	56.25	22	10	68.75
8	-silence -noise -low -aggr -diff	18	14	56.25	23	9	71.88
8	-noise -band -fft -cheb	18	14	56.25	22	10	68.75
8	-silence -band -lpc -cheb	18	14	56.25	21	11	65.62
8	-silence -noise -low -fft -cheb	18	14	56.25	23	9	71.88
8	-noise -bandstop -aggr -cheb	18	14	56.25	25	7	78.12
8	-noise -bandstop -fft -cheb	18	14	56.25	24	8	75
8	-silence -noise -bandstop -aggr -diff	18	14	56.25	25	7	78.12
9	-noise -high -fft -eucl	17	15	53.12	22	10	68.75
9	-noise -high -aggr -eucl	17	15	53.12	20	12	62.5

Table 3. Top Most Accurate Configurations for Spoken Accent Identification, 1st and 2nd Guesses, Mean Clustering (Mokhov (2008d))

- 3 loaders
- strings and n-grams (4)
- noise and silence removal (4)
- 13 preprocessing modules
- 5 feature extractors
- 9 classifiers

Run #	Configuration	$GOOD_{1st}$	BAD_{1st}	$Precision_{1st}$,%	$GOOD_{2nd}$	BAD_{2nd}	$Precision_{2nd}$,%
1	-noise -raw -aggr -cos	23	9	71.88	25	7	78.12
1	-silence -noise -raw -aggr -cos	23	9	71.88	25	7	78.12
2	-raw -aggr -cos	22	10	68.75	25	7	78.12
2	-silence -raw -fft -cos	22	10	68.75	25	7	78.12
2	-silence -noise -raw -fft -cos	22	10	68.75	25	7	78.12
2	-raw -fft -cos	22	10	68.75	25	7	78.12
2	-silence -raw -aggr -cos	22	10	68.75	25	7	78.12
2	-noise -raw -fft -cos	22	10	68.75	25	7	78.12
3	-noise -low -aggr -eucl	21	11	65.62	28	4	87.5
3	-band -aggr -cos	21	11	65.62	25	7	78.12
3	-noise -endp -fft -eucl	21	11	65.62	28	4	87.5
3	-low -aggr -cos	21	11	65.62	26	6	81.25
3	-noise -low -fft -eucl	21	11	65.62	28	4	87.5
3	-noise -norm -aggr -cos	21	11	65.62	26	6	81.25
3	-noise -low -aggr -cos	21	11	65.62	27	5	84.38
4	-silence -low -fft -eucl	20	12	62.5	27	5	84.38
4	-silence -noise -bandstop -fft -cos	20	12	62.5	25	7	78.12
4	-silence -noise -bandstop -fft -diff	20	12	62.5	26	6	81.25
4	-silence -norm -fft -eucl	20	12	62.5	27	5	84.38
4	-silence -bandstop -aggr -cos	20	12	62.5	25	7	78.12
4	-silence -bandstop -fft -cos	20	12	62.5	25	7	78.12
4	-silence -noise -norm -fft -eucl	20	12	62.5	27	5	84.38
4	-silence -bandstop -aggr -cheb	20	12	62.5	28	4	87.5
4	-silence -norm -aggr -eucl	20	12	62.5	27	5	84.38
4	-noise -bandstop -fft -eucl	20	12	62.5	27	5	84.38
4	-silence -norm -fft -diff	20	12	62.5	24	8	75
4	-bandstop -fft -eucl	20	12	62.5	27	5	84.38
4	-noise -bandstop -fft -diff	20	12	62.5	24	8	75
4	-silence -low -aggr -eucl	20	12	62.5	27	5	84.38
4	-silence -bandstop -aggr -diff	20	12	62.5	28	4	87.5
4	-silence -noise -bandstop -fft -cheb	20	12	62.5	26	6	81.25
4	-silence -norm -fft -cheb	20	12	62.5	24	8	75
4	-norm -aggr -cos	20	12	62.5	26	6	81.25
4	-silence -noise -bandstop -aggr -cos	20	12	62.5	25	7	78.12
4	-silence -noise -bandstop -aggr -diff	20	12	62.5	26	6	81.25
4	-noise -bandstop -fft -cheb	20	12	62.5	24	8	75
5	-silence -bandstop -fft -eucl	19	13	59.38	28	4	87.5
5	-bandstop -fft -cos	19	13	59.38	26	6	81.25
5	-silence -norm -fft -cos	19	13	59.38	26	6	81.25
5	-silence -low -aggr -cos	19	13	59.38	25	7	78.12
5	-silence -noise -low -fft -eucl	19	13	59.38	27	5	84.38
5	-silence -norm -aggr -cos	19	13	59.38	26	6	81.25
5	-silence -bandstop -fft -diff	19	13	59.38	27	5	84.38
5	-silence -low -fft -cos	19	13	59.38	25	7	78.12
5	-silence -low -fft -diff	19	13	59.38	23	9	71.88
5	-silence -noise -low -lpc -hamming	19	13	59.38	23	9	71.88
5	-endp -lpc -cheb	19	13	59.38	23	9	71.88
5	-noise -bandstop -aggr -mink	19	13	59.38	24	8	75
5	-silence -noise -band -fft -cheb	19	13	59.38	25	7	78.12
5	-noise -bandstop -aggr -eucl	19	13	59.38	27	5	84.38
5	-silence -noise -norm -fft -cos	19	13	59.38	25	7	78.12
5	-silence -noise -low -aggr -cos	19	13	59.38	25	7	78.12
5	-silence -noise -low -aggr -cheb	19	13	59.38	25	7	78.12
5	-silence -noise -endp -lpc -cos	19	13	59.38	26	6	81.25
5	-noise -raw -aggr -mink	19	13	59.38	24	8	75
5	-silence -low -aggr -cheb	19	13	59.38	23	9	71.88
5	-low -aggr -eucl	19	13	59.38	27	5	84.38
5	-low -fft -cos	19	13	59.38	26	6	81.25
5	-silence -noise -low -fft -cos	19	13	59.38	25	7	78.12
5	-noise -bandstop -aggr -cos	19	13	59.38	21	11	65.62
5	-silence -noise -low -fft -diff	19	13	59.38	25	7	78.12
5	-silence -noise -norm -fft -diff	19	13	59.38	23	9	71.88
5	-raw -aggr -mink	19	13	59.38	23	9	71.88
5	-silence -norm -aggr -diff	19	13	59.38	24	8	75
5	-silence -noise -endp -lpc -cheb	19	13	59.38	26	6	81.25
5	-silence -bandstop -aggr -eucl	19	13	59.38	26	6	81.25
5	-bandstop -aggr -cheb	19	13	59.38	26	6	81.25

Table 4. Top Most Accurate Configurations for Spoken Accent Identification, 1st and 2nd Guesses, Median Clustering (Mokhov (2008d))

Rank #	Configuration	$GOOD_{1st}$	BAD_{1st}	$Precision_{1st}$,%	$GOOD_{2nd}$	BAD_{2nd}	$Precision_{2nd}$,%
1	-noise -high -aggr -mink	26	6	81.25	32	0	100
1	-silence -noise -band -aggr -cheb	26	6	81.25	32	0	100
1	-silence -noise -band -lpc -cos	26	6	81.25	31	1	96.88
1	-silence -noise -band -fft -cheb	26	6	81.25	32	0	100
1	-noise -bandstop -fft -diff	26	6	81.25	32	0	100
1	-noise -bandstop -fft -cheb	26	6	81.25	32	0	100
2	-silence -band -lpc -cos	25	7	78.12	31	1	96.88
2	-silence -noise -bandstop -fft -diff	25	7	78.12	32	0	100
2	-noise -endp -lpc -eucl	25	7	78.12	31	1	96.88
2	-silence -noise -band -aggr -eucl	25	7	78.12	32	0	100
2	-silence -noise -endp -lpc -cheb	25	7	78.12	32	0	100
2	-noise -endp -lpc -diff	25	7	78.12	32	0	100
2	-silence -noise -band -fft -eucl	25	7	78.12	32	0	100
2	-silence -noise -band -aggr -diff	25	7	78.12	32	0	100
2	-silence -noise -bandstop -fft -cheb	25	7	78.12	32	0	100
2	-silence -noise -band -fft -diff	25	7	78.12	32	0	100
2	-noise -bandstop -aggr -cheb	25	7	78.12	32	0	100
3	-noise -band -aggr -cheb	24	8	75	32	0	100
3	-noise -high -fft -eucl	24	8	75	31	1	96.88
3	-noise -high -lpc -cos	24	8	75	30	2	93.75
3	-silence -low -fft -diff	24	8	75	32	0	100
3	-silence -noise -high -lpc -diff	24	8	75	30	2	93.75
3	-silence -noise -low -aggr -cheb	24	8	75	32	0	100
3	-silence -noise -endp -lpc -cos	24	8	75	31	1	96.88
3	-silence -noise -low -fft -diff	24	8	75	32	0	100
3	-silence -noise -norm -fft -diff	24	8	75	32	0	100
3	-silence -noise -norm -aggr -cheb	24	8	75	32	0	100
3	-silence -noise -bandstop -aggr -cheb	24	8	75	32	0	100
3	-silence -noise -endp -lpc -eucl	24	8	75	31	1	96.88
3	-silence -noise -low -aggr -diff	24	8	75	32	0	100
3	-silence -noise -norm -aggr -diff	24	8	75	32	0	100
3	-noise -endp -lpc -cos	24	8	75	31	1	96.88
3	-silence -noise -low -fft -cheb	24	8	75	32	0	100
3	-noise -endp -lpc -hamming	24	8	75	31	1	96.88
3	-silence -noise -bandstop -aggr -diff	24	8	75	32	0	100
3	-noise -endp -lpc -cheb	24	8	75	32	0	100
4	-low -lpc -cheb	23	9	71.88	32	0	100
4	-noise -norm -lpc -cheb	23	9	71.88	32	0	100
4	-noise -low -lpc -cheb	23	9	71.88	32	0	100
4	-endp -lpc -cheb	23	9	71.88	31	1	96.88
4	-noise -band -fft -diff	23	9	71.88	32	0	100
4	-low -lpc -mink	23	9	71.88	31	1	96.88
4	-low -lpc -eucl	23	9	71.88	31	1	96.88
4	-noise -norm -aggr -cheb	23	9	71.88	32	0	100
4	-noise -norm -lpc -mink	23	9	71.88	31	1	96.88
4	-silence -high -lpc -cos	23	9	71.88	32	0	100
4	-noise -low -lpc -mink	23	9	71.88	32	0	100
4	-noise -norm -lpc -eucl	23	9	71.88	31	1	96.88
4	-noise -low -lpc -eucl	23	9	71.88	32	0	100
4	-silence -low -lpc -cheb	23	9	71.88	31	1	96.88
4	-noise -band -lpc -hamming	23	9	71.88	30	2	93.75
4	-noise -band -aggr -diff	23	9	71.88	32	0	100
4	-silence -noise -raw -aggr -cheb	23	9	71.88	32	0	100
4	-endp -lpc -eucl	23	9	71.88	29	3	90.62
4	-low -lpc -diff	23	9	71.88	32	0	100
4	-noise -low -fft -cheb	23	9	71.88	32	0	100
4	-silence -noise -norm -lpc -cheb	23	9	71.88	31	1	96.88
4	-noise -norm -lpc -diff	23	9	71.88	32	0	100
4	-noise -low -lpc -diff	23	9	71.88	32	0	100
4	-endp -lpc -diff	23	9	71.88	31	1	96.88
4	-noise -high -lpc -mink	23	9	71.88	29	3	90.62
4	-noise -high -fft -cheb	23	9	71.88	29	3	90.62
4	-silence -low -fft -cheb	23	9	71.88	32	0	100
4	-silence -noise -high -lpc -cheb	23	9	71.88	30	2	93.75
4	-noise -norm -aggr -diff	23	9	71.88	32	0	100
4	-noise -band -lpc -cos	23	9	71.88	30	2	93.75

Table 5. Top Most Accurate Configurations for Gender Identification, 1st and 2nd Guesses, Mean Clustering (Mokhov (2008d))

Run #	Configuration	$GOOD_{1st}$	BAD_{1st}	$Precision_{1st}$,%	$GOOD_{2nd}$	BAD_{2nd}	$Precision_{2nd}$,%
1	-silence -noise -band -lpc -cos	26	6	81.25	30	2	93.75
1	-silence -noise -endp -lpc -eucl	26	6	81.25	31	1	96.88
2	-silence -band -lpc -cos	25	7	78.12	31	1	96.88
2	-silence -noise -band -aggr -cheb	25	7	78.12	32	0	100
2	-silence -band -lpc -mink	25	7	78.12	32	0	100
2	-endp -lpc -cheb	25	7	78.12	31	1	96.88
2	-silence -noise -band -fft -cheb	25	7	78.12	32	0	100
2	-noise -endp -lpc -eucl	25	7	78.12	31	1	96.88
2	-silence -noise -endp -lpc -cheb	25	7	78.12	32	0	100
2	-silence -noise -band -aggr -diff	25	7	78.12	32	0	100
2	-silence -noise -bandstop -aggr -cheb	25	7	78.12	32	0	100
2	-silence -noise -bandstop -fft -cheb	25	7	78.12	32	0	100
2	-silence -noise -band -fft -diff	25	7	78.12	32	0	100
2	-silence -noise -bandstop -aggr -diff	25	7	78.12	32	0	100
3	-noise -high -aggr -mink	24	8	75	31	1	96.88
3	-low -lpc -cheb	24	8	75	31	1	96.88
3	-silence -noise -bandstop -fft -diff	24	8	75	32	0	100
3	-noise -high -aggr -eucl	24	8	75	30	2	93.75
3	-noise -high -lpc -cos	24	8	75	30	2	93.75
3	-noise -norm -lpc -cheb	24	8	75	31	1	96.88
3	-noise -low -lpc -cheb	24	8	75	32	0	100
3	-noise -bandstop -aggr -eucl	24	8	75	32	0	100
3	-silence -noise -endp -lpc -cos	24	8	75	31	1	96.88
3	-silence -noise -band -lpc -diff	24	8	75	32	0	100
3	-low -lpc -mink	24	8	75	30	2	93.75
3	-low -lpc -eucl	24	8	75	30	2	93.75
3	-noise -norm -lpc -mink	24	8	75	30	2	93.75
3	-noise -low -lpc -mink	24	8	75	30	2	93.75
3	-silence -noise -band -aggr -eucl	24	8	75	32	0	100
3	-noise -norm -lpc -eucl	24	8	75	30	2	93.75
3	-noise -low -lpc -eucl	24	8	75	31	1	96.88
3	-noise -band -lpc -hamming	24	8	75	29	3	90.62
3	-noise -bandstop -fft -diff	24	8	75	32	0	100
3	-noise -endp -lpc -diff	24	8	75	32	0	100
3	-endp -lpc -eucl	24	8	75	30	2	93.75
3	-bandstop -aggr -cos	24	8	75	31	1	96.88
3	-low -lpc -diff	24	8	75	31	1	96.88
3	-silence -noise -low -aggr -eucl	24	8	75	32	0	100
3	-noise -norm -lpc -diff	24	8	75	31	1	96.88
3	-noise -low -lpc -diff	24	8	75	32	0	100
3	-endp -lpc -diff	24	8	75	30	2	93.75
3	-endp -lpc -cos	24	8	75	29	3	90.62
3	-silence -noise -band -lpc -cheb	24	8	75	32	0	100
3	-noise -endp -lpc -cos	24	8	75	31	1	96.88
3	-noise -endp -lpc -hamming	24	8	75	31	1	96.88
3	-noise -bandstop -aggr -cheb	24	8	75	32	0	100
3	-noise -bandstop -fft -cheb	24	8	75	32	0	100
3	-noise -endp -lpc -cheb	24	8	75	32	0	100
4	-noise -norm -lpc -cos	23	9	71.88	30	2	93.75
4	-silence -noise -band -lpc -eucl	23	9	71.88	32	0	100
4	-silence -noise -norm -aggr -cos	23	9	71.88	29	3	90.62
4	-silence -band -lpc -eucl	23	9	71.88	32	0	100
4	-silence -low -fft -cos	23	9	71.88	29	3	90.62
4	-noise -bandstop -fft -eucl	23	9	71.88	32	0	100
4	-silence -noise -norm -fft -cos	23	9	71.88	29	3	90.62
4	-raw -fft -eucl	23	9	71.88	32	0	100
4	-silence -noise -endp -lpc -hamming	23	9	71.88	31	1	96.88
4	-high -aggr -mink	23	9	71.88	32	0	100
4	-noise -low -aggr -diff	23	9	71.88	32	0	100
4	-low -fft -cos	23	9	71.88	29	3	90.62
4	-silence -noise -low -fft -cos	23	9	71.88	29	3	90.62
4	-silence -band -lpc -diff	23	9	71.88	31	1	96.88
4	-noise -bandstop -aggr -cos	23	9	71.88	29	3	90.62
4	-silence -noise -low -fft -diff	23	9	71.88	32	0	100
4	-bandstop -fft -eucl	23	9	71.88	32	0	100

Table 6. Top Most Accurate Configurations for Gender Identification, 1st and 2nd Guesses, Median Clustering (Mokhov (2008d))

Guess	Rank	Configuration	GOOD	BAD	Precision, %
1st	1	-wav -raw -lpc -cheb	147	54	73.13
1st	1	-wav -silence -noise -raw -lpc -cheb	147	54	73.13
1st	1	-wav -noise -raw -lpc -cheb	147	54	73.13
1st	1	-wav -norm -lpc -cheb	147	54	73.13
1st	1	-wav -silence -raw -lpc -cheb	147	54	73.13
1st	2	-wav -silence -norm -fft -cheb	129	72	64.18
1st	3	-wav -bandstop -fft -cheb	125	76	62.19
1st	3	-wav -silence -noise -norm -fft -cheb	125	76	62.19
1st	3	-wav -silence -low -fft -cheb	125	76	62.19
1st	4	-wav -silence -norm -lpc -cheb	124	77	61.69
1st	5	-wav -silence -noise -low -fft -cheb	122	79	60.70
1st	6	-wav -silence -noise -raw -lpc -cos	120	81	59.70
1st	6	-wav -noise -raw -lpc -cos	120	81	59.70
1st	6	-wav -raw -lpc -cos	120	81	59.70
1st	6	-wav -silence -raw -lpc -cos	120	81	59.70
1st	6	-wav -norm -lpc -cos	120	81	59.70
1st	7	-wav -noise -bandstop -fft -cheb	119	82	59.20
1st	7	-wav -silence -noise -bandstop -lpc -cos	119	82	59.20
1st	8	-wav -silence -noise -bandstop -lpc -cheb	118	83	58.71
1st	8	-wav -silence -norm -fft -cos	118	83	58.71
1st	8	-wav -silence -bandstop -fft -cheb	118	83	58.71
1st	9	-wav -bandstop -fft -cos	115	86	57.21
1st	10	-wav -silence -noise -bandstop -fft -cheb	112	89	55.72
1st	11	-wav -noise -raw -fft -cheb	111	90	55.22
1st	11	-wav -silence -noise -raw -fft -cheb	111	90	55.22
1st	11	-wav -silence -raw -fft -cheb	111	90	55.22
1st	11	-wav -raw -fft -cheb	111	90	55.22
1st	12	-wav -silence -noise -raw -fft -cos	110	91	54.73
1st	12	-wav -noise -raw -fft -cos	110	91	54.73
1st	12	-wav -raw -fft -cos	110	91	54.73
1st	12	-wav -silence -raw -fft -cos	110	91	54.73
1st	13	-wav -noise -bandstop -lpc -cos	109	92	54.23
1st	13	-wav -norm -fft -cos	109	92	54.23
1st	13	-wav -norm -fft -cheb	109	92	54.23
1st	14	-wav -silence -low -lpc -cheb	105	96	52.24
1st	14	-wav -silence -noise -norm -lpc -cheb	105	96	52.24
1st	15	-wav -silence -norm -lpc -cos	101	100	50.25
1st	16	-wav -silence -bandstop -fft -cos	99	102	49.25
1st	17	-wav -noise -norm -lpc -cos	96	105	47.76
1st	17	-wav -low -lpc -cos	96	105	47.76
1st	18	-wav -silence -noise -low -fft -cos	92	109	45.77
1st	19	-wav -noise -low -lpc -cos	91	110	45.27
1st	20	-wav -silence -noise -low -lpc -cheb	87	114	43.28
1st	20	-wav -silence -low -fft -cos	87	114	43.28
1st	20	-wav -silence -noise -norm -fft -cos	87	114	43.28
1st	21	-wav -noise -low -fft -cheb	86	115	42.79
1st	22	-wav -silence -low -lpc -cos	85	116	42.29
1st	22	-wav -silence -noise -norm -lpc -cos	85	116	42.29
1st	23	-wav -noise -low -fft -cos	84	117	41.79
1st	23	-wav -low -lpc -cheb	84	117	41.79
1st	23	-wav -noise -norm -lpc -cheb	84	117	41.79
1st	24	-wav -noise -low -lpc -cheb	82	119	40.80
1st	25	-wav -noise -norm -fft -cos	81	120	40.30
1st	25	-wav -low -fft -cos	81	120	40.30
1st	26	-wav -low -fft -cheb	80	121	39.80
1st	26	-wav -noise -norm -fft -cheb	80	121	39.80
1st	26	-wav -noise -bandstop -lpc -cheb	80	121	39.80
1st	27	-wav -silence -noise -bandstop -fft -cos	78	123	38.81
1st	28	-wav -silence -noise -low -lpc -cos	76	125	37.81
1st	29	-wav -noise -bandstop -fft -cos	75	126	37.31
1st	30	-wav -bandstop -lpc -cheb	74	127	36.82
1st	31	-wav -silence -bandstop -lpc -cheb	65	136	32.34
1st	32	-wav -bandstop -lpc -cos	63	138	31.34
1st	33	-wav -silence -bandstop -lpc -cos	54	147	26.87

Table 7. File types identification top results, bigrams (Mokhov & Debbabi (2008))

Certain results were quite encouraging for the first and second best statistics extracts in Table 7 and Table 8, as well as statistics per file type in Table 9. We also collected the worst statistics, where the use of a "raw" loader impacted negatively drastically the accuracy of the results as shown in Table 10 and Table 11; yet, some file types were robustly recognized, as shown in Table 12. This gives a clue to the researchers and investigators in which direction to follow to increase the precision and which ones not to use.

Guess	Rank	Configuration	GOOD	BAD	Precision, %
2nd	1	-wav -raw -lpc -cheb	166	35	82.59
2nd	1	-wav -silence -noise -raw -lpc -cheb	166	35	82.59
2nd	1	-wav -noise -raw -lpc -cheb	166	35	82.59
2nd	1	-wav -norm -lpc -cheb	166	35	82.59
2nd	1	-wav -silence -raw -lpc -cheb	166	35	82.59
2nd	2	-wav -silence -norm -fft -cheb	137	64	68.16
2nd	3	-wav -bandstop -fft -cheb	130	71	64.68
2nd	3	-wav -silence -noise -norm -fft -cheb	140	61	69.65
2nd	3	-wav -silence -low -fft -cheb	140	61	69.65
2nd	4	-wav -silence -norm -lpc -cheb	176	25	87.56
2nd	5	-wav -silence -noise -low -fft -cheb	142	59	70.65
2nd	6	-wav -silence -noise -raw -lpc -cos	142	59	70.65
2nd	6	-wav -noise -raw -lpc -cos	142	59	70.65
2nd	6	-wav -raw -lpc -cos	142	59	70.65
2nd	6	-wav -silence -raw -lpc -cos	142	59	70.65
2nd	6	-wav -norm -lpc -cos	142	59	70.65
2nd	7	-wav -noise -bandstop -fft -cheb	138	63	68.66
2nd	7	-wav -silence -noise -bandstop -lpc -cos	151	50	75.12
2nd	8	-wav -silence -noise -bandstop -lpc -cheb	156	45	77.61
2nd	8	-wav -silence -norm -fft -cos	147	54	73.13
2nd	8	-wav -silence -bandstop -fft -cheb	129	72	64.18
2nd	9	-wav -bandstop -fft -cos	127	74	63.18
2nd	10	-wav -silence -noise -bandstop -fft -cheb	135	66	67.16
2nd	11	-wav -noise -raw -fft -cheb	122	79	60.70
2nd	11	-wav -silence -noise -raw -fft -cheb	122	79	60.70
2nd	11	-wav -silence -raw -fft -cheb	122	79	60.70
2nd	11	-wav -raw -fft -cheb	122	79	60.70
2nd	12	-wav -silence -noise -raw -fft -cos	130	71	64.68
2nd	12	-wav -noise -raw -fft -cos	130	71	64.68
2nd	12	-wav -raw -fft -cos	130	71	64.68
2nd	12	-wav -silence -raw -fft -cos	130	71	64.68
2nd	13	-wav -noise -bandstop -lpc -cos	148	53	73.63
2nd	13	-wav -norm -fft -cos	130	71	64.68
2nd	13	-wav -norm -fft -cheb	121	80	60.20
2nd	14	-wav -silence -low -lpc -cheb	127	74	63.18
2nd	14	-wav -silence -noise -norm -lpc -cheb	127	74	63.18
2nd	15	-wav -silence -norm -lpc -cos	151	50	75.12
2nd	16	-wav -silence -bandstop -fft -cos	135	66	67.16
2nd	17	-wav -noise -norm -lpc -cos	118	83	58.71
2nd	17	-wav -low -lpc -cos	118	83	58.71
2nd	18	-wav -silence -noise -low -fft -cos	146	55	72.64
2nd	19	-wav -noise -low -lpc -cos	115	86	57.21
2nd	20	-wav -silence -noise -low -lpc -cheb	120	81	59.70
2nd	20	-wav -silence -low -fft -cos	143	58	71.14
2nd	20	-wav -silence -noise -norm -fft -cos	143	58	71.14
2nd	21	-wav -noise -low -fft -cheb	130	71	64.68
2nd	22	-wav -silence -low -lpc -cos	111	90	55.22
2nd	22	-wav -silence -noise -norm -lpc -cos	111	90	55.22
2nd	23	-wav -noise -low -fft -cos	128	73	63.68
2nd	23	-wav -low -lpc -cheb	130	71	64.68
2nd	23	-wav -noise -norm -lpc -cheb	130	71	64.68
2nd	24	-wav -noise -low -lpc -cheb	129	72	64.18
2nd	25	-wav -noise -norm -fft -cos	129	72	64.18
2nd	25	-wav -low -fft -cos	129	72	64.18
2nd	26	-wav -low -fft -cheb	115	86	57.21
2nd	26	-wav -noise -norm -fft -cheb	115	86	57.21
2nd	26	-wav -noise -bandstop -lpc -cheb	127	74	63.18
2nd	27	-wav -silence -noise -bandstop -fft -cos	125	76	62.19
2nd	28	-wav -silence -noise -low -lpc -cos	118	83	58.71
2nd	29	-wav -noise -bandstop -fft -cos	123	78	61.19
2nd	30	-wav -bandstop -lpc -cheb	111	90	55.22
2nd	31	-wav -silence -bandstop -lpc -cheb	133	68	66.17
2nd	32	-wav -bandstop -lpc -cos	123	78	61.19
2nd	33	-wav -silence -bandstop -lpc -cos	126	75	62.69

Table 8. File types identification top results, 2nd best, bigrams (Mokhov & Debbabi (2008))

In addition to the previously described options, here we also have: `-wav` that corresponds to a custom loader that translates any files into a WAV-like format. The detail that is not present in the resulting tables are the internal configuration of the loader's *n*-grams loading or raw state.

3. The results in Table 13 represent the classification of the French publications using the same spectral techniques to determine whether a particular article in the French press was published in France or Quebec. The complete description of the related experiments and results can be found in Mokhov (2010a;b).
   In addition to the previously mentioned options, we have: `-title-only` to indicate to work with article titles only instead of main body texts; `-ref` tells the system to validate against reference data supplied by the organizers rather than the training data.

Guess	Rank	File type	GOOD	BAD	Precision, %
1st	1	Mach-O filetype=10 i386	64	0	100.00
1st	2	HTML document text	64	0	100.00
1st	3	TIFF image data; big-endian	64	0	100.00
1st	4	data	64	0	100.00
1st	5	ASCII c program text; with very long lines	64	0	100.00
1st	6	Rich Text Format data; version 1; Apple Macintosh	128	0	100.00
1st	7	ASCII English text	64	0	100.00
1st	8	a /sw/bin/ocamlrun script text executable	516	60	89.58
1st	9	perl script text executable	832	192	81.25
1st	10	NeXT/Apple typedstream data; big endian; version 4; system 1000	255	65	79.69
1st	11	Macintosh Application (data)	48	16	75.00
1st	12	XML 1.0 document text	320	128	71.43
1st	13	ASCII text	242	142	63.02
1st	14	Mach-O executable i386	3651	3325	52.34
1st	15	Bourne shell script text executable	262	2298	10.23
2nd	1	Mach-O filetype=10 i386	64	0	100.00
2nd	2	HTML document text	64	0	100.00
2nd	3	TIFF image data; big-endian	64	0	100.00
2nd	4	data	64	0	100.00
2nd	5	ASCII c program text; with very long lines	64	0	100.00
2nd	6	Rich Text Format data; version 1; Apple Macintosh	128	0	100.00
2nd	7	ASCII English text	64	0	100.00
2nd	8	a /sw/bin/ocamlrun script text executable	529	47	91.84
2nd	9	perl script text executable	960	64	93.75
2nd	10	NeXT/Apple typedstream data; big endian; version 4; system 1000	281	39	87.81
2nd	11	Macintosh Application (data)	64	0	100.00
2nd	12	XML 1.0 document text	366	82	81.70
2nd	13	ASCII text	250	134	65.10
2nd	14	Mach-O executable i386	5091	1885	72.98
2nd	15	Bourne shell script text executable	528	2032	20.62

Table 9. File types identification top results, bigrams, per file type (Mokhov & Debbabi (2008))

8. Conclusion

We presented an overview of MARF, a modular and extensible pattern recognition framework for a reasonably diverse spectrum of the learning and recognition tasks. We outlined the pipeline and the data structures used in this open-source project in a practical manner. We provided some typical results one can obtain by running MARF's implementations for various learning and classification problems.

8.1 Advantages and disadvantages of the approach

The framework approach is both an advantage and a disadvantage. The advantage is obvious - a consistent and uniform environment and implementing platform for comparative studies with a plug-in architecture. However, as the number of algorithms grows it is more difficult to adjust the framework's API itself without breaking all the modules that depend on it.

The coverage of algorithms is as good as the number of them implemented in / contributed to the project. In the results mentioned in Section 7 we could have attained better precision in some cases if better algorithm implementations were available (or any bugs in exiting ones fixed).

Guess	Rank	Configuration	GOOD	BAD	Precision, %
1st	1	-wav -noise -raw -fft -cheb	9	192	4.48
1st	1	-wav -raw -lpc -cheb	9	192	4.48
1st	1	-wav -bandstop -fft -cheb	9	192	4.48
1st	1	-wav -noise -low -fft -cos	9	192	4.48
1st	1	-wav -noise -norm -fft -cos	9	192	4.48
1st	1	-wav -noise -low -fft -cheb	9	192	4.48
1st	1	-wav -silence -noise -raw -lpc -cheb	9	192	4.48
1st	1	-wav -low -fft -cos	9	192	4.48
1st	1	-wav -silence -noise -raw -fft -cos	9	192	4.48
1st	1	-wav -noise -low -lpc -cos	9	192	4.48
1st	1	-wav -silence -noise -low -lpc -cheb	9	192	4.48
1st	1	-wav -noise -bandstop -lpc -cos	9	192	4.48
1st	1	-wav -noise -norm -lpc -cos	9	192	4.48
1st	1	-wav -silence -low -fft -cos	9	192	4.48
1st	1	-wav -silence -noise -raw -fft -cheb	9	192	4.48
1st	1	-wav -silence -low -lpc -cheb	9	192	4.48
1st	1	-wav -silence -noise -norm -fft -cheb	9	192	4.48
1st	1	-wav -silence -raw -fft -cheb	9	192	4.48
1st	1	-wav -silence -noise -bandstop -lpc -cheb	9	192	4.48
1st	1	-wav -noise -raw -fft -cos	9	192	4.48
1st	1	-wav -low -lpc -cos	9	192	4.48
1st	1	-wav -silence -noise -bandstop -fft -cos	9	192	4.48
1st	1	-wav -silence -norm -fft -cheb	9	192	4.48
1st	1	-wav -silence -noise -raw -lpc -cos	9	192	4.48
1st	1	-wav -silence -norm -fft -cos	9	192	4.48
1st	1	-wav -raw -fft -cos	9	192	4.48
1st	1	-wav -silence -low -fft -cheb	9	192	4.48
1st	1	-wav -silence -noise -low -fft -cos	9	192	4.48
1st	1	-wav -silence -bandstop -lpc -cos	9	192	4.48
1st	1	-wav -bandstop -fft -cos	9	192	4.48
1st	1	-wav -noise -raw -lpc -cos	9	192	4.48
1st	1	-wav -noise -bandstop -fft -cheb	9	192	4.48
1st	1	-wav -silence -noise -bandstop -lpc -cos	9	192	4.48
1st	1	-wav -silence -raw -fft -cos	9	192	4.48
1st	1	-wav -raw -lpc -cos	9	192	4.48
1st	1	-wav -silence -norm -lpc -cos	9	192	4.48
1st	1	-wav -silence -noise -low -lpc -cos	9	192	4.48
1st	1	-wav -noise -raw -lpc -cheb	9	192	4.48
1st	1	-wav -low -lpc -cheb	9	192	4.48
1st	1	-wav -raw -fft -cheb	9	192	4.48
1st	1	-wav -silence -bandstop -lpc -cheb	9	192	4.48
1st	1	-wav -norm -lpc -cheb	9	192	4.48
1st	1	-wav -silence -raw -lpc -cos	9	192	4.48
1st	1	-wav -noise -low -lpc -cheb	9	192	4.48
1st	1	-wav -noise -norm -lpc -cheb	9	192	4.48
1st	1	-wav -norm -fft -cos	9	192	4.48
1st	1	-wav -low -fft -cheb	9	192	4.48
1st	1	-wav -silence -bandstop -fft -cheb	9	192	4.48
1st	1	-wav -norm -fft -cheb	9	192	4.48
1st	1	-wav -noise -bandstop -fft -cos	9	192	4.48
1st	1	-wav -noise -norm -fft -cheb	9	192	4.48
1st	1	-wav -silence -noise -norm -fft -cos	9	192	4.48
1st	1	-wav -silence -noise -low -fft -cheb	9	192	4.48
1st	1	-wav -silence -noise -norm -lpc -cheb	9	192	4.48
1st	1	-wav -norm -lpc -cos	9	192	4.48
1st	1	-wav -silence -raw -lpc -cheb	9	192	4.48
1st	1	-wav -silence -noise -bandstop -fft -cheb	9	192	4.48
1st	1	-wav -silence -low -lpc -cos	9	192	4.48
1st	1	-wav -silence -norm -lpc -cheb	9	192	4.48
1st	1	-wav -silence -bandstop -fft -cos	9	192	4.48
1st	1	-wav -silence -noise -norm -lpc -cos	9	192	4.48
1st	1	-wav -noise -bandstop -lpc -cheb	9	192	4.48
1st	1	-wav -bandstop -lpc -cos	9	192	4.48
1st	1	-wav -bandstop -lpc -cheb	9	192	4.48

Table 10. File types identification worst results, raw loader (Mokhov & Debbabi (2008))

8.2 Future work

The general goals of the future and ongoing research include:

- There are a lot more algorithms to implement and test for the existing tasks.
- Apply to more case studies.
- Enhance statistics reporting and details thereof (memory usage, run-time, recall, f-measure, etc.).

- Scalability studies with the General Intensional Programming System (GIPSY) project (see Mokhov & Paquet (2010); Paquet (2009); Paquet & Wu (2005); The GIPSY Research and Development Group (2002–2010); Vassev & Paquet (2008)).

Guess	Rank	Configuration	GOOD	BAD	Precision, %
2nd	1	-wav -noise -raw -fft -cheb	10	191	4.98
2nd	1	-wav -raw -lpc -cheb	10	191	4.98
2nd	1	-wav -bandstop -fft -cheb	10	191	4.98
2nd	1	-wav -noise -low -fft -cos	10	191	4.98
2nd	1	-wav -noise -norm -fft -cos	10	191	4.98
2nd	1	-wav -noise -low -fft -cheb	10	191	4.98
2nd	1	-wav -silence -noise -raw -lpc -cheb	10	191	4.98
2nd	1	-wav -low -fft -cos	10	191	4.98
2nd	1	-wav -silence -noise -raw -fft -cos	10	191	4.98
2nd	1	-wav -noise -low -lpc -cos	10	191	4.98
2nd	1	-wav -silence -noise -low -lpc -cheb	10	191	4.98
2nd	1	-wav -noise -bandstop -lpc -cos	10	191	4.98
2nd	1	-wav -noise -norm -lpc -cos	10	191	4.98
2nd	1	-wav -silence -low -fft -cos	10	191	4.98
2nd	1	-wav -silence -noise -raw -fft -cheb	10	191	4.98
2nd	1	-wav -silence -low -lpc -cheb	10	191	4.98
2nd	1	-wav -silence -noise -norm -fft -cheb	10	191	4.98
2nd	1	-wav -silence -raw -fft -cheb	10	191	4.98
2nd	1	-wav -silence -noise -bandstop -lpc -cheb	10	191	4.98
2nd	1	-wav -noise -raw -fft -cos	10	191	4.98
2nd	1	-wav -low -lpc -cos	10	191	4.98
2nd	1	-wav -silence -noise -bandstop -fft -cos	10	191	4.98
2nd	1	-wav -silence -norm -fft -cheb	10	191	4.98
2nd	1	-wav -silence -noise -raw -lpc -cos	10	191	4.98
2nd	1	-wav -silence -norm -fft -cos	10	191	4.98
2nd	1	-wav -raw -fft -cos	10	191	4.98
2nd	1	-wav -silence -low -fft -cheb	10	191	4.98
2nd	1	-wav -silence -noise -low -fft -cos	10	191	4.98
2nd	1	-wav -silence -bandstop -lpc -cos	10	191	4.98
2nd	1	-wav -bandstop -fft -cos	10	191	4.98
2nd	1	-wav -noise -raw -lpc -cos	10	191	4.98
2nd	1	-wav -noise -bandstop -fft -cheb	10	191	4.98
2nd	1	-wav -silence -noise -bandstop -lpc -cos	10	191	4.98
2nd	1	-wav -silence -raw -fft -cos	10	191	4.98
2nd	1	-wav -raw -lpc -cos	10	191	4.98
2nd	1	-wav -silence -norm -lpc -cos	10	191	4.98
2nd	1	-wav -silence -noise -low -lpc -cos	10	191	4.98
2nd	1	-wav -noise -raw -lpc -cheb	10	191	4.98
2nd	1	-wav -low -lpc -cheb	10	191	4.98
2nd	1	-wav -raw -fft -cheb	10	191	4.98
2nd	1	-wav -silence -bandstop -lpc -cheb	10	191	4.98
2nd	1	-wav -norm -lpc -cheb	10	191	4.98
2nd	1	-wav -silence -raw -lpc -cos	10	191	4.98
2nd	1	-wav -noise -low -lpc -cheb	10	191	4.98
2nd	1	-wav -noise -norm -lpc -cheb	10	191	4.98
2nd	1	-wav -norm -fft -cos	10	191	4.98
2nd	1	-wav -low -fft -cheb	10	191	4.98
2nd	1	-wav -silence -bandstop -fft -cheb	10	191	4.98
2nd	1	-wav -norm -fft -cheb	10	191	4.98
2nd	1	-wav -noise -bandstop -fft -cos	10	191	4.98
2nd	1	-wav -noise -norm -fft -cheb	10	191	4.98
2nd	1	-wav -silence -noise -norm -fft -cos	10	191	4.98
2nd	1	-wav -silence -noise -low -fft -cheb	10	191	4.98
2nd	1	-wav -silence -noise -norm -lpc -cheb	10	191	4.98
2nd	1	-wav -norm -lpc -cos	10	191	4.98
2nd	1	-wav -silence -raw -lpc -cheb	10	191	4.98
2nd	1	-wav -silence -noise -bandstop -fft -cheb	10	191	4.98
2nd	1	-wav -silence -low -lpc -cos	10	191	4.98
2nd	1	-wav -silence -norm -lpc -cheb	10	191	4.98
2nd	1	-wav -silence -bandstop -fft -cos	10	191	4.98
2nd	1	-wav -silence -noise -norm -lpc -cos	10	191	4.98
2nd	1	-wav -noise -bandstop -lpc -cheb	10	191	4.98
2nd	1	-wav -bandstop -lpc -cos	10	191	4.98
2nd	1	-wav -bandstop -lpc -cheb	10	191	4.98

Table 11. File types identification worst results, 2nd guess, raw loader (Mokhov & Debbabi (2008))

Guess	Rank	File type	GOOD	BAD	Precision, %
1st	1	a /sw/bin/ocamlrun script text executable	576	0	100.00
1st	2	Bourne shell script text executable	0	2560	0.00
1st	3	Mach-O filetype=10 i386	0	64	0.00
1st	4	HTML document text	0	64	0.00
1st	5	NeXT/Apple typedstream data; big endian; version 4; system 1000	0	320	0.00
1st	6	Mach-O executable i386	0	6976	0.00
1st	7	ASCII text	0	384	0.00
1st	8	TIFF image data; big-endian	0	64	0.00
1st	9	Macintosh Application (data)	0	64	0.00
1st	10	data	0	64	0.00
1st	11	ASCII c program text; with very long lines	0	64	0.00
1st	12	perl script text executable	0	1024	0.00
1st	13	Rich Text Format data; version 1; Apple Macintosh	0	128	0.00
1st	14	XML 1.0 document text	0	448	0.00
1st	15	ASCII English text	0	64	0.00
2nd	1	a /sw/bin/ocamlrun script text executable	576	0	100.00
2nd	2	Bourne shell script text executable	0	2560	0.00
2nd	3	Mach-O filetype=10 i386	0	64	0.00
2nd	4	HTML document text	0	64	0.00
2nd	5	NeXT/Apple typedstream data; big endian; version 4; system 1000	0	320	0.00
2nd	6	Mach-O executable i386	0	6976	0.00
2nd	7	ASCII text	0	384	0.00
2nd	8	TIFF image data; big-endian	0	64	0.00
2nd	9	Macintosh Application (data)	64	0	100.00
2nd	10	data	0	64	0.00
2nd	11	ASCII c program text; with very long lines	0	64	0.00
2nd	12	perl script text executable	0	1024	0.00
2nd	13	Rich Text Format data; version 1; Apple Macintosh	0	128	0.00
2nd	14	XML 1.0 document text	0	448	0.00
2nd	15	ASCII English text	0	64	0.00

Table 12. File types identification worst results, per file, raw loader (Mokhov & Debbabi (2008))

9. Acknowledgments

This work was funded in part by the Faculty of Engineering and Computer Science (ENCS), Concordia University, Montreal, Canada. We would like to acknowledge the original co-creators of MARF: Stephen Sinclair, Ian Clément, Dimitrios Nicolacopoulos as well as subsequent contributors of the MARF R&D Group, including Lee Wei Huynh, Jian "James" Li, Farid Rassai, and all other contributors. The author would like to also mention the people who inspired some portions of this or the related work including Drs. Leila Kosseim, Sabine Bergler, Ching Y. Suen, Lingyu Wang, Joey Paquet, Mourad Debbabi, Amr M. Youssef, Chadi M. Assi, Emil Vassev, Javad Sadri; and Michelle Khalifé.

10. References

Abdi, H. (2007). Distance, *in* N. J. Salkind (ed.), *Encyclopedia of Measurement and Statistics*, Thousand Oaks (CA): Sage.

Bernsee, S. M. (1999–2005). The DFT "à pied": Mastering the Fourier transform in one day, [online]. http://www.dspdimension.com/data/html/dftapied.html.

Cavalin, P. R., Sabourin, R. & Suen, C. Y. (2010). Dynamic selection of ensembles of classifiers using contextual information, *Multiple Classifier Systems*, LNCS 5997, pp. 145–154.

Clement, I., Mokhov, S. A., Nicolacopoulos, D., Fan, S. & the MARF Research & Development Group (2002–2010). TestLPC - Testing LPC Algorithm Implementation within MARF, Published electronically within the MARF project, http://marf.sf.net. Last viewed February 2010.

Rank #	Guess	Configuration	GOOD	BAD	Precision,%
1	1st	-title-only -ref -silence -noise -norm -aggr -eucl	1714	768	69.06
1	1st	-title-only -ref -silence -noise -norm -fft -eucl	1714	768	69.06
1	1st	-title-only -ref -low -aggr -eucl	1714	768	69.06
1	1st	-title-only -ref -noise -norm -aggr -eucl	1714	768	69.06
1	1st	-title-only -ref -silence -low -aggr -eucl	1714	768	69.06
1	1st	-title-only -ref -noise -norm -fft -eucl	1714	768	69.06
1	1st	-title-only -ref -silence -low -fft -eucl	1714	768	69.06
1	1st	-title-only -ref -low -fft -eucl	1714	768	69.06
2	1st	-title-only -ref -noise -endp -fft -eucl	1701	781	68.53
2	1st	-title-only -ref -noise -endp -aggr -eucl	1701	781	68.53
2	1st	-title-only -ref -silence -noise -endp -fft -eucl	1701	781	68.53
2	1st	-title-only -ref -silence -noise -endp -aggr -eucl	1701	781	68.53
3	1st	-title-only -ref -silence -noise -bandstop -aggr -eucl	1694	788	68.25
3	1st	-title-only -ref -silence -noise -bandstop -fft -eucl	1694	788	68.25
3	1st	-title-only -ref -noise -bandstop -aggr -eucl	1694	788	68.25
3	1st	-title-only -ref -noise -bandstop -fft -eucl	1694	788	68.25
4	1st	-title-only -ref -bandstop -aggr -cos	1691	791	68.13
4	1st	-title-only -ref -bandstop -fft -cos	1691	791	68.13
5	1st	-title-only -ref -silence -bandstop -fft -cos	1690	792	68.09
5	1st	-title-only -ref -silence -bandstop -aggr -cos	1690	792	68.09
6	1st	-title-only -ref -bandstop -fft -eucl	1688	794	68.01
6	1st	-title-only -ref -bandstop -aggr -eucl	1688	794	68.01
7	1st	-title-only -ref -silence -bandstop -fft -eucl	1686	796	67.93
7	1st	-title-only -ref -silence -bandstop -aggr -eucl	1686	796	67.93
8	1st	-title-only -ref -norm -fft -eucl	1678	804	67.61
8	1st	-title-only -ref -norm -aggr -cos	1678	804	67.61
8	1st	-title-only -ref -silence -norm -fft -cos	1678	804	67.61
8	1st	-title-only -ref -norm -aggr -eucl	1678	804	67.61
8	1st	-title-only -ref -norm -fft -cos	1678	804	67.61
8	1st	-title-only -ref -silence -norm -aggr -eucl	1678	804	67.61
8	1st	-title-only -ref -silence -norm -fft -eucl	1678	804	67.61
8	1st	-title-only -ref -silence -norm -aggr -cos	1678	804	67.61
9	1st	-title-only -ref -silence -raw -fft -eucl	1676	806	67.53
9	1st	-title-only -ref -silence -raw -aggr -eucl	1676	806	67.53
9	1st	-title-only -ref -raw -fft -eucl	1676	806	67.53
9	1st	-title-only -ref -noise -raw -fft -eucl	1676	806	67.53
9	1st	-title-only -ref -noise -raw -aggr -eucl	1676	806	67.53
9	1st	-title-only -ref -silence -noise -raw -aggr -eucl	1676	806	67.53
9	1st	-title-only -ref -silence -noise -raw -fft -eucl	1676	806	67.53
9	1st	-title-only -ref -raw -aggr -eucl	1676	806	67.53
10	1st	-title-only -ref -silence -noise -low -aggr -eucl	1670	812	67.28
10	1st	-title-only -ref -silence -noise -low -fft -eucl	1670	812	67.28
11	1st	-title-only -ref -noise -low -fft -eucl	1669	813	67.24
11	1st	-title-only -ref -noise -low -aggr -eucl	1669	813	67.24
12	1st	-title-only -ref -endp -fft -cos	1651	831	66.52
13	1st	-title-only -ref -silence -low -aggr -cheb	1631	851	65.71
13	1st	-title-only -ref -silence -low -fft -cheb	1631	851	65.71
13	1st	-title-only -ref -silence -noise -norm -aggr -cheb	1631	851	65.71
13	1st	-title-only -ref -silence -noise -norm -fft -cheb	1631	851	65.71

Table 13. Geographic location identification using article titles only on reference data (Mokhov (2010b))

Clement, I., Mokhov, S. A. & the MARF Research & Development Group (2002–2010). TestNN - Testing Artificial Neural Network in MARF, Published electronically within the MARF project, http://marf.sf.net. Last viewed February 2010.

Darwin, I. F., Gilmore, J., Collyer, G., McMahon, R., Harris, G., Zoulas, C., Lowth, C., Fischer, E. & Various Contributors (1973–2007). `file` - determine file type, BSD General Commands Manual, file(1), BSD. man file(1).

Darwin, I. F., Gilmore, J., Collyer, G., McMahon, R., Harris, G., Zoulas, C., Lowth, C., Fischer, E. & Various Contributors (1973–2008). `file` - determine file type, [online]. ftp://ftp.astron.com/pub/file/, last viewed April 2008.

Flanagan, D. (1997). *Java in a Nutshell*, second edn, O'Reily & Associates, Inc. ISBN 1-56592-262-X.

Forest, D., Grouin, C., Sylva, L. D. & DEFT (2010). Campagne DÉfi Fouille de Textes (DEFT) 2010, [online], http://www.groupes.polymtl.ca/taln2010/deft.php.

Freeman, E., Freeman, E., Sierra, K. & Bates, B. (2004). *Head First Design Patterns*, first edn, O'Reilly. http://www.oreilly.com/catalog/hfdesignpat/toc.pdf, http://www.oreilly.com/catalog/hfdesignpat/chapter/index.html.

Gamma, E., Helm, R., Johnson, R. & Vlissides, J. (1995). *Design Patterns: Elements of Reusable Object-Oriented Software*, Addison-Wesley. ISBN: 0201633612.

Garcia, E. (2006). Cosine similarity and term weight tutorial, [online]. http://www.miislita.com/information-retrieval-tutorial/cosine-similarity-tutorial.html.

Green, D. (2001–2005). Java reflection API, Sun Microsystems, Inc. http://java.sun.com/docs/books/tutorial/reflect/index.html.

Hamming, R. W. (1950). Error detecting and error correcting codes, *Bell System Technical Journal* 26(2): 147–160. See also http://en.wikipedia.org/wiki/Hamming_ distance.

Haridas, S. (2006). *Generation of 2-D digital filters with variable magnitude characteristics starting from a particular type of 2-variable continued fraction expansion*, Master's thesis, Department of Electrical and Computer Engineering, Concordia University, Montreal, Canada.

Haykin, S. (1988). *Digital Communications*, John Wiley and Sons, New York, NY, USA.

Ifeachor, E. C. & Jervis, B. W. (2002). *Speech Communications*, Prentice Hall, New Jersey, USA.

Jini Community (2007). Jini network technology, [online]. http://java.sun.com/developer/products/jini/index.jsp.

Jurafsky, D. S. & Martin, J. H. (2000). *Speech and Language Processing*, Prentice-Hall, Inc., Pearson Higher Education, Upper Saddle River, New Jersey 07458. ISBN 0-13-095069-6.

Khalifé, M. (2004). *Examining orthogonal concepts-based micro-classifiers and their correlations with noun-phrase coreference chains*, Master's thesis, Department of Computer Science and Software Engineering, Concordia University, Montreal, Canada.

Larman, C. (2006). *Applying UML and Patterns: An Introduction to Object-Oriented Analysis and Design and Iterative Development*, third edn, Pearson Education. ISBN: 0131489062.

Mahalanobis, P. C. (1936). On the generalised distance in statistics, *Proceedings of the National Institute of Science of India 12*, pp. 49–55. Online at http://en.wikipedia.org/wiki/Mahalanobis_distance.

Merx, G. G. & Norman, R. J. (2007). *Unified Software Engineering with Java*, Pearson Prentice Hall. ISBN: 978-0-13-047376-6.

Mokhov, S. A. (2006). On design and implementation of distributed modular audio recognition framework: Requirements and specification design document, [online]. Project report, http://arxiv.org/abs/0905.2459, last viewed April 2010.

Mokhov, S. A. (2007a). Introducing MARF: a modular audio recognition framework and its applications for scientific and software engineering research, *Advances in Computer and Information Sciences and Engineering*, Springer Netherlands, University of Bridgeport, U.S.A., pp. 473–478. Proceedings of CISSE/SCSS'07.

Mokhov, S. A. (2007b). MARF for PureData for MARF, *Pd Convention '07*, artengine.ca, Montreal, Quebec, Canada. http://artengine.ca/~catalogue-pd/32-Mokhov.pdf.

Mokhov, S. A. (2008–2010c). WriterIdentApp – Writer Identification Application, Unpublished.

Mokhov, S. A. (2008a). Choosing best algorithm combinations for speech processing tasks in machine learning using MARF, *in* S. Bergler (ed.), *Proceedings of the 21st Canadian AI'08*, Springer-Verlag, Berlin Heidelberg, Windsor, Ontario, Canada, pp. 216–221. LNAI 5032.

Mokhov, S. A. (2008b). Encoding forensic multimedia evidence from MARF applications as Forensic Lucid expressions, *in* T. Sobh, K. Elleithy & A. Mahmood (eds), *Novel Algorithms and Techniques in Telecommunications and Networking, proceedings of CISSE'08*, Springer, University of Bridgeport, CT, USA, pp. 413–416. Printed in January 2010.

Mokhov, S. A. (2008c). Experimental results and statistics in the implementation of the modular audio recognition framework's API for text-independent speaker identification, *in* C. D. Zinn, H.-W. Chu, M. Savoie, J. Ferrer & A. Munitic (eds), *Proceedings of the 6th International Conference on Computing, Communications and Control Technologies (CCCT'08)*, Vol. II, IIIS, Orlando, Florida, USA, pp. 267–272.

Mokhov, S. A. (2008d). Study of best algorithm combinations for speech processing tasks in machine learning using median vs. mean clusters in MARF, *in* B. C. Desai (ed.), *Proceedings of C3S2E'08*, ACM, Montreal, Quebec, Canada, pp. 29–43. ISBN 978-1-60558-101-9.

Mokhov, S. A. (2008e). Towards security hardening of scientific distributed demand-driven and pipelined computing systems, *Proceedings of the 7th International Symposium on Parallel and Distributed Computing (ISPDC'08)*, IEEE Computer Society, pp. 375–382.

Mokhov, S. A. (2008f). Towards syntax and semantics of hierarchical contexts in multimedia processing applications using MARFL, *Proceedings of the 32nd Annual IEEE International Computer Software and Applications Conference (COMPSAC)*, IEEE Computer Society, Turku, Finland, pp. 1288–1294.

Mokhov, S. A. (2010a). Complete complimentary results report of the MARF's NLP approach to the DEFT 2010 competition, [online]. http://arxiv.org/abs/1006.3787.

Mokhov, S. A. (2010b). L'approche MARF à DEFT 2010: A MARF approach to DEFT 2010, *Proceedings of TALN'10*. To appear in DEFT 2010 System competition at TALN 2010.

Mokhov, S. A. & Debbabi, M. (2008). File type analysis using signal processing techniques and machine learning vs. `file` unix utility for forensic analysis, *in* O. Goebel, S. Frings, D. Guenther, J. Nedon & D. Schadt (eds), *Proceedings of the IT Incident Management and IT Forensics (IMF'08)*, GI, Mannheim, Germany, pp. 73–85. LNI140.

Mokhov, S. A., Fan, S. & the MARF Research & Development Group (2002–2010b). TestFilters – Testing Filters Framework of MARF, Published electronically within the MARF project, http://marf.sf.net. Last viewed February 2010.

Mokhov, S. A., Fan, S. & the MARF Research & Development Group (2005–2010a). MathTestApp – Testing Normal and Complex Linear Algebra in MARF, Published electronically within the MARF project, http://marf.sf.net. Last viewed February 2010.

Mokhov, S. A., Huynh, L.W. & Li, J. (2007). Managing distributed MARF with SNMP, Concordia Institute for Information Systems Engineering, Concordia University, Montreal, Canada. Project Report. Hosted at http://marf.sf.net, last viewed April 2008.

Mokhov, S. A., Huynh, L.W. & Li, J. (2008). Managing distributed MARF's nodes with SNMP, *Proceedings of PDPTA'2008*, Vol. II, CSREA Press, Las Vegas, USA, pp. 948–954.

Mokhov, S. A., Huynh, L.W., Li, J. & Rassai, F. (2007). A Java Data Security Framework (JDSF) for MARF and HSQLDB, Concordia Institute for Information Systems Engineering, Concordia University, Montreal, Canada. Project report. Hosted at http://marf.sf.net, last viewed April 2008.

Mokhov, S. A. & Jayakumar, R. (2008). Distributed modular audio recognition framework (DMARF) and its applications over web services, *in* T. Sobh, K. Elleithy & A. Mahmood (eds), *Proceedings of TeNe'08*, Springer, University of Bridgeport, CT, USA, pp. 417–422. Printed in January 2010.

Mokhov, S. A., Miladinova, M., Ormandjieva, O., Fang, F. & Amirghahari, A. (2008–2010). Application of reverse requirements engineering to open-source, student, and legacy software systems. Unpublished.

Mokhov, S. A. & Paquet, J. (2010). Using the General Intensional Programming System (GIPSY) for evaluation of higher-order intensional logic (HOIL) expressions, *Proceedings of SERA 2010*, IEEE Computer Society, pp. 101–109. Online at http://arxiv.org/abs/0906.3911.

Mokhov, S. A., Sinclair, S., Clement, I., Nicolacopoulos, D. & the MARF Research & Development Group (2002–2010). SpeakerIdentApp - Text-Independent Speaker Identification Application, Published electronically within the MARF project, http://marf.sf.net. Last viewed February 2010.

Mokhov, S. A., Song, M. & Suen, C. Y. (2009). Writer identification using inexpensive signal processing techniques, *in* T. Sobh&K. Elleithy (eds), *Innovations in Computing Sciences and Software Engineering; Proceedings of CISSE'09*, Springer, pp. 437–441. ISBN: 978- 90-481-9111-6, online at: http://arxiv.org/abs/0912.5502.

Mokhov, S. A. & the MARF Research & Development Group (2003–2010a). LangIdentApp – Language Identification Application, Published electronically within the MARF project, http://marf.sf.net. Last viewed February 2010.

Mokhov, S. A. & the MARF Research & Development Group (2003–2010b). Probabilistic-ParsingApp - Probabilistic NLP Parsing Application, Published electronically within the MARF project, http://marf.sf.net. Last viewed February 2010.

Mokhov, S. A. & Vassev, E. (2009a). Autonomic specification of self-protection for Distributed MARF with ASSL, *Proceedings of C3S2E'09*, ACM, New York, NY, USA, pp. 175–183.

Mokhov, S. A. & Vassev, E. (2009b). Leveraging MARF for the simulation of the securing maritime borders intelligent systems challenge, *Proceedings of the Huntsville Simulation Conference (HSC'09)*, SCS. To appear.

Mokhov, S. A. & Vassev, E. (2009c). Self-forensics through case studies of small to medium software systems, *Proceedings of IMF'09*, IEEE Computer Society, pp. 128–141.

Mokhov, S. A., Clement, I., Sinclair, S. & Nicolacopoulos, D. (2002–2003). Modular Audio Recognition Framework, Department of Computer Science and Software Engineering, Concordia University, Montreal, Canada. Project report, http://marf.sf.net, last viewed April 2010.

O'Shaughnessy, D. (2000). *Speech Communications*, IEEE, New Jersey, USA.

Paquet, J. (2009). Distributed eductive execution of hybrid intensional programs, *Proceedings of the 33rd Annual IEEE International Computer Software and Applications Conference (COMPSAC'09)*, IEEE Computer Society, Seattle, Washington, USA, pp. 218–224.

Paquet, J. & Wu, A. H. (2005). GIPSY – a platform for the investigation on intensional programming languages, *Proceedings of the 2005 International Conference on Programming Languages and Compilers (PLC 2005)*, CSREA Press, pp. 8–14.

Press, W. H. (1993). *Numerical Recipes in C*, second edn, Cambridge University Press, Cambridge, UK.

Puckette, M. & PD Community (2007–2010). Pure Data, [online]. http://puredata.org.

Russell, S. J. & Norvig, P. (eds) (1995). *Artificial Intelligence: A Modern Approach*, Prentice Hall, New Jersey, USA. ISBN 0-13-103805-2.

Sinclair, S., Mokhov, S. A., Nicolacopoulos, D., Fan, S. & the MARF Research & Development Group (2002–2010). TestFFT – Testing FFT Algorithm Implementation within MARF, Published electronically within the MARF project, http://marf.sf.net. Last viewed February 2010.

Sun Microsystems, Inc. (1994–2009). The Java website, Sun Microsystems, Inc. http://java.sun.com, viewed in April 2009.

Sun Microsystems, Inc. (2004). Java IDL, Sun Microsystems, Inc. http://java.sun.com/j2se/1.5.0/docs/guide/idl/index.html.

Sun Microsystems, Inc. (2006). The java web services tutorial (for Java Web Services Developer's Pack, v2.0), Sun Microsystems, Inc. http://java.sun.com/webservices/docs/2.0/tutorial/doc/index.html.

The GIPSY Research and Development Group (2002–2010). The General Intensional Programming System (GIPSY) project, Department of Computer Science and Software Engineering, Concordia University, Montreal, Canada. http://newton.cs.concordia.ca/~gipsy/, last viewed February 2010.

The MARF Research and Development Group (2002–2010). The Modular Audio Recognition Framework and its Applications, [online]. http://marf.sf.net and http://arxiv.org/abs/0905.1235, last viewed April 2010.

The Sphinx Group at Carnegie Mellon (2007–2010). The CMU Sphinx group open source speech recognition engines, [online]. http://cmusphinx.sourceforge.net.

Vaillant, P., Nock, R. & Henry, C. (2006). Analyse spectrale des textes: détection automatique des frontières de langue et de discours, *Verbum ex machina: Actes de la 13eme conference annuelle sur le Traitement Automatique des Langues Naturelles (TALN 2006)*, pp. 619–629. Online at http://arxiv.org/abs/0810.1212.

Vassev, E. & Mokhov, S. A. (2009). Self-optimization property in autonomic specification of Distributed MARF with ASSL, *in* B. Shishkov, J. Cordeiro & A. Ranchordas (eds), *Proceedings of ICSOFT'09*, Vol. 1, INSTICC Press, Sofia, Bulgaria, pp. 331–335.

Vassev, E. & Mokhov, S. A. (2010). Towards autonomic specification of Distributed MARF with ASSL: Self-healing, *Proceedings of SERA 2010*, Vol. 296 of *SCI*, Springer, pp. 1–15.

Vassev, E. & Paquet, J. (2008). Towards autonomic GIPSY, *Proceedings of the Fifth IEEE Workshop on Engineering of Autonomic and Autonomous Systems (EASE 2008)*, IEEE Computer Society, pp. 25–34.

Wollrath, A. & Waldo, J. (1995–2005). Java RMI tutorial, Sun Microsystems, Inc. http://java.sun.com/docs/books/tutorial/rmi/index.html.

Zipf, G. K. (1935). *The Psychobiology of Language*, Houghton-Mifflin, New York, NY. See also http://en.wikipedia.org/wiki/Zipf%27s_law.

Zwicker, E. & Fastl, H. (1990). *Psychoacoustics facts and models*, Springer-Verlag, Berlin.

3

Robot Learning of Domain Specific Knowledge from Natural Language Sources

Ines Čeh, Sandi Pohorec, Marjan Mernik and Milan Zorman
University of Maribor
Slovenia

1. Introduction

The belief that problem solving systems would require only processing power was proven false. Actually almost the opposite is true: for even the smallest problems vast amounts of knowledge are necessary. So the key to systems that would aid humans or even replace them in some areas is knowledge. Humans use texts written in natural language as one of the primary knowledge sources. Natural language is by definition ambiguous and therefore less appropriate for machine learning. For machine processing and use the knowledge must be in a formal; machine readable format. Research in recent years has focused on knowledge acquisition and formalization from natural language sources (documents, web pages). The process requires several research areas in order to function and is highly complex. The necessary steps usually are: natural language processing (transformation to plain text, syntactic and semantic analysis), knowledge extraction, knowledge formalization and knowledge representation. The same is valid for learning of domain specific knowledge although the very first activity is the domain definition.

These are the areas that this chapter focuses on; the approaches, methodologies and techniques for learning from natural language sources. Since this topic covers multiple research areas and every area is extensive, we have chosen to segment this chapter into five content segments (excluding introduction, conclusion and references). In the second segment we will define the term *domain* and provide the reader with an overview of domain engineering (domain analysis, domain design and domain implementation). The third segment will present natural language processing. In this segment we provide the user with several levels of natural language analysis and show the process of knowledge acquirement from natural language (NL). Sub segment 3.1 is about theoretical background on syntactic analysis and representational structures. Sub segment 3.2 provides a short summary of semantic analysis as well as current sources for semantic analysis (WordNet, FrameNet). The fourth segment elaborates on knowledge extraction. We define important terms such as *data, information* and *knowledge* and discuss on approaches for knowledge acquisition and representation. Segment five is a practical real world (although on a very small scale) scenario on learning from natural language. In this scenario we limit ourselves on a small segment of *health/nutrition* domain as we acquire, process and formalize knowledge on chocolate consumption. Segment six is the conclusion and segment seven provides the references.

2. Domain engineering

Domain engineering (Czarnecki & Eisenecker, 2000) is the process of collecting, organizing and storing the experiences in domain specific system (parts of systems) development. The intent is to build reusable products or tools for the implementation of new systems within the domain. With the reusable products, new systems can be built both in shorter time and with less expense. The products of domain engineering, such as reusable components, domain specific languages (DSL) (Mernik et al., 2005), (Kosar et al., 2008) and application generators, are used in the application engineering (AE). AE is the process of building a particular domain system in which all the reusable products are used. The link between domain and application engineering, which often run in parallel, is shown on Fig. 1. The individual phases are completed in the order that domain engineering takes precedence in every phase. The outcome of every phase of domain engineering is transferred both to the next step of domain engineering and to the appropriate application engineering phase.

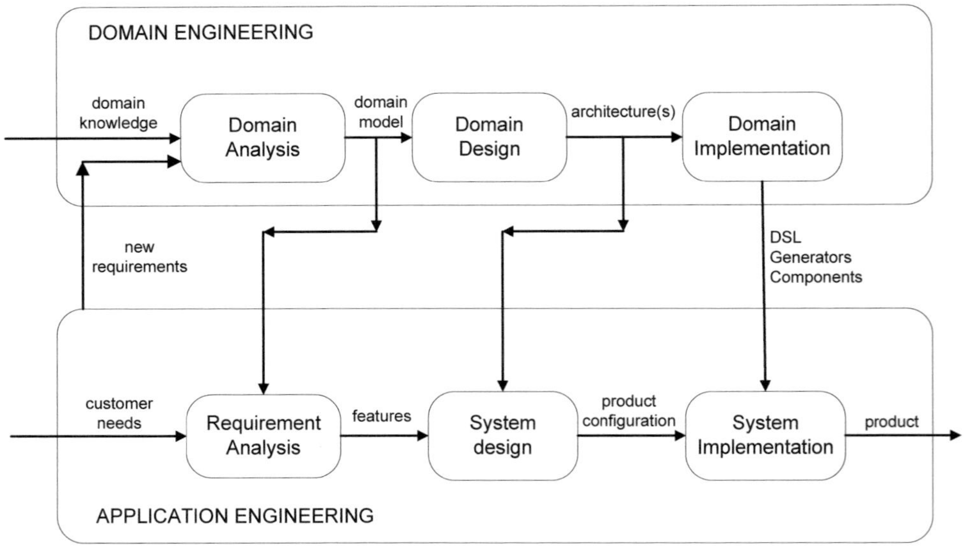

Fig. 1. Software development with domain engineering

The difference between conventional software engineering and domain engineering is quite clear; conventional software engineering focuses on the fulfilment of demands for a particular system while domain engineering develops solutions for the entire family of systems (Czarnecki & Eisenecker, 2000). Conventional software engineering is comprised of the following steps: requirements analysis, system design and the system implementation. Domain engineering steps are: domain analysis, domain design and domain implementation. The individual phases correspond with each other, requirement analysis with domain analysis, system design with domain design and system implementation with domain implementation. On one hand requirement analysis provides requirements for one system, while on the other domain analysis forms reusable configurable requirements for an entire family of systems. System design results in the design of one system while domain design results in a reusable design for a particular class of systems and a production plan. System implementation performs a single system implementation; domain implementation implements reusable components, infrastructure and the production process.

2.1 Concepts of domain engineering

This section will provide a summary of the basic concepts in domain engineering, as summarized by (Czarnecki & Eisenecker, 2000), which are: *domain, domain scope, relationships between domains, problem space, solution space* and *specialized methods* of domain engineering. In the literature one finds many definitions of the term *domain*. Czarnecki & Eisenecker defined *domain* as a knowledge area which is scoped to maximize the satisfaction of the requirements of its stakeholders, which includes a set of concepts and a terminology familiar to the stakeholders in the area and which includes the knowledge to build software system (or parts of systems) in the area.

According to the application systems in the domain two separate domain scope types are defined: horizontal (systems category) and a vertical (per system) scope. The former refers to the question how many different systems exist in the domain; the latter refers to the question which parts of these systems are within the domain. The vertical scope is increased according to the sizes of system parts within the domain. The vertical scope determines *vertical* versus *horizontal* and *encapsulated* versus *diffused* paradigms of domains. This is shown on Fig. 2, where each rectangle represents a system and the shaded areas are the system parts within the domain. While vertical domains contain entire systems, the horizontal ones contain only the system parts in the domain scope. Encapsulated domains are horizontal domains, where system parts are well localized with regard to their systems. Diffused domains are also horizontal domains but contain numerous different parts of each system in the domain scope. The scope of the domain is determined in the process of domain scoping. Domain scoping is a subprocess of domain analysis.

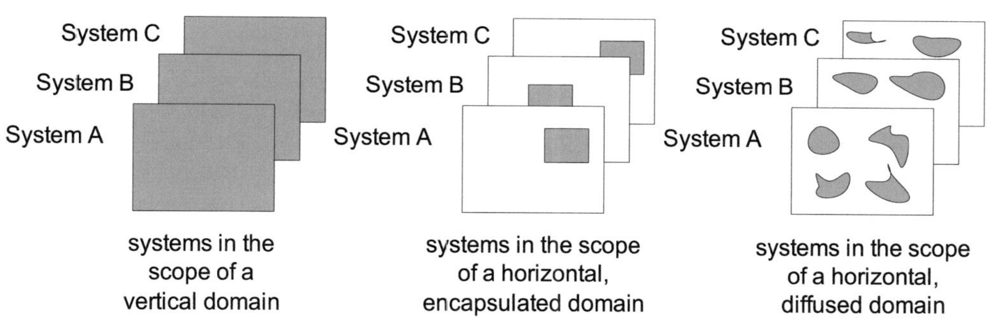

Fig. 2. Vertical, horizontal, encapsulated and diffused domains

Relationships between domains *A* and *B* are of three major types:

- *A* is contained in *B*: All knowledge in domain *A* is also in the domain *B*. We say that *A* is a subdomain of domain *B*.
- *A* uses *B*: Knowledge in domain *A* addresses knowledge in domain *B* in a typical way. For instance it is sensible to represent aspects of domain *A* with terms from the domain *B*. We say that domain *B* is a support domain of domain *A*.
- *A* is analogous to *B*: There are many similarities between *A* and *B*; there is no necessity to express the terms from one domain with the terms from the other. We say that domain *A* is analogous to domain *B*.

A set of valid system specifications in the domain is referred to as the problem space while a set of concrete systems is the solution space. System specifications in the problem space are expressed with the use of numerous DSL, which define domain concepts. The common structure of the solution space is called the target architecture. Its purpose is the definition of a tool for integration of implementation components. One of the domain engineering goals is the production of components, generators and production processes, which automate the mapping between system specifications and concrete systems. Different system types (real-time support, distribution, high availability, tolerance deficiency) demand different (specialized) modelling techniques. This naturally follows in the fact that different domain categories demand different specialized methods of domain engineering.

2.2 Domain engineering process

The domain engineering process is comprised of three phases (Czarnecki & Eisenecker, 2000), (Harsu, 2002): *domain analysis, domain design* and *domain implementation.*

Domain analysis

Domain analysis is the activity that, with the use of the properties model, discovers and formalizes common and variable domain properties. The goal of domain analysis is the selection and definition of the domain and the gathering and integration of appropriate domain information to a coherent domain (Czarnecki & Eisenecker, 2000). The result of domain analysis is an explicit representation of knowledge on the domain; the domain model. The use of domain analysis provides the development of configurable requirements and architectures instead of static requirements which result from application engineering (Kang et al., 2004).

Domain analysis includes domain planning (planning of the sources for domain analysis), identification, scoping and domain modelling. These activities are summarized in greater detail in Table 1.

Domain information sources are: existing systems in the domain, user manuals, domain experts, system manuals, textbooks, prototypes, experiments, already defined systems requirements, standards, market studies and others. Regardless of these sources, the process of domain analysis is not solely concerned with acquisition of existing information. A systematic organization of existing knowledge enables and enhances information spreading in a creative manner.

Domain model is an explicit representation of common and variable systems properties in the domain and the dependencies between variable properties (Czarnecki & Eisenecker, 2000). The domain model is comprised (Czarnecki & Eisenecker, 2000) of the following activities:

- *Domain definition* defines domain scope and characterizes its content with examples from existing systems in the domain as well as provides the generic rules about the inclusion or exclusion of generic properties.
- *Domain lexicon* is a domain dictionary that contains definitions of terms related to the domain. Its purpose is to enhance the communication process between developers and impartial persons by simplifying it and making it more precise.
- *Concept models* describe concepts in the domain in an appropriate modelling formalism.
- *Feature models* define a set of reusable and configurable requirements for domain systems specifications. The requirements are called features. The feature model prescribes which property combinations are appropriate for a given domain. It represents the configurability aspect of reusable software systems.

The domain model is intended to serve as a unified source of references in the case of ambiguity, at the problem analysis phase or later during implementation of reusable components, as a data store of distributed knowledge for communication and learning and as a specification for developers of reusable components (Falbo et al., 2002).

Domain Analysis major process components	Domain analysis activities
Domain characterization (domain planning and scoping)	*Select domain* Perform business analysis and risk analysis in order to determine which domain meets the business objectives of the organization.
	Domain description Define the boundary and the contents of the domain.
	Data source identification Identify the sources of domain knowledge.
	Inventory preparation Create inventory of data sources.
Data collection (domain modelling)	*Abstract recovery* Recover abstraction
	Knowledge elicitation Elicit knowledge from experts
	Literature review
	Analysis of context and scenarios
Data analysis (domain modelling)	*Identification of entities, operations, and relationships*
	Modularization Use some appropriate modelling technique, e.g. object-oriented analysis or function and data decomposition. Identify design decisions.
	Analysis of similarity Analyze similarities between entities, activities, events, relationship, structures, etc.
	Analysis of variations Analyze variations between entities, activities, events, relationship, structures, etc.
	Analysis of combinations Analyze combinations suggesting typical structural or behavioural patterns.
	Trade-off analysis Analyze trade-offs that suggest possible decompositions of modules and architectures to satisfy incompatible sets of requirements found in the domain.
Taxonomic classification (domain modelling)	*Clustering* Cluster descriptions.
	Abstraction Abstract descriptions.
	Classification Classify description.
	Generalization Generalize descriptions.
	Vocabulary construction
Evaluation	*Evaluate the domain model.*

Table 1. Common Domain Analysis process by Arango (Arango, 1994)

Domain analysis can incorporate different methodologies. These differentiate by the degree of formality in the method, products or information extraction techniques. Most known methodologies are: Domain Analysis and Reuse Environment - DARE (Frakes et al., 1998), Domain-Specific Software Architecture – DSSA (Taylor et al., 1995), Family-Oriented Abstractions, Specification, and Translation - FAST (Weiss & Lai, 1999), Feature Reuse-Driven Software Engineering Business - FeatureRSEB (Griss et al., 1998), Feature-Oriented Domain Analysis - FODA (Kang et al., 1990), Feature-Oriented Reuse Method – FORM (Kang et al., 2004), Ontology-Based Domain Engineering - ODE (Falbo et al., 2002) and Organization Domain Modelling - ODM (Simons & Anthony, 1998).

FODA has proved to be the most appropriate (Alana & Rodriguez, 2007) and we will shortly examine it in the following. FODA is a method of domain analysis that was developed by the Software Engineering Institute (SEI). It is known for its models and feature modelling.

FODA process is comprised of two phases: context analysis and domain modelling. The goal of context analysis is to determine the boundaries (scope) of the analyzed domain and the goal of domain modelling is to develop a domain model (Czarnecki & Eisenecker, 2000). FODA domain modelling phase in comprised of the following steps (Czarnecki & Eisenecker, 2000):

- *Information analysis* with the main goal of retrieving domain knowledge in the form of domain entities and links between them. Modelling techniques used in this phase can be in the form of semantic networks, entity-relationship modelling or object oriented modelling. The result of information analysis is an information model that matches the conceptual model.
- *Features analysis* covers application capabilities in the domain as viewed by the project contractor and the final user. Common and variable features that apply to the family of systems are simply called features. They are contained in the features model.
- *Operational analysis* results in the operational model. It shows how the application works and covers the relations between objects in the informational model and the features in the feature model.

An important product from this phase is the domain dictionary that defines the terminology used in the domain (along with the definitions of domain concepts and properties). As we mentioned FODA methodology is known by its feature modelling. Properties can be defined as the system characteristics visible to the end user (Harsu, 2002).They are categorized into: mandatory, alternative and optional. They are visualized on a feature diagram, which is a key element of the domain model. The feature concept is further explained and presented in (Czarnecki & Eisenecker, 2000).

Domain design

Domain design takes the domain model built in the process of domain analysis and tries to create a general architecture that all the domain elements are compliant with (Czarnecki & Eisenecker, 2000). Domain design focuses on the domain space for solution planning (solution space). It takes the configuration requirements, developed in the domain analysis phase and produces a standardized solution for a family of systems that is configurable. Domain design tries to create architectural patterns that try to solve common problem for the family of systems in the domain, despite different configuration requirements (Czarnecki & Eisenecker, 2000). Beside the pattern development the engineers have to carefully determine the scope of individual pattern and the level of context at which the pattern applies. Scope limitation is crucial: too much context is reflected in a pattern that is not acceptable to many systems, too little context on the other hand is reflected in a pattern that lacks capability to an extent that it is not usable. A usable pattern has to be applicable to many systems and of high quality (Buschmann et al., 2007).

Domain implementation

Domain implementation covers the implementation of the architecture, components and tools designed in the phase of domain design.

3. Natural language processing

The term natural language is used to describe human languages (English, German, Chinese, ...). Processing these languages includes both written and spoken language (text and speech). In general the term refers to processing written language since the speech processing has evolved into a separate field of research. According to the term this segment will focus on the written language. To implement a program to acquire knowledge from natural language requires that we transform the language to a formal language (format) that is machine readable. In order to perform such a task it is vital that we are able to understand the natural language. Major problems with language understanding are that a large amount of knowledge is required to understand the meaning of complex passages. Because of this the first programs to understand natural language were limited to a minute environment. One of the earliest was Terry Winograd's SHRDLU (Winograd, 1972) which was able to formulate conversations about a blocks world. In order to work on a larger scale where a practical application is possible language analysis is required. Generally speaking there are several levels of natural language analysis (Luger, 2005):

- *Prosody* analyses rhythm and intonation. Difficult to formalize, important for poetry, religious chants, children wordplay and babbling of infants.
- *Phonology* examines sounds that are combined to form language. Important for speech recognition and generation.
- *Morphology* examines word components (morphemes) including rules for word formation (for example: prefixes and suffixes which modify word meaning). Morphology determines the role of a word in a sentence by its tense, number and part-of-speech (POS).
- *Syntax* analysis studies the rules that are required for the forming of valid sentences.
- *Semantics* studies the meaning of words and sentences and the means of conveying the meaning.
- *Pragmatics* studies ways of language use and its effects on the listeners.

When considering means to acquire knowledge from natural language sources the analysis is a three step process: syntactic analysis, meaning analysis (semantic interpretation; generally in two phases) and the forming of the final structure that represents the meaning of the text. The process is shown on Fig. 3. In the next sections (3.1 and 3.2) we will provide an overview of the syntactic and semantic analysis while the practical overview with resources and approaches specific to the learning of domain specific knowledge will be discussed in the following sections.

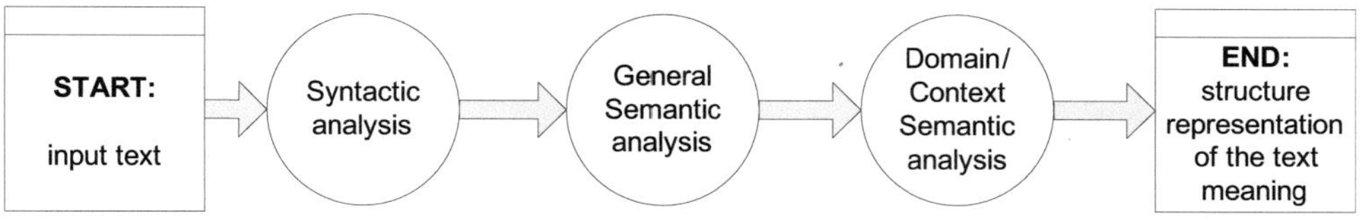

Fig. 3. Natural language analysis process

3.1 Theoretical overview of the syntactic analysis and representational structures

The goal of syntactic analysis is to produce the *parse tree*. The parse tree is a breakdown of natural language (mostly on the level of sentences) to their syntactic structure. It identifies the linguistic relations. Syntactic analysis can be achieved with context-free or context sensitive grammars. The theoretical background for context-free grammars was outlined by Partee et al., 1993. An example of a system built on context-free grammars is presented in Alshawi, 1992. Perhaps the simplest implementation of a context-free grammar is the use of production (rewrite) rules with a series of rules with terminals (words from natural language) and non terminals (linguistic concepts: noun phrase, verb, sentence...). An example of the parse three with the rewrite rules is shown on Fig. 4.

An alternative approach is in the form of transition network parsers which although they themselves are not sufficient for natural language they do form the basis for augmented transition networks (Woods, 1970).

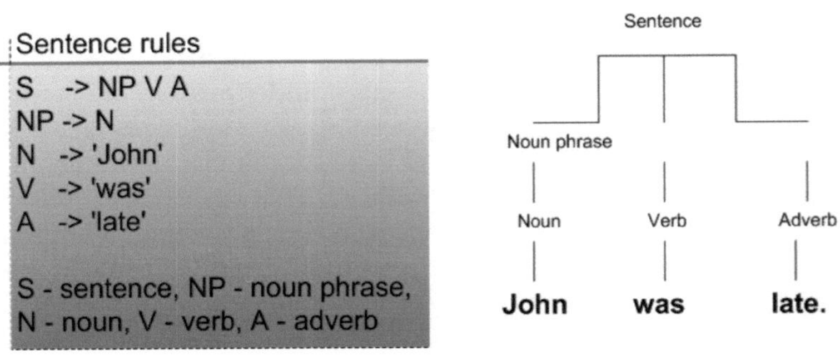

Fig. 4. Small set of rewrite rules and the result of syntax analysis, a parse tree

The shortcoming of context-free grammars is evident in the name itself; they lack the context that is necessary for proper sentence analysis. Although they can be extended to take context into consideration a more native approach to the problems seems to be the use of grammars that are natively context aware. The main difference between the context-free (CF) and context-sensitive (CS) grammars is that the CS grammars allow more than one symbol on the left side of a rule and enable the definition of a context in which that rule can be applied. CS grammars are on a higher level on the Chomsky grammar hierarchy (Chomsky, 1956) presented on Fig. 5 than CF grammars and they are able to represent some language structures that the CF grammars are unable but they do have several significant shortcomings (Luger, 2005):

- they dramatically increase the number of rules and non-terminals,
- they obscure the phrase structure of the language,
- the more complicated semantic consistency checks lose the separation of syntactic and semantic components of the language and
- they do not address the problem of building a semantic representation of the text meaning.

It appears that despite their native context awareness CS grammars have proven to be too complicated and they are usable only for the validation of sentence structure. For the purpose of acquiring knowledge from natural language sources they are not usable at all since they do not address the building of a semantic representation of the text meaning.

Various researchers have focused on enhancing context-free grammars. A new class of grammars emerged; the augmented context-free (ACF) grammars. The approach replaces

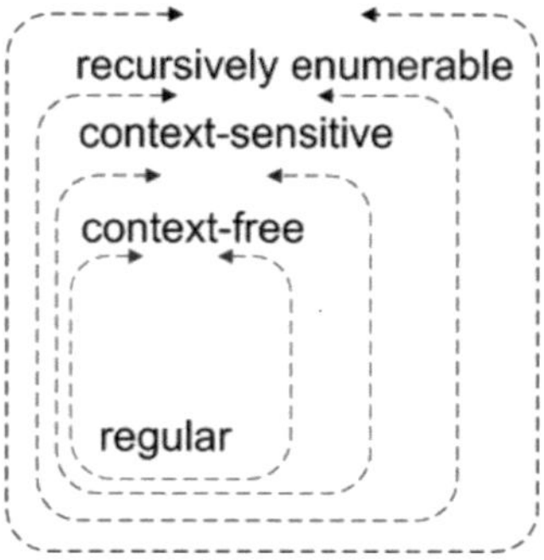

Fig. 5. Chomsky grammar hierarchy

the usage of the grammar to describe the number, tense and person. These terms become features attached to terminals and nonterminals. Most important types of ACF grammars are augmented phase structure grammars (Heidorn, 1975), augmentations of logic grammars (Allen, 1987) and augmented transition networks.

3.2 Semantic analysis

We have tried to give a broad overview of the complexity of syntactic analysis of natural language in the previous section because syntactic analysis is tightly coupled with semantic analysis. Semantic analysis tries to determine the meaning at the level of various language structures (words, sentences, passages). In other words semantic analysis is the process in which words are assigned their *sense*. Semantic analysis is a component of a large number of scientific research areas (Sheth et al., 2005): Information retrieval, Information Extraction, Computational Linguistics, Knowledge Representation, Artificial Intelligence and Data Management. Since the research areas are very different each has a very different definition of cognition, concepts and meaning (Hjorland, 1998). Sheth et al. organized the different views to three forms of semantics: *Implicit*, *Formal* and *Powerful* (Soft). Techniques based on the analysis of unstructured texts and document repositories with loosely defined and less formal structure in the fields of Information Retrieval, Information Extraction and Computational Linguistics have data sources of the *implicit* type.

Knowledge Representation, Artificial Intelligence and Data Management fields have a more formal data form. Information and knowledge is presented in the form of well defined syntactic structures (and rules by which the structures can be combined to represent the meaning of complex syntactic structures) with definite semantic interpretations associated (Sheth et al., 2005). According to the aforementioned properties these fields rely on Formal Semantics. Semantic web in the future will be annotated with knowledge from different sources so it is important that the systems would be able to deal with inconsistencies. They should also be able to increase the expressiveness of formalisms. These are the features that would require *soft* (powerful) semantics (Sheth et al.)

The datasets that contain meanings of words are called sense sets. The first sense set, "WordNet®"was created at Princeton (Miller, 1995). WordNet is a lexical database that contains nouns, verbs, adjectives and adverbs of the English language. Words are grouped into sets of cognitive synonyms (sysnets). Each sysnet expresses a concept. Interlinked sysnets form a network of related words and concepts. The network is organized in hierarchies which are defined by either a *generalization* or *specialization*. An example of a WordNet hierarchy is presented on Fig. 6.

A global repository of wordnets in languages other than English (more than fifty are available) is available on the Global WordNet Association webpage (http://www.globalwordnet.org/).
Similar project is being conducted at Berkeley University; their FrameNet (http://framenet.icsi.berkeley.edu/ is based on frame semantics. Frame semantics is a development of case grammar. Essentially to understand a word one has to know all essential knowledge that relates to that word. A semantic frame is a structure of concepts interconnected in such a way that without knowing them all one lacks knowledge of anyone in particular. A frame describes a situation or an event. Currently FrameNet contains more than 11.600 lexical units (6800 fully annotated) in more than 960 semantic frames.

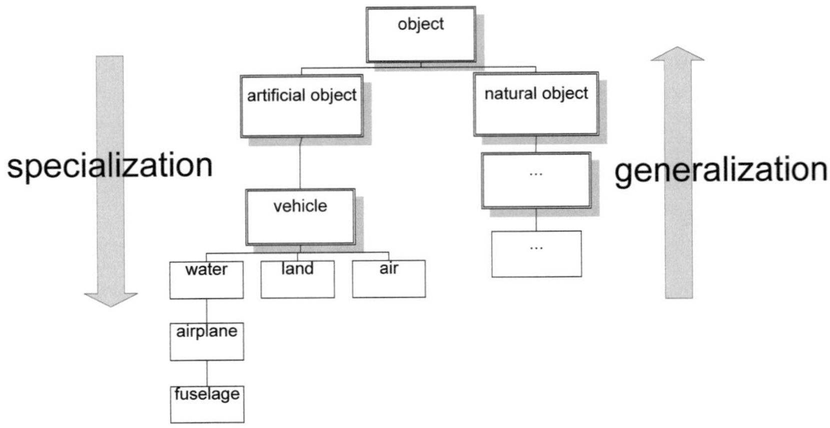

Fig. 6. Example of WordNet network of interlinked sysnets in the form of a directed acyclic graph

4. Knowledge extraction

Knowledge extraction is a long standing goal of research in the areas within artificial intelligence (Krishnamoorthy & Rajeev, 1996), (Russell & Norvig, 2003). Numerous sources, such as philosophy, psychology, linguistics, have contributed to a wealth of ideas and a solid foundation in applied science. In the early years there was a general consensus that machines will be able to solve any problem as efficiently as the world foremost experts. Scientist believed that there is the theoretical possibility of creating a machine designed for problem solving that could take on any problem with a minimum amount of information. The machine would use its enormous computing power to solve the problem. Only when the work began on building such a machine, everyone realized that the solution to problem solving lies in knowledge, not computing power. Actual machines require excessive amount of knowledge to perform even the most basic intelligent tasks. The knowledge must be in a structural form so that it can be stored and used when necessary. These machines are known as *expert systems*. Actually they are knowledge based systems (KBS) (Kendal & Creen, 2007); expert systems are just a part of knowledge based systems.
Knowledge engineers quickly realized that acquisition of quality knowledge appropriate for quality and robust systems is a time consuming activity. Consequentially knowledge acquisition was designated the bottleneck of expert system implementation. Because of this knowledge acquisition became the primary research area of knowledge engineering (Kendal

& Creen, 2007). Knowledge engineering is the process of developing knowledge systems in any field, public or private sector, sales or industry (Debenham, 1989).
In knowledge engineering it is essential that one understands these terms: *data, information* and *knowledge*. Their hierarchy is presented on Fig. 7.
Before we can begin to understand "knowledge" we must first understand the terms data and information. Literature provides many definitions of these terms (Kendal & Green, 2007), (Zins, 2007). Their meaning becomes clear only when we look for the differences between them. There exist no universal definition of *data* or *information* and no definition is applicable in all situations. Data becomes information when their creator supplements them with an added value. Different ways in which this can occur is presented in (Valente, 2004).
When we examine some of the definitions of knowledge, such as:"knowledge is the result of information understanding" (Hayes, 1992), "knowledge is information with context and value that make it usable" (Gandon, 2000), it becomes clear that knowledge is something that one has after he understands information.
So as information derives from knowledge, knowledge also derives from information. During the derivation one of the following transformations (Gandon, 2000) takes place: comparison (how can the information on this situation be compared to another familiar situation), consequences (what consequences does the information have on decisions and courses of action), connections (how this part of knowledge connects to other parts) and conversation (what is the people's opinion on this information). It should be clear that data, information and knowledge are not static by nature; they are the stages in a process of applying data and its transformation to knowledge. From the knowledge engineering standpoint it is positive to handle knowledge as something that is expressed as a rule or is usable for decision support. For instance: "IF it rains, THEN use an umbrella". The value of data increases as it is transformed into knowledge as knowledge enables the making of useful decisions. Knowledge can be regressed to information and data. Davenport and Prusak (Davenport & Prusak, 1998) called this process „de-knowledging". It occurs when there is too much knowledge and the knowledge worker can no longer grasp the sense of it.

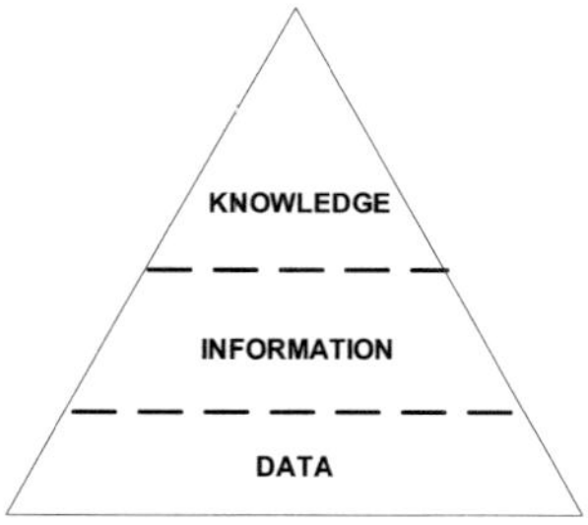

Fig. 7. Data, information and knowledge

Knowledge engineer usually works with three types of knowledge: declarative, procedural and meta-knowledge. Declarative knowledge describes the objects (facts and rules), that are in the experts systems scope, and the relations between them. Procedural knowledge provides alternative actions, which are based on the use of facts for knowledge acquirement. Meta-knowledge is knowledge about knowledge that helps us understand how experts use knowledge for their decisions.
Knowledge engineers have to be able to distinguish between these three knowledge types and to understand how to encode different knowledge types into a specific form of knowledge based systems.

Knowledge based systems (KBS) are computer programs that are intended to mimic the work of specific knowledge areas experts (Kendal & Creen 2007). They incorporate vast amounts of knowledge, rules and mechanisms in order to successfully solve problems. The main types of knowledge systems are: expert systems, neural networks, case-based reasoning, genetic algorithms, intelligent agents, data mining and intelligent tutoring systems. These types are presented in detail in (Kendal & Creen, 2007). KBS can be used on many tasks, which were once in the domain in humans. Compared to human counterparts they have some advantages as well as disadvantages. For example while human knowledge is expensive, KBS are relatively cheap. On the other side humans have a wider focus and understanding; KBS are limited to a particular problem and cannot be applied on other domains.

Since mid eighties knowledge engineers have developed several principles, methods and tools for the improvement of the knowledge acquirement process. These principles cover the use of knowledge engineering on actual world problems. Some key principles that are discussed in detail in (Shadbolt & Milton, 1999), are that different types of knowledge, experts (expertise), knowledge representation and knowledge usage exist and that structural methods should be used in order to increase efficiency.

Development of knowledge based applications is difficult for the knowledge engineers. Knowledge based projects cannot be handled with the techniques for software engineering. Life-cycle of knowledge based application and software applications are different in several aspects. With the intent to achieve impartiality in knowledge engineering the life-cycle of applications focuses on the six critical phases presented on Fig. 8.

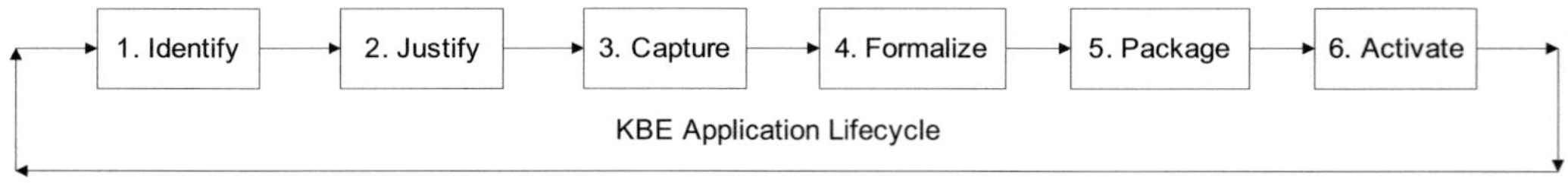

Fig. 8. Knowledge based engineering application lifecycle

According to the specifics of each principle element, numerous knowledge engineering techniques have been developed. Well known, used in many projects, techniques are: Methodology and tools Oriented to Knowledge-Based Engineering Applications - MOKA (Stokes, 2001), Structured Process Elicitation Demonstrations Environment - SPEDE (Pradorn, 2007) and Common Knowledge Acquisition and Design System - CammonKADS (Schreiber et al., 1999).

Knowledge acquisition is difficult, both for humans and machines. Phrase "knowledge acquisition" generally refers to gathering knowledge from knowledge rich sources and the appropriate classification to a knowledge base. As well as this it also refers to improving knowledge in existing knowledge bases. The process of knowledge acquisition can be manual or automatic. In the manual mode the knowledge engineer receives knowledge from one or more domain experts. In automatic mode a machine learning system is used for autonomous learning and improvement of real world knowledge.

Manual knowledge acquirement is difficult because of two reasons. First, the knowledge engineer has to maintain contact with the experts for a substantial amount of time, in some cases several years. And second because in some cases the experts cannot formally express their knowledge. These problems can be avoided with autonomous knowledge encoding with the use of machine learning. The approach is presented on Fig. 9. The database is formed with the use of experts and various reasoning/inference systems. Machine learning uses the data in the database to infer new knowledge. This newly found knowledge is then transformed into a knowledge base.

Knowledge representation is concerned with researching knowledge formalization and machine processing. Automation inference techniques enable computer system to infer conclusions from machine readable knowledge. It is the goal of knowledge representation and inference to plan computer systems, that would, similar as humans, infer on machine interpretable representations of the real world.

An overview of state of the art technologies of the semantic web and the use cases clearly show that knowledge representation is in many different formats. Most widely used representations are semantic networks, rules and logic. We continue with a short examination of these representations, a more detailed presentation can be found in (Grimm et al., 2007).

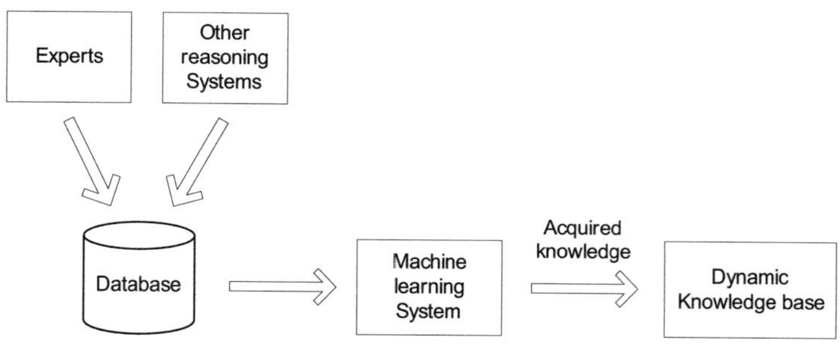

Fig. 9. Principles of automated knowledge acquisition

The term *semantic network* encompasses a family of graph-based representations which share a common set of assumptions and concerns. A visual representation is that of a graph where node connections are the relations between concepts. Nodes and connections are labelled to provide the necessary information about the concept and type of association. Fig. 10 shows an example of a semantic network for a domain of animals. The concepts are represented by ellipses and the connections are arrows. The network is a representation of this natural language passage:

„Mammals and reptiles are animals. Dogs and dolphins are mammals, snakes and crocodiles are reptiles. Snakes are reptiles without legs; crocodiles are reptiles with four legs. While dolphins live in the sea, the dogs live on land. Dogs have four legs. Labrador retriever is a medium sized dog." The nouns in this text refer to concepts; the verbs are links between them.

Newer models of a network representation language are conceptual graphs. A conceptual graph is (Luger 2005) a finite, connected, bipartite graph. The nodes in the graph are either concepts or conceptual relations. Conceptual graphs do not use labeled arcs; instead the conceptual relation nodes represent relations between concepts. Because conceptual graphs are bipartite, concepts only have arcs to relations, and vice versa. Example shown on Fig. 11 a) represents a simple proposition "Cat's color is white". A more complex graph on Fig. 11 b) represents the sentence "John bought Joan a large ice cream" indicates how conceptual graphs are used to formalize natural language.

Semantic networks are especially appropriate for the extraction of taxonomic structures or domain objects categories and for the expression of general sentences on the domain of

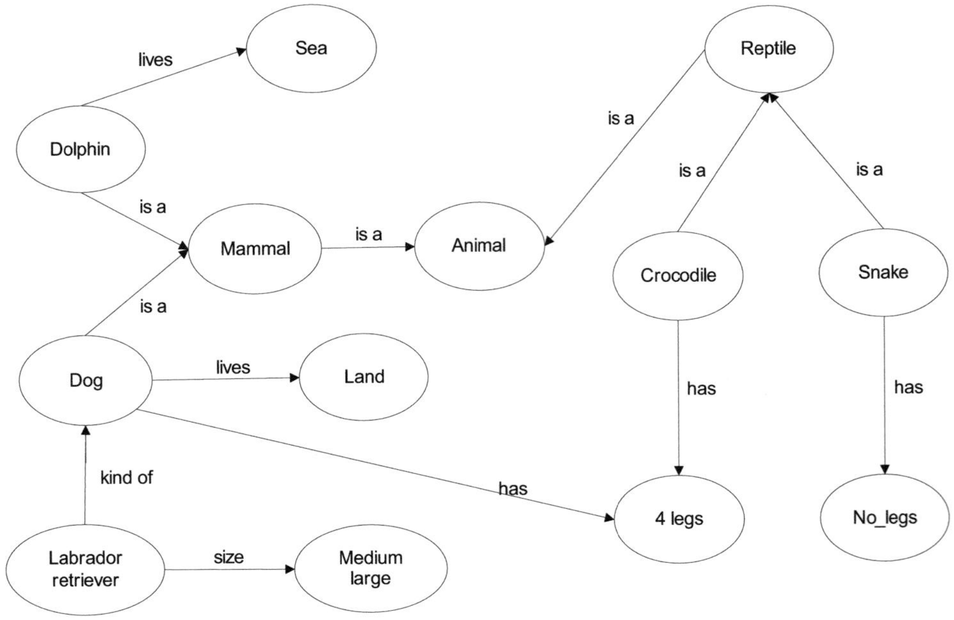

Fig. 10. Semantic net: animals

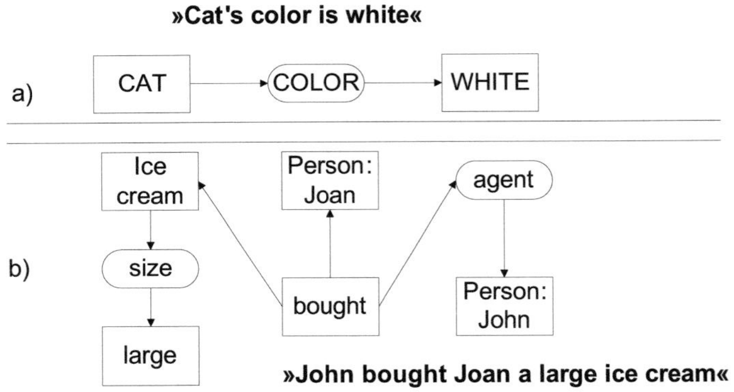

Fig. 11. Conceptual graphs of "Cat's colour is white" and "John bought Joan a large ice cream"

interest. Inheritance and other relations between these kinds of categories can be represented and inferred from the hierarchies the network naturally contains. Individual representatives or even data values like numbers or strings are not compatible with the idea of semantic networks (Grimm, 2007).

Another natural form of knowledge expression is expression with *rules* that mimic the principle of consequence. They are in the form of IF-THEN constructs and support the expression of various complex sentences.

Rules are found in logic programming systems, such as the well known programming language Prolog (Sterling & Shapiro, 1994), deductive data bases (Minker, 1987) or business rules systems (Grimm, 2007). „IF" part of the rule is the body, while the„THEN" part is the head of the rule. An example of a rule that refers to Fig. 10 is:

IF something is a Labrador retriever **THEN** it is also a dog.

Because rules in natural language are not appropriate for machine processing these kinds of phrases are formalized with the use of predicates and object variables in the domain of interest. Formalized, the example above would be written like this:

Dogs(?t) :- Labrador retriever (?t).

In most logical programming languages the rule is read as an inverse implication, which starts with the head followed by the body. It is identified with the „:-" symbol that is a synonym for the reversed arrow (Grimm, 2007).
Afore mentioned forms, semantic networks and rules, are formalized with logic that provides the exact semantics. Without that kind of precise formalization they would be ambiguous and consequently not appropriate for machine processing. The most featured and fundamental logical formalism that is typically used for knowledge representation is the first order logic (Gašević et al., 2006). First order logic provides means to describe the domain of interest as a composition of objects and the construction of logical formulas around those objects. The objects are formed with the use of predicates, functions, variables and logic connectives.
Similar to semantic networks, most natural language sentences can be expressed with terms from logic sentences about the objects in the target domain with the appropriate choice of predicates and function symbols (Grimm, 2007).
Axiomatising parts of the semantic network on Fig. 10 will be used to demonstrate the use of logic for knowledge representation. For instance, subsumption on Fig. 12 can be directly expressed with logical implication which is formulated in (1):

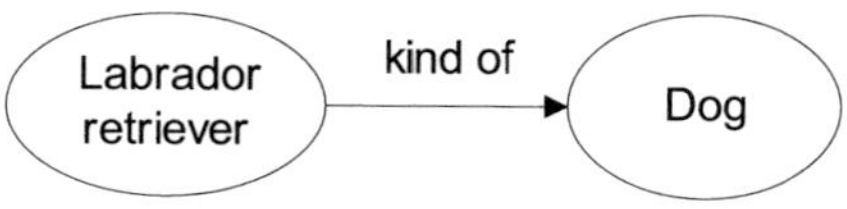

Fig. 12. Example of subsumption

$$\forall x : (Labrador\_retriever(x) \rightarrow Dogs(x)) \tag{1}$$

Logic can also be used to represent rules. IF-THEN rules can be expressed as a logical implication with universal quantity variables. For instance the basic formalization of the rule: „IF something is a Labrador retriever THEN it is also a dog" is also translated to the same logic formula (1).

5. Practical case of learning from natural language

This section will focus on a chronological sequence of learning from natural text. It will present a short example on how to use the aforementioned methodologies, approaches and techniques on a small example. We have to stress that this is only a short practical example and so the approaches chosen in it are somewhat simplified to allow for better understanding of the example. The example is not intended to be a cookbook for learning from natural language; it is merely used to present the user with a real world scenario with a chronological sequence of the steps and actions necessary for the incorporation of natural language knowledge in a formalized fashion. We will use the health/nutrition domain and we will be focusing on the consumption of chocolate and its influence on patients. The scenario will outline the entire process of learning in the proper order. The sequence of actions is the following:

- Definition of the target domain.
- Acquisition of natural language resources and pre-processing.
- Knowledge extraction and formalization.

5.1 Domain definition

The first step cannot be automated. A knowledge engineer has to determine what the boundaries of the target domain are. He accomplishes this with an extensive examination of the target domain in order to familiarize himself with the domain concepts. Almost exclusively a knowledge engineer is someone with background in computer science and with the exception that the target domain falls within his area of expertise he usually has only the most basic understanding of the target domain. To be able to successfully incorporate his skills in the entire process it is vital that he understands the target domain at least to a certain degree. This first step is concluded when the domain is firmly, formally defined in such a way that there are no ambiguities on the question what falls inside the domain and what lies on the outside. In our example a short definition of the domain would be the following: The main two entities in the domain are chocolate and patients. The domain scope will be limited to milk, sweet and dark chocolate only. The goal of the learning will be the positive and negative effect of chocolate consumption with regard to quantity. Fig. 13 shows a simplified model of the domain. Additionally the source of learning will be the news reporting on studies being done by the research community. The news selection policy will be based on top level breadth-first policy; if the title contains a keyword from the domain the news is included in the knowledge base.

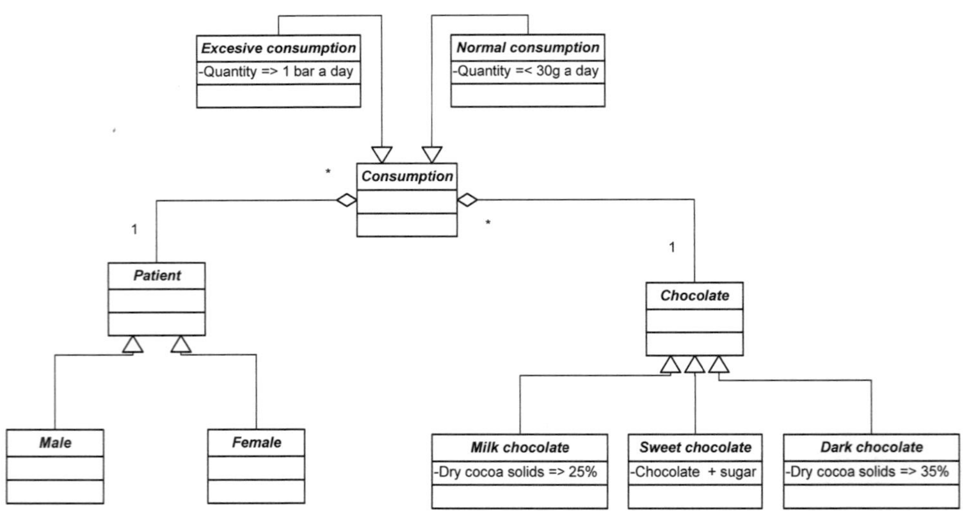

Fig. 13. Domain model for chocolate consumption

5.2 Acquisition of natural language resources and pre-processing

In this step the knowledge engineer determines which natural language sources are available to him and which can be added during the process. He has to determine the source format (documents, web pages...) and the necessary processing for the transformation to the final format. For the example which we are providing we have chosen reports on research projects and studies as the primary source of data. The data will be acquired by RSS feeds from selected health websites. A snippet of the XML file compliant with the RSS 2.0 specification is shown on Fig. 14. News, published by CNN, titled *"Daily chocolate may keep the heart doctor away"* is selected because it contains keyword from the domain model ("chocolate"). On a similar principle other news are selected and inserted to a relational database for local storage and queued for further processing. The collection of domain documents can be enhanced with periodical download of the RSS feeds.

Pre-processing of the selected news is comprised from:

- the download of the full news,
- transformation to plaintext (stripping of HTML tags) and
- sentence level tokenization.

The download of the full news is necessary because the RSS feeds contain only short content (title, short description...) and the target web address of the news.


```
<item>
    <title>Sleep Apnea Linked to Eyelid Disorder</title>
    <link>http://news.health.com/2010/04/02/sleep-apnea-linked-eyelidisorder/</link>
    <pubDate>Sat, 03 Apr 2010 02:08:37 +0000</pubDate>
        ...
</item>
<item>
    <title>Daily chocolate may keep the heart doctor away</title>
    <link>http://rss.cnn.com/~r/rss/cnn_latest/~3/E-6aM9zPrqE/index.html/</link>
    <pubDate>Sat, 03 Apr 2010 02:08:37 +0000</pubDate>
        ...
</item>
```


Fig. 14. Snippet from the news feed

5.3 Knowledge extraction and formalization

The first step in knowledge extraction is the part-of-speech (POS) analysis. It can be performed with the use of existing POS taggers, for example the TnT (Brants, 2000) or TreeTagger (Schmid, 1994). The latter achieved 96% accuracy on the Penn-Treebank data. In the example we are following, the news has been fully downloaded, the text transformed to plaintext and tokenized to individual sentences. The sentences to be used can be classified by a simple TFIDF (Term Frequency Inverse Document Frequency) metric. For our purposes the documents in the formula are sentences. The metric is defined as follows:

$$d^{(i)} = TF(W_i, d) IDF(W_i) \tag{2}$$

The IDF is defined:

$$IDF(W_i) = \log \frac{D}{DF(W_i)} \tag{3}$$

D is the number of documents, DF(W) is the number of documents in which the word (W) occurs at least once and TF(W, d) is the number of word W occurrences in the document d.

Additionally the metric can be normalized so that the TFIDF of individual words is divided by the square root of the sum of all TFIDF word frequencies as follows:

$$nTFIDF = \frac{TFIDF_{i,j}}{\sqrt{\sum_i TFIDF_{i,j}^2}} \tag{4}$$

The very first sentence provides useful knowledge and we will follow the example on this sentence. It is stated as:

"Eating as little as a quarter of an ounce of chocolate each day may lower your risk of experiencing heart attack or stroke!". The POS analysis provides the tags listed in.

This is processed by semantic interpretation that uses existing domain knowledge (defined in the domain definition phase) to produce a representation of the meaning. Fig. 15 shows an internal representation in the form of a conceptual graph. Semantic interpretation uses both the knowledge about word meanings (within the domain) and linguistic structure.

Word	Tag	Word	Tag	Word	Tag
Eating	VBG	*as*	RB	*little*	JJ
as	IN	*a*	DT	*quarter*	NN
of	IN	*an*	DT	*ounce*	NN
of	IN	*chocolate*	NN	*each*	DT
day	NN	*may*	MD	*lower*	VB
your	PRP$	*risk*	NN	*of*	IN
experiencing	VBG	*a*	DT	*heart*	NN
attack	NN	*or*	CC	*stroke*	VB
Legend: IN - Preposition or subordinating conjunction, JJ - Adjective, MD - Modal, NN - Noun, singular or mass, PRP$ - Possessive pronoun, RB - Adverb, VB - Verb, base form, VBG - Verb, gerund or present participle					

Table 2. POS tags of a news sentence

The sentence is separated into two distinct categories: cause (IF) and effect (THEN). Both are associated with the object. In the figure the application used knowledge that *ounce* is a unit of amount, *day* is a unit of time and that a person normally eats chocolate not the other way around. So combining this knowledge produced the resulting representation of knowledge in the sentence. The agent (the one that influences) is *chocolate*, the object (the recipient of the action) is the word *your* and the action (agent to object) is *eating*. Combining that *to eat* is associated with the domain concept of amount and that *ounce* is a unit of amount the application can effectively reason that the meaning of the cause part (Fig. 15 segment A) of the sentence is: object that *eats* a 0.25 *ounce* of *chocolate* in a period of *one day*. The effect side (Fig. 15 segment C) has the meaning of: the object experiences the influence of *reduced* possibility of a disease of type *heart attack/stroke*. This internal representation is then generalized with the addition of known concepts. The object *yours* is a possessive pronoun and therefore is mapped to a person which is marked as *"patient„* in the domain.

The amount of quarter of an ounce is mapped to the primary unit for amount in the domain, (grams) with the use of a conversion factor. So ¼ of an ounce becomes 7.08738078 grams. The resulting semantic net with the additional information is the final interpretation of the domain specific world knowledge learned from this sentence. These representations can

transform to a rule base which can then be automatically evaluated and used by the final application (the one that uses the knowledge learned).
For the example we have been following a rule would be in the following form:

RULE	chocolate *consumption influence*
IF	typeof (object) IS patient
AND	typeof (action) IS eat
AND	action::target IS chocolate
AND	quantityof (action) IS 7g
AND	timespan (action) IS 24h
THEN	typeof(consequence) IS influence
AND	consequence::target IS disease
AND	typeof(disease) IS heart attack/stroke
AND	relationship (consequence, consequence::target) IS reduced risk

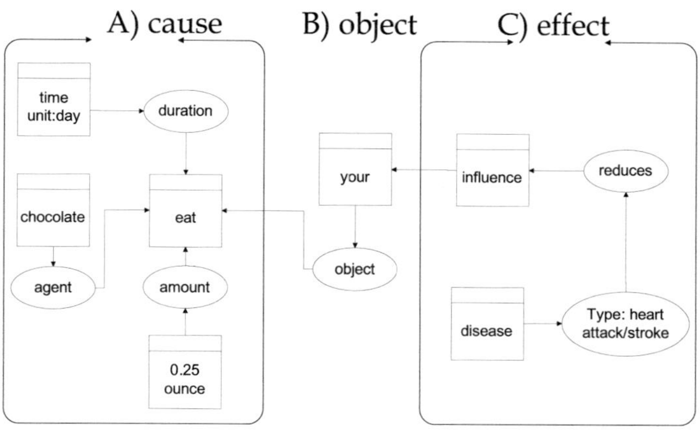

Fig. 15. Internal representation of the meaning of the sentence

This is the final formalization of acquired knowledge. In this form the knowledge is fully machine readable, providing there are inferring rules that define how to evaluate the value entities (typeof, quantityof,...). This format can be stored and used as need arises.

6. Conclusion

We have presented the major research areas that are vital to learning domain specific knowledge. The practical example shows the chronological sequence of the learning process. We have shown that it is vital to formally define the target domain. Also in order for the knowledge engineers to effectively determine the domain and evaluate the progress of the project they have to have a more than superficial knowledge of the domain. Incorporation of existing knowledge (dictionaries, semantic annotations etc.) is very important since every task is very time consuming and repeating existing work is not efficient.
Knowledge extraction should have a much higher success rate if it is done on smaller documents. It is for this reason that the practical example uses news feeds. Their content is already summarized in the form of the short description. The full text of the news can then be used to provide facts that show how and why the summary is correct. So in the example we are counting on the title and short description to provide the new facts while the news

body is used as the supporting information. This provides an efficient example of knowledge learning from natural language.

7. References

Alana, E. & Rodriguez, A. I. (2007). Domain Engineering Methodologies Survey, available on *http://www.pnp-software.com/cordet/download/pdf/GMV-CORDET-RP-001_Iss1.pdf*

Allen, J. (1994). *Natural Language Understanding (2nd Edition),* Addison Wesley, ISBN-10: 0805303340

Alshawi, H. (1992). *The Core Language Engine,* The MIT Press, ISBN-10: 0262011263, USA

Arango, G. (1994). Domain Analysis Methods. In *Software Reusability,* Schafer, W.; Prieto-Díaz, R. & M. Matsumoto (Ed.), page numbers (17-49), Ellis Horwood

Brants, T. (2000). TnT – A Statistical Part-of-Speech Tagger, *Proceedings of the sixth conference on Applied Natural Language Processing,* pp. 224-231, ISBN-10: 1558607048, Seattle, Washington, April – May 2000, Morristown, NJ, USA

Buschmann, F.; Henney, K. & Schmidt, D. C. (2007). *Pattern-Oriented Software Architecture: On Patterns and Pattern Languages,* John Wiley & Sons, ISBN-10: 0471486480, England

Chomsky, N. (1956). Three Models for the Description of Language, *IRE Transactions on Information Theory,* Vol. 2, page numbers (113-124

Czarnecki, K. & Eisenecker, U. (2000). *Generative Programming: Methods, Tools andApplications,* ACM Press/Addison-Wesley Publishing Co., ISBN-10: 0201309777, New York, NY, USA

Davenport, T. H. & Prusak, L. (1998). *Working Knowledge: How Organizations Manage What They Know,* Harvard Bussiness Press, ISBN-10: 0875846556, United States of America

Debenham, J. K. (1989). *Knowledge systems design,* Prentice Hall, ISBN-10: 0135164281

Falbo, R; Guizzardi, G & Duarte, K. C. (2002). An ontological approach to domain engineering, *Proceedings of the 14th international conference on Software engineering and knowledge engineering,* pp. 351-358, ISBN-10: 1581135564, Ischia, Italy, July 2002, ACM, New York, NY, USA

Frakes, W.; Prieto-Diaz, R. & Fox, C. (1998). DARE: Domain analysis and reuse environmrent, *Annals of Software Engineering,* Vol. 5, No. 1, (January 1998) page numbers (125-141), ISSN: 1573-7489

Gandon, F. (2000). Distributed Artifical Intelligence and Knowledge Management: Ontologies and Multi-Agent systems for a Corporate Semantic Web. *Scientific Philosopher Doctorate Thesis in Informatics,* INRIA and University of Nice.

Gašević, D.; Djurić, D. & Devedžić, V. (2006). *Model Driven Architecture and Ontology Development,* Springer-Verlag Berlin Heidelberg, ISBN-10: 3540321802, Germany

Grimm, S.; Hitzler, P. & Abecker, A. (2007). Knowledge Representation and Ontologies, In: *Semantic Web Services,* Studer, R.; Grimm, S. & Abecker, A., (Ed.), page numbers (51-105), Springer Berlin Heidelberg New Vork, ISBN-13: 9783540708940, Online edition

Griss, M.L.; Favaro, J. & d' Alessandro M. (1998). Integrating Feature Modeling with the RSEB, *Proceedings of the 5th Internarional Conference on Software Reuse,* pp. 76, ISBN-10: 0818683775, Victoria, British Columbia, Canada, IEEE Computer Society Washington, DC, USA

Harsu, M. (2002). A survey on domain engineering. *Report 31*, Institute of Software Systems, Tempere University of Technology

Hayes, R. (1992). Measurement of information, *Information Processing & Management*, Vol. 29, No. 1, (January-February 1993), page numbers (1-11), ISSN: 0306-4573

Heidorn, G. E. (1975). Augmented phrase structure grammars, *Proceedings of the 1975 Workshop on Theoretical issues in natural language processing*, pp. 1-5, Cambridge, Massachusetts, June 1975, Association for Computational Linguistics, Morristown, NJ, USA

Hjorland, B. (1998). Information retrieval, text composition and semantics, *Knowledge Organization*, Vol. 25, No. 1-2, (1998), page numbers (16-31), ISSN: 0943-7444

Kang, K.; Cohen, S.; Hess, J.; Novak, W. & Peterson, S. (1990). Feature-Oriented Domain Analysis (FODA) Feasibility Study, *Technical CMU/SEI-90-TR-21*, Software Engineering Institute, Carnegie Mellon University

Kang, K. C.; Kim, S.; Lee, J.; Kim, K.; Shin, E. & Huh, M. (2004). FORM: A feature-oriented reuse method with domain-specific reference architectures, *Annals of Software Engineering*, Vol. 5, No. 1, (January 1998) page numbers (143-168), ISSN: 1573-7489

Kendal, S. & Creen, M. (2007). *An Introduction to Knowledge Engineering*, Springer, ISBN: 1846284759, United States of America

Kosar, T.; Martinez Lopez, P. E.; Barrientos, P. A. & Mernik, M. (2008), A preliminary study on various implementation approaches of domain-specific language, *Information and Software Technology*, Vol. 50, No. 5, (April 2008) page numbers (390-405), ISSN: 0950-5849

Krishnamoorthy, C. S. & Rajeev, S. (1996). *Artifical Intelligence and Experts Systems for Engineers*, CRC-Press, ISBN-10: 0849391253, USA

Luger, G. F. (2005). *Artificial intelligence, Structure and Strategies for Complex Problem Solving (Fifith Edition)*, Pearson Education Limited, ISBN-10: 0321263189, USA

Mernik, M.; Heering, J. & Sloane, A. M. (2005). When and how to develop domain-specific languages, *ACM Computing Surveys (CSUR)*, Vol. 37, No. 4, (December 2005), page numbers (316-344), ISSN: 0360-0300

Miller, G. A. (1995). WordNet: A Lexical Database for English, *Communications of the ACM*, Vol. 38, No. 11, (November 1995) page numbers (39-41), ISSN: 0001-0782

Minker, J. (1987). *Foundations of Deductive Databases and Logic Programming*, Morgan Kaufmann Pub, ISBN: 0934613400, United States

Partee, B. H.; ter Meulen, A. & Wall, R.E. (1993). *Mathematical methods in linguistics*, Kluwer Academic Publishers, ISBN-10: 9027722454, Netherlands

Pradorn, S.; Nopasit, C.; Yacine, O.; Gilles, N. & Abdelaziz, B. (2007). Knowledge Engineering Technique for Cluster Development, Springer, ISBN-13: 9783540767183

Russell, S. & Norvig, P. (2003). *Artifical Intelligence A Modern Approach*, Prentice Hall, ISBN: 0131038052, United States of America

Schmid, G. (1994). TreeTagger - a language independent part-of-speech tagger, available on *http://www.ims.uni-stuttgart.de/Tools/DecisionTreeTagger.html*

Schreiber, G.; Akkermans, H.; Anjewierden, A.; de Hoog, R.; Ahadbolt, N.; Van de Velde, W. & Wielinga, B. (1999). *Knowledge Engineering and Management: The CommonKADS Methodology*, The MIT Press, ISBN: 0262193000, USA

Shadbolt, N. & Milton, N. (1999). From Knowledge Engineering to Knowledge Management, *British Journal of Management*, Vol. 10, No. 4, (December 1999), page numbers (309-322), IISN: 1045-3172

Sheth, A.; Ramakrishnan, C. & Thomas, C. (2005). Semantics for the Semantic Web: The Implicit, the Formal and the Powerful, *International Journal on Semantic Web and Information Systems,* Vol. 1, No. 1, (January-March 2005), page numbers (1-18), ISSN: 1552-6283

Simons, M. & Anthony, J. (1998). Weaving the Model Web: A Multi-Modeling Approach to Concepts and Features in Domain Engineering, *Proceedings of the 5th International Conference on Software Reuse,* pp. 94-102, ISBN: 0818683775, Victoria, DC, Canada, June 1998, IEEE Computer Society Washington, DC, USA

Sterling, L. & Shapiro, E. (1994). *The Art of Prolog, Second Edition: Advanced Programming Tecniques (Logic Programming),* The MIT Press, ISBN: 0262193388, USA

Stokes, M. (2001). *Managing Engineering Knowledge. MOKA - Methodology for Knowledge-Based Engineering Applications,* John Wiley & Sons Australia, Limited, ISBN: 1860582958

Taylor, N. R.; Tracz, W. & Coglianse, L. (1995). Software development using domain-specific software architectures, *ACM SIGSOFT Software Engineering Notes,* Vol. 20, No. 5, (December 1995) page numbers (27-38), ISSN: 0163-5948

Valente, G. (2004). Artifical Intelligence methods in Operational Knowledge Management, Ph.D. Dissertation, University of Turin

Winograd, T. (1972). *Understanding natural language,* Academic Pr, ISBN-10: 0127597506, Orlando, Florida, USA

Weiss, D. M. & Lai, C. T. R. (1999). *Software Product-Line Engineering: A Family-Based Software Development Process,* Addison-Wesley Professional, ISBN: 0201694387

Woods, W.A. (1970). Transition network grammars for natural language analysis, *Communciations of the ACM,* Vol. 13, No. 10, (October 1970), page numbers 591-606, ISSN: 0001-0782

Zins, C. (2007). Conceptual approaches for defining data, information and knowledge, *Journal of the American Society for Information Science and Technology,* Vol. 58, No. 4, (February 2007), page numbers (479-493), ISSN: 1532-2882

4

Uncertainty in Reinforcement Learning — Awareness, Quantisation, and Control

Daniel Schneegass, Alexander Hans, and Steffen Udluft
Siemens AG, Corporate Research & Technologies, Intelligent Systems & Control
Germany

1. Introduction

Reinforcement learning (RL) (Sutton & Barto, 1998) is the machine learning answer to the optimal control problem and has been proven to be a promising solution to a wide variety of industrial application domains (e.g., Schaefer et al., 2007; Stephan et al., 2000), including robot control (e.g., Merke & Riedmiller, 2001; Abbeel et al., 2006; Lee et al., 2006; Peters & Schaal, 2008).

In contrast to many classical approaches, building upon extensive domain knowledge, RL aims to derive an optimal policy (i.e., control strategy) from observations only, acquired by the exploration of an unknown environment. For a limited amount of observations the collected information may not be sufficient to fully determine the environment's properties. Assuming the environment to be a Markov decision process (MDP), it is in general only possible to create estimators for the MDP's transition probabilities and the reward function. As the true parameters remain uncertain, the derived policy that is optimal w.r.t. the estimators is in general not optimal w.r.t. the real MDP and may even perform insufficiently. This is unacceptable in industrial environments with high requirements not only on performance, but also robustness and quality assurance.

To overcome this problem, we incorporate the uncertainties of the estimators into the derived Q-function, which is utilised by many RL methods. In order to guarantee a minimal performance with a given probability, as a solution to quality assurance, we present an approach using statistical uncertainty propagation (UP) (e.g., D'Agostini, 2003) on the Bellman iteration to obtain Q-functions together with their uncertainty. In a second step, we introduce a modified Bellman operator, jointly optimising the Q-function and minimising its uncertainty. This method leads to a policy that is no more optimal in the conventional meaning, but maximizes the guaranteed minimal performance and hence optimises the quality requirements. In addition, we show that the approach can be used for efficient exploration as well. In the following we apply the technique exemplarily on discrete MDPs.

This chapter is organised as follows. Within the introduction we give an overview of RL and uncertainty and report on related work. The key section 2 discusses how to bring the concepts of RL and uncertainty together. We explain the application of uncertainty propagation to the Bellman iteration for policy evaluation and policy iteration for discrete MDPs and proceed with section 3, where we introduce the concept of certain-optimality. We further discuss the important observation that certain-optimal policies are stochastic in general (section 4), having a direct impact on the algorithmic solution. Our approach provides a general framework for different statistical paradigms, we elaborate on this generic view as well as important examples and their advantages and disadvantages in section 5. Section 6 focuses on a possible solution to asymptotically improve the algorithm's time and space complexity and section 7 explains how the proposed concepts can be used to effectively rise to the exploration-exploitation dilemma by seeking uncertain areas of the environment. Finally, in section 8, we focus on the three main application fields quality assurance, exploration, and performance improvement and prove our claims with artificial and industrial benchmarks.

1.1 Reinforcement learning

In (RL) the main objective is to achieve a policy that optimally moves an agent within a Markov decision process (MDP), which is given by state and action spaces S and A as well as the dynamics, defined by a transition probability distribution $P_T: S \times A \times S \rightarrow [0,1]$ depending on the the current state, the chosen action, and the successor state. The agent collects rewards while transiting, whose expected discounted future sum

$$V^{\pi}(s) = \mathrm{E}_s^{\pi}\left(\sum_{i=0}^{\infty} \gamma^i R\left(s^{(i)}, \pi\left(s^{(i)}\right), s^{(i+1)}\right)\right), \tag{1}$$

the value function, has to be maximised over the policy space $\Pi = \{\pi | \pi: S \rightarrow A\}$ for all possible states s, where $0 < \gamma < 1$ is the discount factor, s' the successor state of s, $\pi \in \Pi$ the used policy, and $s = \{s', s'', \ldots, s^{(i)}, \ldots\}$. As an intermediate step one constructs a so-called Q-function $Q^{\pi}(s,a)$ depending on the current state and the chosen action. The optimal $Q^* = Q^{\pi^*}$ is determined by a solution of the Bellman optimality equation

$$Q^*(s,a) = \mathrm{E}_{s'}\left(R(s,a,s') + \gamma V^*(s')\right) \tag{2}$$

$$= \mathrm{E}_{s'}\left(R(s,a,s') + \gamma \max_{a'} Q^*(s',a')\right). \tag{3}$$

Therefore the best policy is $\pi^*(s) = \arg\max_a Q^*(s, a)$. We define the Bellman operator T as $(TQ)(s, a) = \mathrm{E}_{s'}(R(s, a, s') + \gamma \max_{a'} Q(s', a'))$ for any Q. The fixed point of $Q = \mathbf{Solve}(TQ)$, i.e., the Bellman operator followed by its projection on the Q-function's hypothesis space, is the approached solution (Sutton & Barto, 1998; Lagoudakis & Parr, 2003; Munos, 2003). Given the parameters of the MDP, i.e., the definitions of the state and the action space, the transition probabilities, and the reward function, this solution can be found using dynamic programming.

For further details and a more broad and general introduction to RL we refer to Sutton & Barto (1998) or Kaelbling et al. (1996).

1.2 Uncertainty

Statistical uncertainty is a crucial issue in many application fields of statistics including the machine learning domain. It is well accepted that any measurement in nature and any conclusion from measurements are affected by an uncertainty. The International Organization for Standardization (ISO) defines uncertainty to be

> "a parameter, associated with the result of a measurement, that characterizes the dispersion of the values that could reasonably be attributed to the measurand" (ISO, 1993).

We focus on the determination, quantisation, and minimisation of uncertainty of the measurements' conclusions in the context of RL, i.e., the uncertainties of Q-functions and policies. The reason for uncertainty in RL is the ignorance about the true environment, i.e., the true MDP. The more observations are collected, the more certain the observer is about the MDP. And the larger the stochasticity, the more uncertainty remains about the MDP for a given amount of observations. And indeed, if the MDP is known to be completely deterministic, everything is known about a state-action pair if it is observed once. There is no uncertainty left. If in contrast the system is highly stochastic, the risk of obtaining a low long-term return in expectation is large.

Note that the mentioned uncertainty is therefore qualitatively different from the MDP's stochasticity leading to the risk of obtaining a low long-term return in the single run. The main difference is that the latter considers the inherent stochasticity of the MDP, whereas uncertainty considers the stochasticity of choosing an MDP from a set of MDPs.

The uncertainty of the measurements, i.e., the transitions and rewards, are propagated to the conclusions, e.g., the Q-function, by uncertainty propagation (UP), which is a common concept in statistics (D'Agostini, 2003). We determine the uncertainty of values $f(\mathrm{x})$ with $f: \mathbb{R}^m \rightarrow \mathbb{R}^n$ given the uncertainty of their arguments x as

$$\mathrm{Cov}(f) = \mathrm{Cov}(f, f) = D\mathrm{Cov}(\mathrm{x})D^T, \tag{4}$$

where $D_{i,j} = \frac{\partial f_i}{\partial \mathrm{x}_j}$ is the Jacobian matrix of f w.r.t. x and Cov(x) = Cov(x,x) the covariance matrix of the arguments x holding the uncertainty of x.

In the following, we usually work on multi-dimensional objects, having several indices, rather than vectors like f or x, having a single index. Therefore, those objects have to be appropriately vectorised. This can be done by any enumeration and is only of technical importance.

1.3 Related work

There have already been several contributions to estimate generalisation, confidence, and performance bounds in RL. We consider the work of Bertsekas & Tsitsiklis (1996), who gave lower-bounds on the policy's performance by using policy iteration techniques, which were substantially improved by Munos (2003). Kearns et al. (2000) discussed error-bounds for a theoretical policy search algorithm based on trajectory trees. Capacity results on policy evaluation are given by Peshkin & Mukherjee (2001). Antos et al. (2006) provided a broad capacity analysis of Bellman residual minimisation in batch RL. Incorporating prior knowledge about confidence and uncertainty directly into the approached policy were already applied in former work as well in the context of Bayesian RL. We especially mention the work of Engel et al. (2003; 2005), Gaussian process temporal difference learning (GPTD), and a similar approach by Rasmussen & Kuss (2003). They applied Gaussian processes and hence a prior distribution over value functions in RL, which is updated to posteriors by observing samples from the MDP. Ghavamzadeh & Engel recently developed algorithms for Bayesian policy gradient RL (2006) and Bayesian actor-critic RL (2007) as further model-free approaches to Bayesian RL. In all these methods Gaussian processes are applied to obtain the value function and the policy's gradient, respectively.

In model-based approaches, however, one starts with a natural local measure of the uncertainty of the transition probabilities and rewards. One of the first contributions in the context of RL is provided by Dearden et al. (1998; 1999), who applied Q-learning in a Bayesian framework with an application to the exploration-exploitation trade-off. Poupart et al. (2006) present an approach for efficient online learning and exploration in a Bayesian context, they ascribe Bayesian RL to POMDPs. Besides, statistical uncertainty consideration is similar to, but strictly demarcated from other issues that deal with uncertainty and risk consideration. Consider the work of Heger (1994) and of Geibel (2001). They deal with risk in the context of undesirable states. Mihatsch & Neuneier (2002) developed a method to incorporate the inherent stochasticity of the MDP. Most related to our approach is the recent independent work by Delage & Mannor (2007), who solved the percentile optimisation problem by convex optimization and applied it to the exploration-exploitation trade-off. They suppose special priors on the MDP's parameters, whereas the present work has no such requirements and can be applied in a more general context of RL methods.

2. Bellman iteration and uncertainty propagation

Our concept of incorporating uncertainty into RL consists in applying UP to the Bellman iteration (Schneegass et al., 2008)

$$Q^m(s_i,a_j) \quad := \quad (TQ^{m-1})(s_i,a_j) \tag{5}$$

$$= \quad \sum_{k=1}^{|S|} P(s_k \mid s_i,a_j)(R(s_i,a_j,s_k)+\gamma V^{m-1}(s_k)), \tag{6}$$

here for discrete MDPs. For policy evaluation we have $V^m(s) = Q^m(s,\pi(s))$, with π the used policy, and for policy iteration $V^m(s) = \max_{a \in A} Q^m(s, a)$ (section 1.1). Thereby we assume a finite number of states s_i, $i \in \{1, \ldots, |S|\}$, and actions a_j, $j \in \{1, \ldots, |A|\}$. The Bellman iteration converges, with $m \to \infty$, to the optimal Q-function, which is appropriate to the estimators P and R. In the general stochastic case, which will be important later, we set $V^m(s) = \sum_{i=1}^{|A|} \pi(s,a_i) Q^m(s,a_i)$ with $\pi(s, a)$ the probability of choosing a in s. To obtain the uncertainty of the approached Q-function, the technique of UP is applied in parallel to the Bellman iteration. With given covariance matrices Cov(P), Cov(R), and Cov(P,R) for the transition probabilities and the rewards, we obtain the initial complete covariance matrix

$$\mathrm{Cov}(Q^0,P,R) = \begin{pmatrix} 0 & 0 & 0 \\ 0 & \mathrm{Cov}(P) & \mathrm{Cov}(P,R) \\ 0 & \mathrm{Cov}(P,R)^T & \mathrm{Cov}(R) \end{pmatrix} \tag{7}$$

and the complete covariance matrix after the mth Bellman iteration

$$\mathrm{Cov}(Q^m,P,R) \quad := \quad D^{m-1}\mathrm{Cov}\left(Q^{m-1},P,R\right)\left(D^{m-1}\right)^T \tag{8}$$

with the Jacobian matrix

$$D^m = \begin{pmatrix} D^m_{Q,Q} & D^m_{Q,P} & D^m_{Q,R} \\ 0 & \mathrm{I} & 0 \\ 0 & 0 & \mathrm{I} \end{pmatrix}, \tag{9}$$

$$\begin{aligned}(D^m_{Q,Q})_{(i,j),(k,l)} &= \gamma\pi(s_k,a_l)P(s_k \mid s_i,a_j),\\ (D^m_{Q,P})_{(i,j),(l,n,k)} &= \delta_{i,l}\delta_{j,n}\left(R(s_i,a_j,s_k)+\gamma V^m(s_k)\right),\\ (D^m_{Q,R})_{(i,j),(l,n,k)} &= \delta_{i,l}\delta_{j,n}P(s_k \mid s_i,a_j).\end{aligned}$$

In combination with the expanded Bellman iteration

$$\begin{pmatrix}Q^m & P & R\end{pmatrix}^T := \begin{pmatrix}TQ^{m-1} & P & R\end{pmatrix}^T \tag{10}$$

the presented uncertainty propagation allows to obtain the covariances between Q-function and P and R, respectively. All parameters of Q^m are linear in Q^m, altogether it is a bi-linear function. Therefore, UP is indeed approximately applicable in this setting (D'Agostini, 2003). Having identified the fixed point consisting of Q^* and its covariance $\mathrm{Cov}(Q^*)$, the uncertainty of each individual state-action pair is represented by the square root of the diagonal entries $\sigma Q^* = \sqrt{\mathrm{diag}(\mathrm{Cov}(Q^*))}$, since the diagonal comprises the Q-values' variances.

Finally, with probability $P(\xi)$ depending on the distribution class of Q, the function

$$Q^*_u(s,a) = (Q^* - \xi\sigma Q^*)(s,a) \tag{11}$$

provides the guaranteed performance expectation applying action a in state s strictly followed by the policy $\pi^*(s) = \mathrm{argmax}_a\, Q^*(s, a)$. Suppose exemplarily Q to be distributed normally, then the choice $\xi = 2$ would lead to the guaranteed performance with $P(2) \approx 0.977$. The appendix provides a proof of existence and uniqueness of the fixed point consisting of Q^* and $\mathrm{Cov}(Q^*)$.

3. Certain-optimality

The knowledge of uncertainty may help in many areas, e.g., improved exploration (see section 7), a general understanding of quality and risks related to the policy's actual usage, but it does not help to improve the guaranteed performance in a principled manner. By applying $\pi(s) = \mathrm{argmax}_a\, Q^*_u(s, a)$, the uncertainty would not be estimated correctly as the agent is only allowed once to decide for another action than the approached policy suggests. To overcome this problem, we want to approach a so-called certain-optimal policy, which maximises the guaranteed performance. The idea is to obtain a policy π that is optimal w.r.t. a specified confidence level, i.e., which maximises $Z(s, a)$ for all s and a such that

$$P\left(\bar{Q}^\pi(s,a) > Z(s,a)\right) > P(\xi) \tag{12}$$

is fulfilled, where $\bar{Q}^\pi$ denotes the true performance function of π and $P(\xi)$ being a prespecified probability. We approach such a solution by approximating Z by Q^π_u and solving

$$\pi^\xi(s) = \arg\max_\pi \max_a Q^\pi_u(s,a) \tag{13}$$

$$= \arg\max_\pi \max_a (Q^\pi - \xi\sigma Q^\pi)(s,a) \tag{14}$$

under the constraints that $Q^{\pi^\xi} = Q^\xi$ is the valid Q-function for π^ξ, i.e.,

$$Q^\xi(s_i,a_j) = \sum_{k=1}^{|S|} P(s_k \mid s_i,a_j)(R(s_i,a_j,s_k) + \gamma Q^\xi(s_k,\pi^\xi(s_k))). \tag{15}$$

Relating to the Bellman iteration, Q shall be a fixed point not w.r.t. the value function as the maximum over all Q-values, but the maximum over the Q-values minus its weighted uncertainty. Therefore, one has to choose

$$\pi^m(s) \quad := \quad \arg\max_a \,(Q^m - \xi\sigma Q^m)(s,a) \tag{16}$$

after each iteration, together with an update of the uncertainties according to the modified policy π^m.

4. Stochasticity of certain-optimal policies

Policy evaluation can be applied to obtain deterministic or stochastic policies. In the framework of MDPs an optimal policy which is deterministic always exists (Puterman, 1994). For certain-optimal policies, however, the situation is different. Particularly, for $\xi > 0$ there is a bias on $\xi\sigma Q(s,\pi(s))$ being larger than $\xi\sigma Q(s, a)$, $a \neq \pi(s)$, if π is the evaluated policy, since $R(s,\pi(s), s')$ depends stronger on $V(s') = Q(s',\pi(s'))$ than $R(s, a, s')$, $a \neq \pi(s)$. The value function implies the choice of action $\pi(s)$ for all further occurrences of state s. Therefore, the (deterministic) joint iteration is not necessarily guaranteed to converge. I.e., switching the policy π to π' with $Q(s,\pi'(s)) - \xi\sigma Q(s,\pi'(s)) > Q(s,\pi(s)) - \xi\sigma Q(s,\pi(s))$ could lead to a larger uncertainty of π' at s and hence to $Q'(s,\pi'(s)) - \xi\sigma Q'(s,\pi'(s)) < Q'(s,\pi(s)) - \xi\sigma Q'(s,\pi(s))$ for Q' at the next iteration. This causes an oscillation.

Additionally, there is another effect causing an oscillation when there is a certain constellation of Q-values and corresponding uncertainties of concurring actions. Consider two actions a_1 and a_2 in a state s with similar Q-values but different uncertainties, a_1 having an only slightly higher Q-value but a larger uncertainty. The uncertainty-aware policy improvement step (equation (16)) would alter π^m to choose a_2, the action with the smaller uncertainty. However, the fact that this action is inferior might only become obvious in the next iteration when the value function is updated for the altered π^m (and now implying the choice of a_2 in s). In the following policy improvement step the policy will be changed back to choose a_1 in s, since now the Q-function reflects the inferiority of a_2. After the next update of the Q-function, the values for both actions will be similar again, because now the value function implies the choice of a_1 and the bad effect of a_2 affects $Q(s, a_2)$ only once.

It is intuitively apparent that a certain-optimal policy should be stochastic in general if the gain in value must be balanced with the gain in certainty, i.e., with a decreasing risk of having estimated the wrong MDP. The risk to obtain a low expected return is hence reduced by diversification, a well-known method in many industries and applications.

The value ξ decides about the cost of certainty. If $\xi > 0$ is large, certain-optimal policies tend to become more stochastic, one pays a price for the benefit of a guaranteed minimal performance, whereas a small $\xi \leq 0$ guarantees deterministic certain-optimal policies and uncertainty takes on the meaning of the chance for a high performance. Therefore, we finally define a stochastic uncertainty incorporating Bellman iteration as

$$\begin{pmatrix} Q^m \\ C^m \\ \pi^m \end{pmatrix} := \begin{pmatrix} TQ^{m-1} \\ D_{m-1} C^{m-1} D_{m-1}^T \\ \Lambda(\pi^{m-1}, TQ^{m-1}, m) \end{pmatrix} \tag{17}$$

with

$$\Lambda(\pi, Q, t)(s,a) = \begin{cases} \min(\pi(s,a) + \frac{1}{t}, 1) & : \quad a = a_Q(s) \\ \frac{\max(1 - \pi(s, a_Q(s)) - \frac{1}{t}, 0)}{1 - \pi(s, a_Q(s))} \pi(s,a) & : \quad \text{otherwise} \end{cases} \tag{18}$$

and $a_Q(s) = \text{argmax}_a\, (Q - \xi\sigma Q)(s, a)$. The harmonically decreasing change rate of the stochastic policies guarantees reachability of all policies on the one hand and convergence on the other hand. Algorithm 1 summarises the joint iteration.[1]

Algorithm 1 Uncertainty Incorporating Joint Iteration for Discrete MDPs

Require: given estimators P and R for a discrete MDP, initial covariance matrices $\text{Cov}(P)$, $\text{Cov}(R)$, and $\text{Cov}(P,R)$ as well as a scalar ξ

Ensure: calculates a certain-optimal Q-function Q and policy π under the assumption of the observations and the posteriors given by $\text{Cov}(P)$, $\text{Cov}(R)$, and $\text{Cov}(P,R)$

set $C = \begin{pmatrix} 0 & 0 & 0 \\ 0 & \text{Cov}(P) & \text{Cov}(P,R) \\ 0 & \text{Cov}(P,R)^T & \text{Cov}(R) \end{pmatrix}$

set $\forall i,j : Q(s_i, a_j) = 0$, $\forall i,j : \pi(s_i, a_j) = \frac{1}{|A|}$, $t = 0$

while the desired precision is not reached **do**

  set $t = t + 1$

  set $\forall i,j : (\sigma Q)(s_i, a_j) = \sqrt{C_{i|A|+j, i|A|+j}}$

  find $\forall i : a_{i,\max} = \text{argmax}_{a_j} (Q - \xi\sigma Q)(s_i, a_j)$

  set $\forall i : d_{i,\text{diff}} = \min(\frac{1}{t}, 1 - \pi(s_i, a_{i,\max}))$

  set $\forall i : \pi(s_i, a_{i,\max}) = \pi(s_i, a_{i,\max}) + d_{i,\text{diff}}$

  set $\forall i : \forall a_j \neq a_{i,\max} : \pi(s_i, a_j) = \frac{1 - \pi(s_i, a_{i,\max})}{1 - \pi(s, a_{i,\max}) + d_{i,\text{diff}}} \pi(s_i, a_j)$

  set $\forall i,j : Q'(s_i, a_j) = \sum_{k=1}^{|S|} P(s_k | s_i, a_j) \left(R(s_i, a_j, s_k) + \gamma \sum_{l=1}^{|A|} \pi(s_k, a_l) Q(s_k, a_l) \right)$

  set $Q = Q'$

  set $D = \begin{pmatrix} D_{Q,Q} & D_{Q,P} & D_{Q,R} \\ 0 & I & 0 \\ 0 & 0 & I \end{pmatrix}$

  set $C = DCD^T$

end while

return $Q - \xi\sigma Q$ and π

[1] Sample implementations of our algorithms and benchmark problems can be found at: http: //ahans.de/publications/robotlearning2010uncertainty/

The function $Q_u^{\xi}(s, a)=(Q_x - \xi\sigma Q_x)(s, a)$ with (Q_x, C_x, π_x) as the fixed point of the (stochastic) joint iteration for given ξ provides, with probability $P(\xi)$ depending on the distribution class of Q, the guaranteed performance applying action a in state s strictly followed by the stochastic policy π_x. First and foremost, π_x maximises the guaranteed performance and is therefore called a certain-optimal policy.

5. The initial covariance matrix – statistical paradigms

The initial covariance matrix

$$\mathrm{Cov}((P,R)) = \begin{pmatrix} \mathrm{Cov}(P,P) & \mathrm{Cov}(P,R) \\ \mathrm{Cov}(P,R)^T & \mathrm{Cov}(R,R) \end{pmatrix} \tag{19}$$

has to be designed by problem dependent prior belief. If, e.g., all transitions from different state-action pairs and the rewards are assumed to be mutually independent, all transitions can be modelled as multinomial distributions. In a Bayesian context one supposes a priorly known distribution (D'Agostini, 2003; MacKay, 2003) over the parameter space $P(s_k \mid s_i, a_j)$ for given i and j. The Dirichlet distribution with density

$$P(P(s_1 \mid s_i,a_j),\ldots,P(s_{|S|} \mid s_i,a_j))_{\alpha_{1,i,j},\ldots,\alpha_{|S|,i,j}} = \frac{\Gamma(\alpha_{i,j})}{\prod_{k=1}^{|S|}\Gamma(\alpha_{k,i,j})}\prod_{k=1}^{|S|}P(s_k \mid s_i,a_j)^{\alpha_{k,i,j}-1} \tag{20}$$

and $\alpha_{i,j} = \sum_{k=1}^{|S|}\alpha_{k,i,j}$ is a conjugate prior in this case with posterior parameters

$$\alpha_{k,i,j}^d = \alpha_{k,i,j} + n_{s_k|s_i,a_j} \tag{21}$$

in the light of the observations occurring $n_{s_k|s_i,a_j}$ times a transition from s_i to s_k by using action a_j. The initial covariance matrix for P then becomes

$$(\mathrm{Cov}(P))_{(i,j,k),(l,m,n)} = \delta_{i,l}\delta_{j,m}\frac{\alpha_{k,i,j}^d(\delta_{k,n}\alpha_{i,j}^d - \alpha_{n,i,j}^d)}{(\alpha_{i,j}^d)^2(\alpha_{i,j}^d+1)}, \tag{22}$$

assuming the posterior estimator $P(s_k \mid s_i,a_j) = \alpha_{k,i,j}^d / \alpha_{i,j}^d$. Similarly, the rewards might be distributed normally with the normal-gamma distribution as a conjugate prior.

As a simplification or by using the frequentist paradigm, it is also possible to use the relative frequency as the expected transition probabilities with their uncertainties

$$(\mathrm{Cov}(P))_{(i,j,k),(l,m,n)} = \delta_{i,l}\delta_{j,m}\frac{P(s_k \mid s_i,a_j)(\delta_{k,n} - P(s_n \mid s_i,a_j))}{n_{s_i,a_j} - 1} \tag{23}$$

with n_{s_i,a_j} observed transitions from the state-action pair (s_i, a_j).

Similarly, the rewards expectations become their sample means and $\mathrm{Cov}(R)$ a diagonal matrix with entries

$$\mathrm{Cov}(R(s_i,a_j,s_k)) = \frac{\mathrm{Var}(R(s_i,a_j,s_k))}{n_{s_k|s_i,a_j} - 1}. \tag{24}$$

The frequentist view and the conjugate priors have the advantage of being computationally feasible, nevertheless, the method is not restricted to them, any meaningful covariance matrix $\mathrm{Cov}((P,R))$ is allowed. Particularly, applying covariances between the transitions starting from different state-action pairs and between states and rewards is reasonable and interesting, if there is some measure of neighbourhood over the state-action space. Crucial is finally that the prior represents the user's belief.

6. Improving asymptotic performance

The proposed algorithm's time complexity per iteration is of higher order than the standard Bellman iteration's one, which needs $O(|S|^2|A|)$ time ($O(|S|^2|A|^2)$ for stochastic policies). The bottleneck is the covariance update with a time complexity of $O((|S||A|)^{2.376})$ (Coppersmith & Winograd, 1990), since each entry of Q depends only on $|S|$ entries of P and R. The overall complexity is hence bounded by these magnitudes.
This complexity can limit the applicability of the algorithm for problems with more than a few hundred states. To circumvent this issue, it is possible to use an approximate version of the algorithm that considers only the diagonal of the covariance matrix. We call this variant the *diagonal approximation of uncertainty incorporating policy iteration* (DUIPI) (Hans & Udluft, 2009). Only considering the diagonal neglects the correlations between the state-action pairs, which in fact are small for many RL problems, where on average different state-action pairs share only little probability to reach the same successor state.
DUIPI is easier to implement and, most importantly, lies in the same complexity class as the standard Bellman iteration. In the following we will derive the update equations for DUIPI. When neglecting correlations, the uncertainty of values $f(x)$ with $f : \mathbb{R}^m \to \mathbb{R}^n$, given the uncertainty of the arguments x as σx, is determined as

$$(\sigma f)^2 = \sum_i \left(\frac{\partial f}{\partial x_i}\right)^2 (\sigma x_i)^2. \tag{25}$$

This is equivalent to equation (4) of full-matrix UP with all non-diagonal elements set equal to zero.
The update step of the Bellman iteration,

$$Q^m(s,a) := \sum_{s'} P(s'|s,a)\left[R(s,a,s') + \gamma V^{m-1}(s')\right], \tag{26}$$

can be regarded as a function of the estimated transition probabilities P and rewards R, and the Q-function of the previous iteration Q^{m-1} (V^{m-1} is a subset of Q^{m-1}), that yields the updated Q-function Q^m. Applying UP as given by equation (25) to the Bellman iteration, one obtains an update equation for the Q-function's uncertainty:

$$\begin{aligned}(\sigma Q^m(s,a))^2 \quad := \quad & \sum_{s'} (D_{Q,Q})^2 (\sigma V^{m-1}(s'))^2 + \\ & \sum_{s'} (D_{Q,P})^2 (\sigma P(s'|s,a))^2 + \\ & \sum_{s'} (D_{Q,R})^2 (\sigma R(s,a,s'))^2,\end{aligned} \tag{27}$$

$$D_{Q,Q} = \gamma P(s'|s,a),\ D_{Q,P} = R(s,a,s') + \gamma V^{m-1}(s'),\ D_{Q,R} = P(s'|s,a). \tag{28}$$

V^m and σV^m have to be set depending on the desired type of the policy (stochastic or deterministic) and whether policy evaluation or policy iteration is performed. E.g., for policy evaluation of a stochastic policy π

$$V^m(s) = \sum_a \pi(a|s) Q^m(s,a), \tag{29}$$

$$(\sigma V^m(s))^2 = \sum_a \pi(a|s)^2 (\sigma Q^m(s,a))^2. \tag{30}$$

For policy iteration, according to the Bellman optimality equation and resulting in the Q-function Q^* of an optimal policy, $V^m(s) = \max_a Q^m(s, a)$ and $(\sigma V^m(s))^2 = (\sigma Q^m(s, \arg\max_a Q^m(s, a)))^2$.

Using the estimators P and R with their uncertainties σP and σR and starting with an initial Q-function Q^0 and corresponding uncertainty σQ^0, e.g., $Q^0 := 0$ and $\sigma Q^0 := 0$, through the update equations (26) and (27) the Q-function and corresponding uncertainty are updated in each iteration and converge to Q^π and σQ^π for policy evaluation and Q^* and σQ^* for policy iteration.

Like the full-matrix algorithm DUIPI can be used with any choice of estimator, e.g., a Bayesian setting using Dirichlet priors or the frequentist paradigm (see section 5). The only requirement is the possibility to access the estimator's uncertainties σP and σR. In Hans & Udluft (2009) and section 8.2 we give results of experiments using the full-matrix version and DUIPI and compare the algorithms for various applications.

Algorithm 2 Diagonal Approximation of Uncertainty Incorporating Policy Iteration

Require: estimators P and R for a discrete MDP, their uncertainties σP and σR, a scalar ξ
Ensure: calculates a certain-optimal policy π
set $\forall i,j : Q(s_i,a_j) = 0,\ (\sigma Q)^2(s_i,a_j) = 0$
set $\forall i,j : \pi(s_i,a_j) = \frac{1}{|A|},\ t = 0$
while the desired precision is not reached **do**
  set $t = t + 1$
  set $\forall s : a_{s,\max} = \arg\max_a Q(s,a) - \xi\sqrt{(\sigma Q)^2(s,a)}$
  $\forall s : d_s = \min(1/t, 1 - \pi(a_{s,\max}|s))$
  set $\forall s : \pi(a_{s,\max}|s) = \pi(a_{s,\max}|s) + d_s$
  set $\forall s : \forall a \neq a_{s,\max} : \pi(a|s) = \frac{1-\pi(a_{s,\max}|s)}{1-\pi(a_{s,\max}|s)+d_s}\pi(a|s)$
  set $\forall s : V(s) = \sum_a \pi(s,a) Q(s,a)$
  set $\forall s : (\sigma V)^2(s) = \sum_a \pi(s,a)(\sigma Q)^2(s,a)$
  set $\forall s,a : Q'(s,a) = \sum_{s'} P(s'|s,a)[R(s,a,s') + \gamma V(s')]$
  set $\forall s,a : (\sigma Q')^2(s,a) =$
   $\sum_s (D_{Q,Q})^2(\sigma V)^2(s') + (D_{Q,P})^2(\sigma P)^2(s'|s,a) + (D_{Q,R})^2(\sigma R)^2(s,a,s')$
  set $Q = Q',\ (\sigma Q)^2 = (\sigma Q')^2$
end while
return π

7. Uncertainty-based exploration

Since RL is usually used with an initially unknown environment, it is necessary to explore the environment in order to gather knowledge. In that context the so-called *exploration-exploitation dilemma* arises: when should the agent stop trying to gain more information (explore) and start to act optimally w.r.t. already gathered information (exploit)? Note that this decision does not have to be a binary one. A good solution of the exploration-exploitation problem could also gradually reduce the amount of exploration and increase the amount of exploitation, perhaps eventually stopping exploration altogether.
The algorithms proposed in this chapter can be used to balance exploration and exploitation by combining existing (already gathered) knowledge and uncertainty about the environment to further explore areas that seem promising judging by the current knowledge. Moreover, by aiming at obtaining high rewards and decreasing uncertainty at the same time, good online performance is possible (Hans & Udluft, 2010).

7.1 Efficient exploration in reinforcement learning

There have been many contributions considering efficient exploration in RL. E.g., Dearden et al. (1998) presented *Bayesian Q-learning*, a Bayesian model-free approach that maintains probability distributions over Q-values. They either select an action stochastically according to the probability that it is optimal or select an action based on *value of information*, i.e., select the action that maximises the sum of Q-value (according to the current belief) and expected gain in information. They later added a Bayesian model-based method that maintains a distribution over MDPs, determines value functions for sampled MDPs, and then uses those value functions to approximate the true value distribution (Dearden et al., 1999). In *model-based interval estimation* (MBIE) one tries to build confidence intervals for the transition probability and reward estimates and then optimistically selects the action maximising the value within those confidence intervals (Wiering & Schmidhuber, 1998; Strehl & Littman, 2008). Strehl & Littman (2008) proved that MBIE is able to find near-optimal policies in polynomial time. This was first shown by Kearns & Singh (1998) for their E^3 algorithm and later by Brafman & Tennenholtz (2003) for the simpler *R-Max* algorithm. R-Max takes one parameter C, which is the number of times a state-action pair (s, a) must have been observed until its actual Q-value estimate is used in the Bellman iteration. If it has been observed fewer times, its value is assumed as $Q(s, a) = R_{\max}/(1 - \gamma)$, which is the maximum possible Q-value ($R_{\max}$ is the maximum possible reward). This way exploration of state-action pairs that have been observed fewer than C times is fostered. Strehl & Littman (2008) presented an additional algorithm called *model-based interval estimation with exploration bonus* (MBIE-EB) for which they also prove its optimality. According to their experiments, it performs similarly to MBIE. MBIE-EB alters the Bellman equation to include an exploration bonus term $\beta / \sqrt{n_{s,a}}$, where β is a parameter of the algorithm and $n_{s,a}$ the number of times state-action pair (s, a) has been observed.

7.2 Uncertainty propagation for exploration

Using full-matrix uncertainty propagation or DUIPI with the parameter ξ set to a negative value it is possible to derive a policy that balances exploration and exploitation:

$$\pi^{\xi}(s) := \arg\max_a (Q^* - \xi\sigma Q^*)(s,a). \tag{31}$$

However, like in the quality assurance context, this would allow to consider the uncertainty only for one step. To allow the resulting policy to plan the exploration, it is necessary to include the uncertainty-aware update of the policy in the iteration as described in section 3. Section 3 proposes to update the policy π^m using Q^m and σQ^m in each iteration and then using π^m in the next iteration to obtain Q^{m+1} and σQ^{m+1}. This way Q-values and uncertainties are not mixed, the Q-function remains the valid Q-function of the resulting policy. Another possibility consists in modifying the Q-values in the iteration with the ξ-weighted uncertainty. However, this leads to a Q-function that is no longer the Q-function of the policy, as it contains not only the sum of (discounted) rewards, but also uncertainties. Therefore, using a Q and σQ obtained this way it is not possible to reason about expected rewards and uncertainties when following this policy. Moreover, when using a negative ξ for exploration the Q-function does not converge in general for this update scheme, because in each iteration the Q-function is increased by the ξ-weighted uncertainty, which in turn leads to higher uncertainties in the next iteration. On the other hand, by choosing ξ and γ to satisfy $\xi + \gamma < 1$ we were able to keep Q and σQ from diverging. Used with DUIPI this update scheme gives rise to a DUIPI variation called *DUIPI with Q-modification* (DUIPI-QM) which has proven useful in our experiments (section 8.2), as DUIPI-QM works well even for environments that exhibit high correlations between different state-action pairs, because through this update scheme of mixing Q-values and uncertainties the uncertainty is propagated through the Q-values.

8. Applications

The presented techniques offer at least three different types of application, which are important in various practical domains.

8.1 Quality assurance and competitions

With a positive ξ one aims at a guaranteed minimal performance of a policy. To optimise this minimal performance, we introduced the concept of certain-optimality. The main practical motivation is to avoid delivering an inferior policy. To simply be aware of the quantification of uncertainty helps to appreciate how well one can count on the result. If the guaranteed Q-value for a specified start state is insufficient, more observations must be provided in order to reduce the uncertainty.

If the exploration is expensive and the system critical such that the performance probability has definitely to be fulfilled, it is reasonable to bring out the best from this concept. This can be achieved by a certain-optimal policy. One abandons "on average" optimality in order to perform as good as possible at the specified confidence level.

Another application field, the counter-part of quality assurance, are competitions, which is symmetrical to quality assurance by using negative ξ. The agent shall follow a policy that gives it the chance to perform exceedingly well and thus to win. In this case, certain-optimality comes again into play as the performance expectation is not the criterion, but the percentile performance.

8.1.1 Benchmarks

For demonstration of the quality assurance and competition aspects as well as the properties of certain-optimal policies, we applied the joint iteration on (fixed) data sets for two simple classes of MDPs. Furthermore, we sampled over the space of allowed MDPs from their (fixed) prior distribution. As a result we achieve a posterior of the possible performances for each policy.

We have chosen a simple bandit problem with one state and two actions and a class of two-state MDPs with each two actions. The transition probabilities are assumed to be distributed multinomially for each start state, using the maximum entropy prior, i.e., the Beta distribution with $\alpha = \beta = 1$. For the rewards we assumed a normal distribution with fixed variance $\sigma_0 = 1$ and a normal prior for the mean with $\mu = 0$ and $\sigma = 1$. Transition probabilities and rewards for different state-action-pairs are assumed to be mutually independent. For the latter benchmark, for instance, we defined to have made the following observations (states **s**, actions **a**, and rewards **r**) over time:

$$\mathbf{s} = (1, 1, 1, 1, 1, 2, 2, 2, 2, 2,2), \quad (32)$$

$$\mathbf{a} = (1, 1, 2, 2, 1, 1, 1, 2, 2,2), \quad (33)$$

$$\mathbf{r} = (1.35, 1, 1, 1, 1, 1, 0, 0, 1, -1). \quad (34)$$

On the basis of those observations we deployed the joint Bellman iteration for different values of ξ, each leading to a policy π^{ξ} that depends on ξ only. The estimates for P and R as well as the initial covariance matrix C^0 are chosen in such a way, that they exactly correspond with the above mentioned posterior distributions. Concurrently, we sampled MDPs from the respective prior distribution. On each of these MDPs we tested the defined policies and weighted their performance probabilities with the likelihood to observe the defined observations given the sampled MDP.

8.1.2 Results

Figure 1 shows the performance posterior distributions for different policies on the two-state MDP problem. Obviously, expectation and variance adopt different values per policy. The expectation-optimal policy reaches the highest expectation whereas the certain and stochastic policies show a lower variance and the competition policy has a wider performance distribution. Each of these properties is exactly the precondition for the aspired behaviour of the respective policy type.

The figures 2 left (bandit problem) and 2 right (two-state MDP problem) depict the percentile performance curves of different policies. In case of the two-state MDP benchmark, these are the same policies as in figure 1 (same colour, same line style), enriched by additional ones. The cumulative distribution of the policies' performances is exactly the inverse function of the graphs in figure 2. Thereby we facilitate a comparison of the performances on different percentiles. The right figure clearly states that the fully stochastic policy shows superior performance at the 10th percentile whereas a deterministic policy, different from the expectation-optimal one, achieves the best performance at the 90th percentile.

In table 1 we listed the derived policies and the estimated percentile performances (given by the Q-function) for different ξ for the two-state MDP benchmark. They approximately match the certain-optimal policies on each of the respective percentiles. With increasing ξ (decreasing percentile) the actions in the first state become stochastic at first and later on the actions in the second state as well. For decreasing ξ the (deterministic) policy switches its action in the first state at some threshold whereas the action in the second state stays the same. These observations can be comprehended from both the graph and the table.

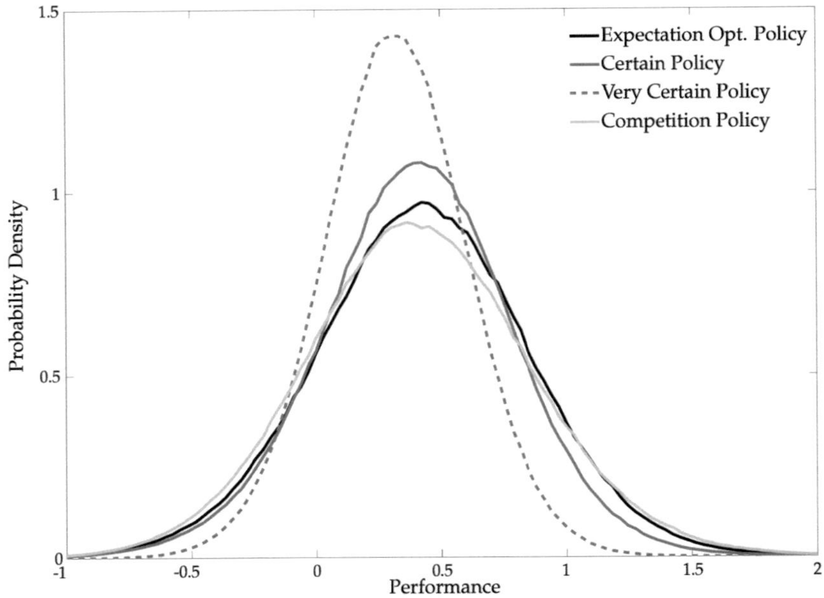

Fig. 1. Performance distribution for different (stochastic) policies on a class of simple MDPs with two states and two actions. The performances are approximately normally distributed. The expectation is highest for the expectation-optimal policy whereas the certain and most stochastic policy features the lowest variance and the highest percentile performance below a certain threshold.

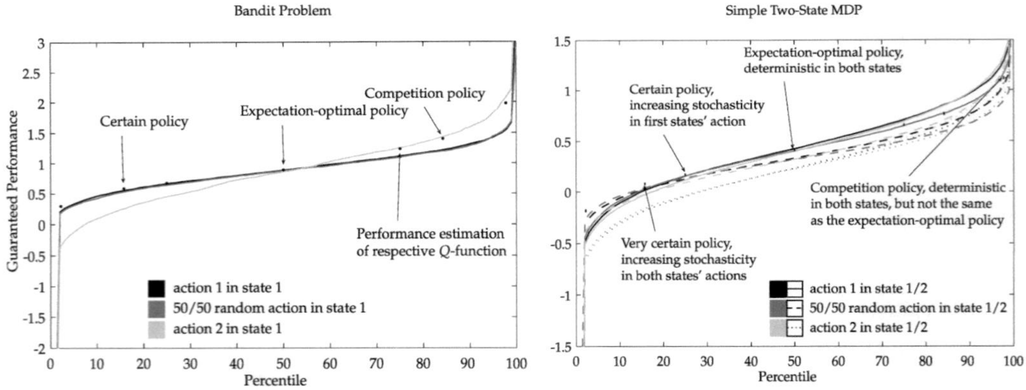

Fig. 2. Percentile performance for simple MDPs and joint iteration results. The different graphs show the percentile performance curves achieved by different policies (i.e., the inverse of the cumulative performance distribution). The grey scale value and the line style depict what action to choose on the state/both states. The dots show the estimated Q-values for the derived certain-optimal policies at the specified percentile. Q-values are distributed normally. The percentiles have been specified by values of $\xi \in \{2, 1$ (*certain policy*), $2/3, 0$ (*expectation-optimal policy*), $-2/3, -1$ (*competition policy*), $-2\}$ for the bandit problem and $\xi \in \{2, 1.5$ (*very certain policy*), $1, 2/3$ (*certain policy*), 0 (*expectation-optimal policy*), $-2/3, -1, -1.5$ (*competition policy*), $-2\}$ on the simple two-state MDP.

ξ	Percentile Performance	$\pi(1,1)$	$\pi(1,2)$	$\pi(2,1)$	$\pi(2,2)$	Entropy
4	− 0.663	0.57	0.43	0.52	0.48	0.992
3	− 0.409	0.58	0.42	0.55	0.45	0.987
2	− 0.161	0.59	0.41	0.60	0.40	0.974
1	0.106	0.61	0.39	0.78	0.22	0.863
2/3	0.202	0.67	0.33	1	0	0.458
0	0.421	1	0	1	0	0
− 2/3	0.651	1	0	1	0	0
− 1	0.762	1	0	1	0	0
− 2	1.103	1	0	1	0	0
− 3	1.429	0	1	1	0	0
− 4	1.778	0	1	1	0	0

Table 1. Derived certain-optimal policies for different values of ξ on the above mentioned dataset (equations (32), (33) and (34)) and the assumed prior for the two-state MDP benchmark problem. In addition the estimated percentile performances and the policies' entropies are given. The results are consistent with figure 2 (right), i.e., the derived policies approximately match the actually certain-optimal policies on the respective percentiles.

8.2 Exploration

As outlined in section 7 our approach can also be used for efficient exploration by using a negative ξ. This leads to a policy that explores state-action pairs where $Q_u^{\xi}(s,a)$ is large more intensively, since the estimator of the Q-value is already large but the true performance of the state-action pair could be even better as the uncertainty is still large as well.
To demonstrate the functionality of our approach for exploration we conducted experiments using two benchmark applications from the literature. We compare the full-matrix version, classic DUIPI, DUIPI with Q-function modification, and two established algorithms for exploration, R-Max (Brafman & Tennenholtz, 2003) and MBIE-EB (Strehl & Littman, 2008). Furthermore, we present some insight of how the parameter ξ influences the agent's behaviour. Note that the focus here is not only gathering information about the environment but also balancing exploration and exploitation in order to provide good online performance.

8.2.1 Benchmarks

The first benchmark is the *RiverSwim* domain from Strehl & Littman (2008), which is an MDP consisting of six states and two actions. The agent starts in one of the first two states (at the beginning of the row) and has the possibility to swim to the left (with the current) or to the right (against the current). While swimming to the left always succeeds, swimming to the right most often leaves the agent in the same state, sometimes leads to the state to the right, and occasionally (with small probability) even leads to the left. When swimming to the left in the very left state, the agent receives a small reward. When swimming to the right in the very right state, the agent receives a very large reward, for all other transitions the reward is zero. The optimal policy thus is to always swim to the right. See figure 3 for an illustration.
The other benchmark is the *Trap* domain from Dearden et al. (1999). It is a maze containing 18 states and four possible actions. The agent must collect flags and deliver them to the goal. For each flag delivered the agent receives a reward. However, the maze also contains a trap

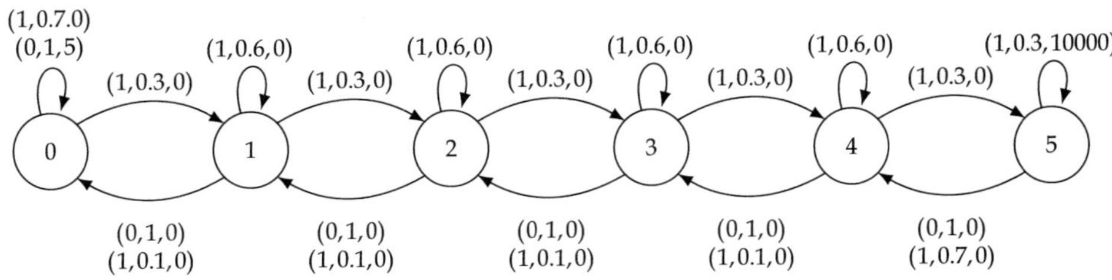

Fig. 3. Illustration of the RiverSwim domain. In the description (a, b, c) of a transition a is the action, b the probability for that transition to occur, and c the reward.

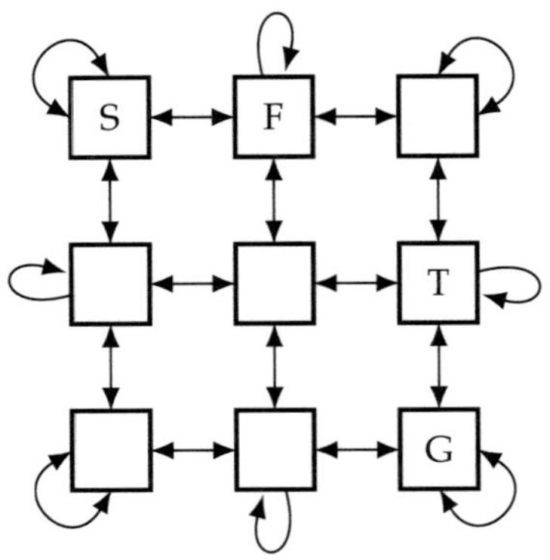

Fig. 4. Illustration of the Trap domain. Starting in state S the agent must collect the flag from state F and deliver it to the goal state G. Once the flag is delivered to state G, the agent receives a reward and is transferred to the start state S again. Upon entering the trap state T a large negative reward is given. In each state the agent can move in all four directions. With probability 0.9 it moves in the desired direction, with probability 0.1 it moves in one of the perpendicular directions with equal probability.

state. Entering the trap state results in a large negative reward. With probability 0.9 the agent's action has the desired effect, with probability 0.1 the agent moves in one of the perpendicular directions with equal probability. See figure 4 for an illustration.

For each experiment we measured the cumulative reward for 5000 steps. The discount factor was set $\gamma = 0.95$ for all experiments. For full-matrix UP, DUIPI, and DUIPI-QM we used Dirichlet priors (section 5). The algorithms were run whenever a new observation became available, i.e., in each step.

8.2.2 Results

Table 2 summarises the results for the considered domains and algorithms obtained with the respective parameters set to the optimal ones found.

For RiverSwim all algorithms except classic DUIPI perform comparably. By considering only the diagonal of the covariance matrix, DUIPI neglects the correlations between different state-action pairs. Those correlations are large for state-action pairs that have a significant probability of leading to the same successor state. In RiverSwim many state-action pairs have this property. Neglecting the correlations leads to an underestimation of the uncertainty, which prevents DUIPI from correctly propagating the uncertainty of Q-values of the right most state to states further left. Thus, although Q-values in state 5 have a

	RiverSwim	Trap
R-Max	$3.02 \pm 0.03 \times 10^6$	469 ± 3
MBIE-EB	$3.13 \pm 0.03 \times 10^6$	558 ± 3
full-matrix UP	$2.59 \pm 0.08 \times 10^6$	521 ± 20
DUIPI	$0.62 \pm 0.03 \times 10^6$	554 ± 10
DUIPI-QM	$3.16 \pm 0.03 \times 10^6$	565 ± 11

Table 2. Best results obtained using the various algorithms in the RiverSwim and Trap domains. Shown is the cumulative reward for 5000 steps averaged over 50 trials for full-matrix UP and 1000 trials for the other algorithms. The used parameters for R-Max were C = 16 (RiverSwim) and C = 1 (Trap), for MBIE-EB $\beta = 0.01$ (RiverSwim) and $\beta = 0.01$ (Trap), for full-matrix UP $\alpha = 0.3$, $\xi = -1$ (RiverSwim) and $\alpha = 0.3$, $\xi = -0.05$ (Trap), for DUIPI $\alpha = 0.3$, $\xi = -2$ (RiverSwim) and $\alpha = 0.1$, $\xi = -0.1$ (Trap), and for DUIPI-QM $\alpha = 0.3$, $\xi = -0.049$ (RiverSwim) and $\alpha = 0.1$, $\xi = -0.049$ (Trap).

large uncertainty throughout the run, the algorithm settles for exploiting the action in the left most state giving the small reward if it has not found the large reward after a few tries. DUIPI-QM does not suffer from this problem as it modifies Q-values using uncertainty. In DUIPI-QM, the uncertainty is propagated through the state space by means of the Q-values. In the Trap domain the correlations of different state-action pairs are less strong. As a consequence, DUIPI and DUIPI-QM perform equally well. Also the performance of MBIE-EB is good in this domain, only R-Max performs worse than the other algorithms. R-Max is the only algorithm that bases its explore/exploit decision solely on the number of executions of a specific state-action pair. Even with its parameter set to the lowest possible value, it often visits the trap state and spends more time exploring than the other algorithms.

8.2.3 Discussion

Figure 5 shows the effect of ξ for the algorithms. Except DUIPI-QM the algorithms show "inverted u"-behaviour. If ξ is too large (its absolute value too small), the agent does not explore much and quickly settles on a suboptimal policy. If, on the other hand, ξ is too small (its absolute value too large), the agent spends more time exploring. We believe that DUIPI-QM would exhibit the same behaviour for smaller values for ξ, however, those are not usable as they would lead to a divergence of Q and σQ.

Figure 6 shows the effect ξ using DUIPI in the Trap domain. While with large ξ the agent quickly stops exploring the trap state and starts exploiting, with small ξ the uncertainty keeps the trap state attractive for more time steps, resulting in more negative rewards.

Using uncertainty as a natural incentive for exploration is achieved by applying uncertainty propagation to the Bellman equation. Our experiments indicate that it performs at least as good as established algorithms like R-Max and MBIE-EB. While most other approaches to exploration assume a specific statistical paradigm, our algorithm does not make such assumptions and can be combined with any estimator. Moreover, it does not rely on state-action pair counters, optimistic initialisation of Q-values, or explicit exploration bonuses. Most importantly, when the user decides to stop exploration, the same method can be used to obtain certain-optimal policies for quality assurance by setting ξ to a positive value.

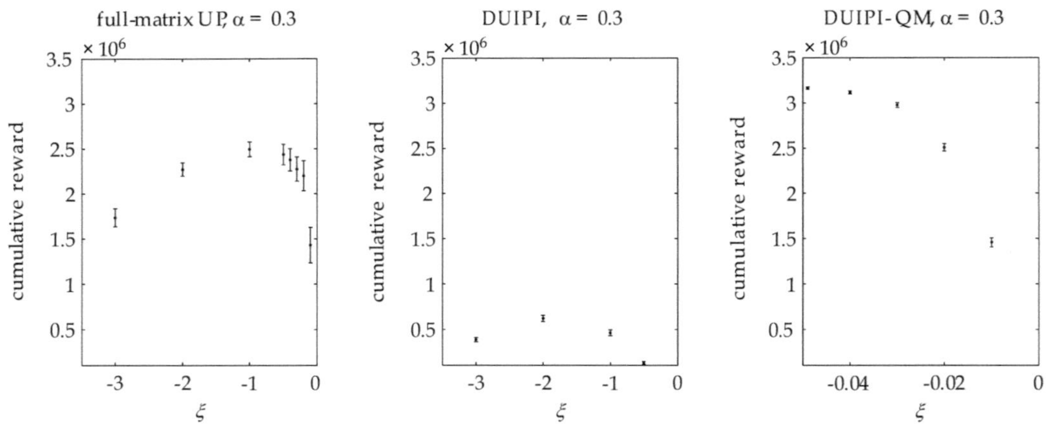

Fig. 5. Cumulative rewards for RiverSwim obtained by the algorithms for various values of ξ. The values for full-matrix UP are averaged over 50 trials, for the values for DUIPI and DUIPI-QM 1000 trials of each experiment were performed.

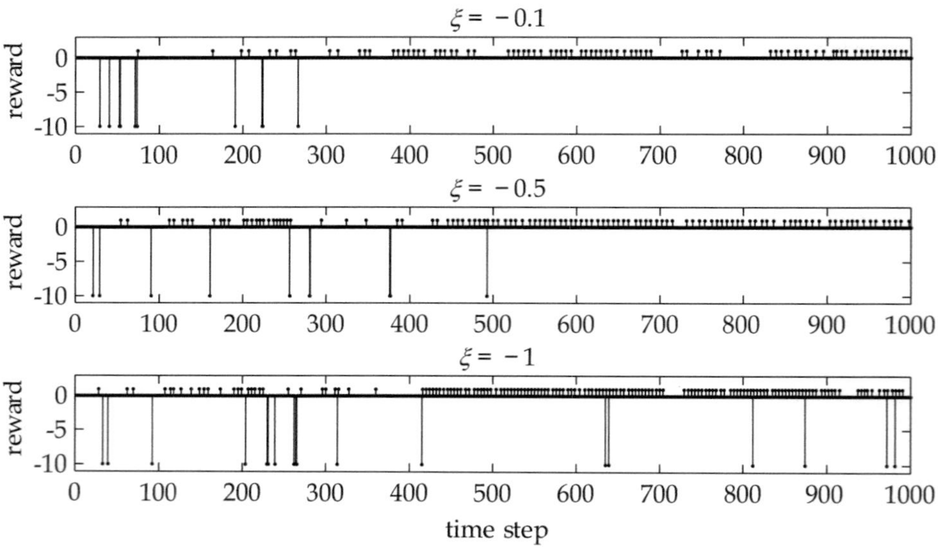

Fig. 6. Immediate rewards of exemplary runs using DUIPI in the Trap domain. When delivering a flag, the agent receives reward 1, when entering the trap state it receives -10. While with $\xi = -0.1$ after less than 300 steps the trap state does not seem worth exploring anymore, setting $\xi = -0.5$ makes the agent explore longer due to uncertainty. With $\xi = -1$ the agent does not stop exploring the trap state in the depicted 1000 time steps.

	full-matrix UP	**DUIPI**	**DUIPI-QM**
time	7 min	14 s	14 s

Table 3. Computation time for 5000 steps in the RiverSwim domain using a single core of an Intel Core 2 Quad Q9550 processor. The policy was updated in every time step.

While the full-matrix UP is the more fundamental and theoretically more sound method, its computational cost is considerable (see table 3). If used with care, however, DUIPI and DUIPI-QM constitute valuable alternatives that proved well in practice. Although our experiments are rather small, we expect DUIPI and DUIPI-QM to also perform well on larger problems.

8.3 Increasing the expected performance

Incorporating uncertainty in RL can even improve the expected performance for concrete MDPs in many practical and industrial environments, where exploration is expensive and only allowed within a small range. The available amount of data is hence small and exploration takes place in an, in part extremely, unsymmetrical way. Data is particularly collected in areas where the operation is already preferable. Many of the insufficiently explored so-called on-border states are undesirable in expectation, but might, by chance, give a high reward in the singular case. If the border is sufficiently large this might happen at least a few times and such an outlier might suggest a high expected reward. Note that in general the size of the border region will increase with the dimensionality of the problem. Carefully incorporating uncertainty avoids the agent to prefer those outliers in its final operation.

We applied the joint iteration on a simple artificial archery benchmark with the "border phenomenon". The state space represents an archer's target (figure 7). Starting in the target's middle, the archer has the possibility to move the arrowhead in all four directions and to shoot the arrow. The exploration has been performed randomly with short episodes. The dynamics were simulated with two different underlying MDPs. The arrowhead's moves are either stochastic (25 percent chance of choosing another action) or deterministic. The event of making a hit after shooting the arrow is stochastic in both settings. The highest probability for a hit is with the arrowhead in the target's middle. The border is explored quite rarely, such that a hit there misleadingly causes the respective estimator to estimate a high reward and thus the agent to finally shoot from this place.

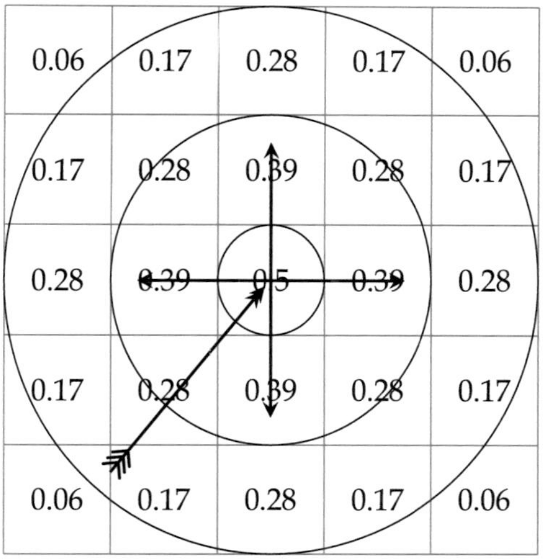

Fig. 7. Visualisation of the archery benchmark. The picture shows the target consisting of its 25 states, together with their hitting probabilities.

Setting	**Model**	**Discr.**	**# Obs.**	$\xi = 0$	$\xi = 0.5$	$\xi = 1$	$\xi = 2$	$\xi = 3$	$\xi = 4$	$\xi = 5$
Archery	Frequentist		100	0.14	**0.16**	0.13	0.05	0.05	0.04	0.04
(Stochastic)			500	0.17	0.20	**0.25**	0.22	0.10	0.05	0.04
			1000	0.21	0.26	**0.29**	0.27	0.22	0.11	0.07
			2500	0.27	0.29	**0.31**	**0.31**	0.30	0.28	0.24
Archery	Deterministic		100	0.35	**0.38**	0.23	0.17	0.12	0.11	0.09
(Deterministic)	Dirichlet Prior		500	0.32	0.38	0.39	**0.41**	0.27	0.18	0.11
	$\forall i : \alpha_i = 0$		1000	0.35	0.41	0.44	**0.45**	0.44	0.30	0.14
			2500	0.44	0.46	0.48	0.49	**0.50**	**0.50**	0.48
Turbine	Frequentist	coarse	10^4	0.736	0.758	0.770	0.815	0.837	0.848	0.855
		medium	10^4	0.751	0.769	0.784	0.816	**0.833**	0.830	0.815
		fine	10^4	0.767	0.785	0.800	0.826	0.837	**0.840**	0.839
Turbine	Maximum Entropy	coarse	10^4	0.720	0.767	0.814	0.848	0.851	**0.854**	**0.854**
	Dirichlet Prior	medium	10^4	0.713	0.731	0.749	0.777	**0.787**	0.780	0.771
	$\forall i : \alpha_i = 1$	fine	10^4	0.735	0.773	0.789	**0.800**	**0.800**	0.786	0.779
	For Comparison			RefCon	RQL	RPS	RFuzzy	RNRR	RPGNRR	RCNN
Turbine		coarse	10^5		0.680	0.657	0.662			
		medium	10^5	0.53	0.687	0.745	0.657	0.851	0.861	0.859
		fine	10^5		0.717	0.729	0.668			

Table 4. Average reward for the archery and gas turbine benchmark.

In table 4 the performance, averaged over 50 trials (two digits precision), for the frequentist setting (in the stochastic case) and the deterministic prior (in the deterministic case) for the transition probabilities are listed.
The table shows that the performance indeed increases with ξ until a maximum and then decreases rapidly. The position of the maximum apparently increases with the number of observations. This can be explained by the decreasing uncertainty. The performance of the theoretical optimal policy is 0.31 for the stochastic archery benchmark and 0.5 for the deterministic one. They are achieved in average by the certain-optimal policy based on 2500 observations with $1 \leq \xi \leq 2$ in the stochastic case and for $3 \leq \xi \leq 4$ in the deterministic case.

8.4 An industrial application

We further applied the uncertainty propagation together with the joint iteration on an application to gas turbine control (Schaefer et al., 2007) with a continuous state and a finite action space, where it can be assumed that the "border phenomenon" appears as well. We discretised the internal state space with three different precisions (coarse ($4^4 = 256$ states), medium ($5^4 = 625$ states), fine ($6^4 = 1296$ states)), where the high-dimensional state space has already been reduced to a four-dimensional approximate Markovian state space, called "internal state space". A detailed description of the problem and the construction of the internal state space can be found in Schaefer et al. (2007). Note that the Bellman iteration and the uncertainty propagation is computationally feasible even with 6^4 states, since P and $\mathrm{Cov}((P,R))$ are sparse.
We summarise the averaged performances (50 trials with short random episodes starting from different operating points, leading to three digits precision) in table 4 on the same uninformed priors as used in section 8.3. The rewards were estimated with an uninformed normal-gamma distribution as conjugate prior with $\sigma = \infty$ and $\alpha = \beta = 0$.
In contrary to the archery benchmark, we left the number of observations constant and changed the discretisation. The finer the discretisation, the larger is the uncertainty. Therefore the position of the maximum tends to increase with decreasing number of states. The performance is largest using the coarse discretisation. Indeed, averaged over all discretisations, the results for the frequentist setting tend to be better than for the maximum entropy prior. The overall best performance can be achieved with the coarse discretisation and the frequentist setting with $\xi = 5$, but using the maximum entropy prior leads to comparable results even with $\xi = 3$.
The theoretical optimum is not known, but for comparison we show the results of the recurrent Q-learning (RQL), prioritised sweeping (RPS), fuzzy RL (RFuzzy), neural rewards regression (RNRR), policy gradient NRR (RPGNRR), and control neural network (RCNN) (Schaefer et al., 2007; Appl & Brauer, 2002; Schneegass et al., 2007). The highest observed performance is 0.861 using 10^5 observations, which has almost been achieved by the best certain-optimal policy using 10^4 observations.

9. Conclusion

A new approach incorporating uncertainty in RL is presented, following the path from *awareness* to *quantisation* and *control*. We applied the technique of uncertainty propagation (awareness) not only to understand the reliability of the obtained policies (quantisation) but also to achieve certain-optimality (control), a new optimality criterion in RL and beyond. We exemplarily implemented the methodology on discrete MDPs, but want to stress on its generality, also in terms of the applied statistical paradigm. We demonstrated how to realistically deal with large-scale problems without a substantial loss of performance. In addition, we have shown that the method can be used to guide exploration (control). By changing a single parameter the derived policies change from certain-optimal policies for quality assurance to policies that are certain-optimal in a reversed sense and can be used for information-seeking exploration.

Current and future work considers several open questions as the application to other RL paradigms and function approximators like neural networks and support vector machines. Another important issue is the utilisation of the information contained in the full covariance matrix rather than only the diagonal. This enhancement can be seen as a generalisation of the local to a global measure of uncertainty. It can be shown that the guaranteed minimal performance for a specific selection of states depends on the covariances between the different states, i.e., the non-diagonal entries of the covariance matrix.

Last but not least the application to further industrial environments is strongly aspired. Definitely, as several laboratory conditions, such as the possibility of an extensive exploration or the access on a sufficiently large number of observations, are typically not fulfilled in practice, we conclude that the knowledge of uncertainty and its intelligent utilisation in RL is vitally important to handle control problems of industrial scale.

10. References

Abbeel, P., Coates, A., Quigley, M. & Ng, A. Y. (2006). An application of reinforcement learning to aerobatic helicopter flight, *Proc. of the 20th Conference on Neural Information Processing Systems*, MIT Press, pp. 1–8.

Antos, A., Szepesvári, C. & Munos, R. (2006). Learning near-optimal policies with Bellman-residual minimization based fitted policy iteration and a single sample path, *Proc. of the Conference on Learning Theory*, pp. 574–588.

Appl, M. & Brauer, W. (2002). Fuzzy model-based reinforcement learning, *Advances in Computational Intelligence and Learning*, pp. 211–223.

Bertsekas, D. P. & Tsitsiklis, J. N. (1996). *Neuro-Dynamic Programming*, Athena Scientific.

Brafman, R. I. & Tennenholtz, M. (2003). R-Max - a general polynomial time algorithm for near-optimal reinforcement learning, *Journal of Machine Learning Research* 3: 213–231.

Coppersmith, D. & Winograd, S. (1990). Matrix multiplication via arithmetic progressions, *Journal of Symbolic Computation* 9: 251–280.

D'Agostini, G. (2003). *Bayesian Reasoning in Data Analysis: A Critical Introduction*, World Scientific Publishing.

Dearden, R., Friedman, N. & Andre, D. (1999). Model based Bayesian exploration, *Proc. of the Conference on Uncertainty in Artificial Intelligence*, pp. 150–159.

Dearden, R., Friedman, N. & Russell, S. J. (1998). *Bayesian Q-learning, Proc. of the Innovative Applications of Artificial Intelligence Conference of the Association for the Advancement of Artificial Intelligence*, pp. 761–768.

Delage, E. & Mannor, S. (2007). Percentile optimization in uncertain Markov decision processes with application to efficient exploration, *Proc. of the International Conference on Machine Learning*, pp. 225–232.

Engel, Y., Mannor, S. & Meir, R. (2003). Bayes meets Bellman: The Gaussian process approach to temporal difference learning, *Proc. of the International Conference on Machine Learning*, pp. 154–161.

Engel, Y., Mannor, S. & Meir, R. (2005). Reinforcement learning with Gaussian processes, *Proc. of the International Conference on Machine learning*, pp. 201–208.

Geibel, P. (2001). Reinforcement learning with bounded risk, *Proc. of the 18th International Conference on Machine Learning*, Morgan Kaufmann, San Francisco, CA, pp. 162–169.

Ghavamzadeh, M. & Engel, Y. (2006). Bayesian policy gradient algorithms, *Advances in Neural Information Processing Systems 19*, pp. 457–464.

Ghavamzadeh, M. & Engel, Y. (2007). Bayesian actor-critic algorithms, *Proc. of the International Conference on Machine learning*, pp. 297–304.

Hans, A. & Udluft, S. (2009). Efficient uncertainty propagation for reinforcement learning with limited data, *Proc. of the International Conference on Artificial Neural Networks*, Springer, pp. 70–79.

Hans, A. & Udluft, S. (2010). Uncertainty propagation for efficient exploration in reinforcement learning, *Proc. of the European Conference on Artificial Intelligence*

Heger, M. (1994). Consideration of risk in reinforcement learning, *Proc. 11th International Conference on Machine Learning*, Morgan Kaufmann, pp. 105–111.

ISO (1993). *Guide to the Expression of Uncertainty in Measurement*, International Organization for Standardization.

Kaelbling, L. P., Littman, M. L. & Moore, A. W. (1996). Reinforcement learning: A survey, *Journal of Artificial Intelligence Research* 4: 237–285.

Kearns, M., Mansour, Y. & Ng, A. Y. (2000). Approximate planning in large POMDPs via reusable trajectories, *Advances in Neural Information Processing Systems 12*.

Kearns, M. & Singh, S. (1998). Near-optimal reinforcement learning in polynomial time, *Proceedings of the 15th International Conference on Machine Learning*, pp. 260–268.

Lagoudakis, M. G. & Parr, R. (2003). Least-squares policy iteration, *Journal of Machine Learning Research* pp. 1107–1149.

Lee, H., Shen, Y., Yu, C.-H., Singh, G. & Ng, A. Y. (2006). Quadruped robot obstacle negotiation via reinforcement learning, *Proc. of the 2006 IEEE International Conference on Robotics and Automation, ICRA 2006, May 15-19, 2006, Orlando, Florida, USA*, pp. 3003–3010.

MacKay, D. J. C. (2003). *Information Theory, Inference, and Learning Algorithms*, Cambridge University Press, Cambridge.

Merke, A. & Riedmiller, M. A. (2001). Karlsruhe brainstormers - a reinforcement learning approach to robotic soccer, *RoboCup 2001: Robot Soccer World Cup V*, Springer, pp. 435- 440.

Mihatsch, O. & Neuneier, R. (2002). Risk-sensitive reinforcement learning, *Machine Learning* 49(2–3): 267–290.

Munos, R. (2003). Error bounds for approximate policy iteration., *Proc. of the International Conference on Machine Learning*, pp. 560–567.

Peshkin, L. & Mukherjee, S. (2001). Bounds on sample size for policy evaluation in Markov environments, *Proc. of Annual Conference on Computational Learning Theory, COLT and the European Conference on Computational Learning Theory*, Vol. 2111, Springer, Berlin, pp. 616–629.

Peters, J. & Schaal, S. (2008). Reinforcement learning of motor skills with policy gradients, *Neural Networks* 21(4): 682–697.

Poupart, P., Vlassis, N., Hoey, J. & Regan, K. (2006). An analytic solution to discrete Bayesian reinforcement learning, *Proc. of the International Conference on Machine Learning*, pp. 697–704.

Puterman, M. L. (1994). *Markov Decision Processes*, John Wiley & Sons, New York.

Rasmussen, C. E. & Kuss, M. (2003). Gaussian processes in reinforcement learning, *Advances in Neural Information Processing Systems 16*, pp. 751–759.

Schaefer, A. M., Schneegass, D., Sterzing, V. & Udluft, S. (2007). A neural reinforcement learning approach to gas turbine control, *Proc. of the International Joint Conference on Neural Networks*.

Schneegass, D., Udluft, S. & Martinetz, T. (2007). Improving optimality of neural rewards regression for data-efficient batch near-optimal policy identification, *Proc. of the International Conference on Artificial Neural Networks*, pp. 109–118.

Schneegass, D., Udluft, S. & Martinetz, T. (2008). Uncertainty propagation for quality assurance in reinforcement learning, *Proc. of the International Joint Conference on Neural Networks*, pp. 2589–2596.

Stephan, V., Debes, K., Gross, H.-M., Wintrich, F. & Wintrich, H. (2000). A reinforcement learning based neural multi-agent-system for control of a combustion process, *Proc. of the International Joint Conference on Neural Networks*, pp. 217–222.

Strehl, A. L. & Littman, M. L. (2008). An analysis of model-based interval estimation for Markov decision processes., *Journal of Computer and System Sciences* 74(8): 1309–1331.

Sutton, R. S. & Barto, A. G. (1998). *Reinforcement Learning: An Introduction*, MIT Press, Cambridge.

Wiering, M. & Schmidhuber, J. (1998). Efficient model-based exploration, *Proceedings of the 5th International Conference on Simulation of Adaptive Behavior: From Animals to Animats 5*, MIT Press/Bradford Books, Montreal, pp. 223–228.

Appendix

Theorem 1 *Suppose a finite MDP $M = (S,A,P,R)$ with discount factor $0 < \gamma < 1$ and C^0 an arbitrary initial symmetric and positive definite covariance matrix. Then the function*

$$\left(Q^m,C^m\right)=\left(TQ^{m-1},D^{m-1}C^{m-1}(D^{m-1})^T\right) \tag{35}$$

provides a unique fixed point (Q^*,C^*) almost surely, independent of the initial Q, for policy evaluation and policy iteration.

Proof: It has already been shown that $Q^m = TQ^{m-1}$ converges to a unique fixed point Q^* (Sutton & Barto, 1998). Since Q^m does not depend on C^k or the Jacobi matrix D^k for any iteration $k<m$, it remains to show that C^* unambiguously arises from the fixed point iteration. We obtain

$$C^m = \prod_{i=0}^{m-1} D^i C^0 \prod_{i=0}^{m-1} (D^i)^T \tag{36}$$

after m iterations. Due to convergence of Q^m, D^m converges to D^* as well, which leads to

$$C^* = \prod_{i=0}^{\infty} D^* C_{\text{conv}} \prod_{i=0}^{\infty} (D^*)^T \tag{37}$$

with C_{conv} the covariance matrix after convergence of Q. By successive matrix multiplication we obtain

$$(D^*)^n = \begin{pmatrix} (D^*)^n_{Q,Q} & \sum_{i=0}^{n} (D^*)^i_{Q,Q} (D^*)_{Q,P} & \sum_{i=0}^{n} (D^*)^i_{Q,Q} (D^*)_{Q,R} \\ 0 & \mathrm{I} & 0 \\ 0 & 0 & \mathrm{I} \end{pmatrix} \tag{38}$$

eventually leading to

$$(D^*)^\infty = \begin{pmatrix} (D^*)^\infty_{Q,Q} & \sum_{i=0}^{\infty} (D^*)^i_{Q,Q} (D^*)_{Q,P} & \sum_{i=0}^{\infty} (D^*)^i_{Q,Q} (D^*)_{Q,R} \\ 0 & \mathrm{I} & 0 \\ 0 & 0 & \mathrm{I} \end{pmatrix} \tag{39}$$

$$= \begin{pmatrix} 0 & (\mathrm{I} - (D^*)_{Q,Q})^{-1} (D^*)_{Q,P} & (\mathrm{I} - (D^*)_{Q,Q})^{-1} (D^*)_{Q,R} \\ 0 & \mathrm{I} & 0 \\ 0 & 0 & \mathrm{I} \end{pmatrix} \tag{40}$$

since all eigenvalues of $(D^*)_{Q,Q}$ are strictly smaller than 1 and $\mathrm{I} - (D^*)_{Q,Q}$ is invertible for all but finitely many $(D^*)_{Q,Q}$. Therefore, almost surely, $(D^*)^\infty$ exists, which implies that C^* exists as well. We finally obtain

$$C^*_{Q,Q} = (\mathrm{I} - (D^*)_{Q,Q})^{-1} \left((D^*)_{Q,P} \quad (D^*)_{Q,R} \right) \tag{41}$$

$$\begin{pmatrix} \mathrm{Cov}(P,P) & \mathrm{Cov}(P,R) \\ \mathrm{Cov}(P,R)^T & \mathrm{Cov}(R,R) \end{pmatrix} \begin{pmatrix} (D^*)^T_{Q,P} \\ (D^*)^T_{Q,R} \end{pmatrix} \left((\mathrm{I} - (D^*)_{Q,Q})^{-1} \right)^T . \tag{42}$$

The fixed point C^* depends on the initial covariance matrices Cov(P), Cov(R), and Cov(P,R) solely, but not on Cov(Q,Q), Cov(Q,P), or Cov(Q,R) and is therefore independent of the operations necessary to reach the fixed point Q^*. □

5

Anticipatory Mechanisms of Human Sensory-Motor Coordination Inspire Control of Adaptive Robots: A Brief Review

Alejandra Barrera
Mexico's Autonomous Technological Institute (ITAM)
Mexico City,
Mexico

1. Introduction

Sensory-motor coordination involves the study of how organisms make accurate goal-directed movements based on perceived sensory information. There are two problems associated to this process: sensory feedback is noisy and delayed, which can make movements inaccurate and unstable, and the relationship between a motor command and the movement it produces is variable, as the body and the environment can both change. Nevertheless, we can observe everyday our ability to perform accurate movements, which is due to a nervous system that adapts to those existing limitations and continuously compensates for them. How does the nervous system do it? By means of anticipating the sensory consequences of motor commands.

The idea that anticipatory mechanisms guide human behaviour, i.e., that predictions about future states directly influence current behavioural decision making, has been increasingly appreciated over the last decades. Various disciplines have explicitly recognized anticipations. In cognitive psychology, the ideo-motor principle states that an action is initiated by the anticipation of its effects, and before this advanced action mechanism can be used, a learning phase has to take place, advising the actor about several actions and their specific effects (Stock and Stock, 2004). In biorobotics, anticipation plays a major role in the coordination and performance of adaptive behaviour (Butz et al., 2002), being interested on designing artificial animals (*animats*) able to adapt to environmental changes efficiently by learning and drawing inferences.

What are the bases of human anticipation mechanisms? Internal models of the body and the world. Internal models can be classified into (Miall & Wolpert, 1996):

a. forward models, which are predictive models that capture the causal relationship between actions and outcome, translating the current system state and the current motor commands (efference copy) into predictions of the future system state, and
b. inverse models, which generate from inputs about the system state and state transitions, an output representing the causal events that produced that state.

Forward models are further divided into (Miall & Wolpert, 1996):

i. forward dynamic models, estimating future system states after current motor commands,

ii. forward sensory models, predicting sensory signals resultant from a given current state, and
iii. forward models of the physical properties of the environment, anticipating the behaviour of the external world.

Hence, by cascading accurate forward dynamic and forward sensory models, transformation of motor commands into sensory consequences can be achieved, producing a lifetime of calibrated movements. The accuracy of forward models is maintained through adaptive processes driven by sensory prediction errors.

Plenty of neuroscientific studies in humans suggest evidence of anticipatory mechanisms based on the concept of internal models, and several robotic implementations of predictive behaviors have been inspired on those biological mechanisms in order to achieve adaptive agents. This chapter provides an overview of such neuroscientific evidences, as well as the state of the art relative to corresponding implementations in robots.

The chapter starts by reviewing several behavioral studies that have demonstrated anticipatory and adaptive mechanisms in human sensory-motor control based on internal models underlying tasks such as eye–hand coordination, object manipulation, eye movements, balance control, and locomotion. Then, after providing a description of neuroscientific bases that have pointed to the cerebellum as a site where internal models are learnt, allocated and maintained, the chapter summarizes different computational systems that may be developed to achieve predictive robot architectures, and presents specific implementations of adaptive behaviors in robots including anticipatory mechanisms in vision, object manipulation, and locomotion.

The chapter also provides a discussion about the implications involved in endowing a robot with the capability of exhibiting an integral predictive behavior while performing tasks in real-world scenarios, in terms of several anticipatory mechanisms that should be implemented to control the robot.

Finally, the chapter concludes by suggesting an open challenge in the biorobotics field: to design a computational model of the cerebellum as a unitary module able to learn and operate diverse internal models necessary to support advanced perception-action coordination of robots, showing a human-like robust reactive behavior improved by integral anticipatory and adaptive mechanisms, while dynamically interacting with the real world during typical real life tasks.

2. Neuroscientific bases of anticipatory and adaptive mechanisms

This section reviews diverse neuroscientific evidences of human anticipatory and adaptive mechanisms in sensory-motor control, including the consideration of the cerebellum as a prime candidate module involved in sensory prediction.

2.1 Behavioral evidences

Several behavioural studies have demonstrated anticipatory and adaptive mechanisms in human sensory-motor control based on internal models underlying tasks such as eye–hand coordination (Ariff et al., 2002; Nanayakkara & Shadmehr, 2003; Kluzik et al., 2008), object manipulation (Johansson, 1998; Witney et al., 2004; Danion & Sarlegna, 2007), eye movements (Barnes & Asselman, 1991), balance control (Huxham et al., 2001), and locomotion (Grasso et al., 1998), as described in the following subsections.

2.1.1 Eye–hand coordination

Evidence of access to a forward dynamic model of the arm from the saccadic eye movement system is shown in (Ariff et al., 2002). In this study, subjects performed reaching movements having their arms hidden and tracking the position of their unseen hand with their eyes.
Ariff et al. (2002) found that in unperturbed reaching movements, saccade occurrence at any time t consistently provided an estimate of hand position at t+196 ms. However, the ability of the brain to guide saccades to the future position of the hand failed when a force pulse unexpectedly changed the arm dynamics immediately after perturbation. Thus, saccades were suppressed for 100 ms and then accurate predictive saccades re-emerged. The saccade inhibition period that followed the hand perturbation was suggested as the time length it takes to recompute the estimate of the future hand position.
In a further study, the arm dynamics was altered by applying various external force fields (Nanayakkara & Shadmehr, 2003). Eyes were able to make accurate predictive saccades after the force pulse only when the externally imposed arm dynamics was predictable, indicating that the saccadic system is able to use new information on arm dynamics to improve its performance.
In the context of reaching adaptation, Kluzik et al. (2008) studied subjects performing goal-directed reaching movements while holding the handle of a robotic arm that produced forces perturbing trajectories. Authors compared subjects' adaptation between three trial conditions: with robot forces turned off in unannounced manner, with robot forces turned off in announced manner, and free-space trials holding the handle but detached from the robot. When forces increased abruptly and in a single step, subjects made large errors in reaching. In contrast, in a gradual case with small force changes from one trial to the next one, subjects reported smaller performance errors. These results allowed authors to conclude that, although practice with a novel tool caused the formation of an internal model of the tool, it also appeared to produce a transient change in the internal model of the subject's arm.

2.1.2 Object manipulation

In (Johansson, 1998), a control scheme of object grasping and manipulation is proposed. In this scheme, both visual and somatosensory inputs are used in conjunction with internal models for parametric adjustment of fingertip forces to object properties in anticipation of the upcoming force requirements.
At the heart of this control is the comparison of somatosensory inflow with the predicted afferent input. Detection of a mismatch between predicted and actual sensory input triggers corrective responses along with an update of the relevant internal model and thus a change in parameter specification.
Witney et al. (2004) confirmed that feedback from cutaneous afferents is critical for successful feedforward control of grip force. Feedback is not only essential for the acquisition of the internal model, but constant uninterrupted feedback is also necessary to maintain previously acquired forward models.
In analyzing whether the human brain anticipates in real time the consequences of movement corrections, Danion and Sarlegna (2007) monitored grip force while subjects transported a hand-held object to a visual target that could move unexpectedly. They found that subjects triggered fast arm movement corrections to bring the object to the new target location, and initiated grip force adjustments before or in synchrony with arm movement corrections. Throughout the movement, grip force anticipated the mechanical consequences

resulting from arm motion, even when it was substantially corrected. Moreover, the predictive control of grip force did not interfere with the on-line control of arm trajectory. Those results allowed authors to confirm that motor prediction is an automatic, real-time process operating during movement execution and correction.

2.1.3 Eye movements

The purpose of smooth pursuit eye movements is to minimize retinal slip, i.e., target velocity projected onto the retina, stabilizing the image of the moving object on the fovea. It has been demonstrated that the brain uses predictions to execute this task and that a typical value is about 200 ms (Barnes & Asselman, 1991).

In (Barnes & Asselman, 1991), experiments were conducted on human subjects required to actively pursue a small target or stare passively at a larger display as it moved in the horizontal plane. Results indicated that prediction is carried out through the storage of information about both the magnitude and timing of eye velocity. Repeated exposure to the moving target leads to update that information. Initially, the response occurred with a latency of approximately 100 ms after the onset of target exposure, but after three or four exposures, the smooth eye movement has increased in peak velocity by a factor of 1.5-2.

Authors stressed the important role of visual feedback to check the validity of the velocity estimate in the predictive process. When a conflict between the estimate and the current visual input occurs, the estimation system is shut down, and the pursuit system falls back on the use of conventional visual feedback in order to build up a new estimate of velocity. In doing so, the reaction time to peak response is increased to 300 ms for the initial response, but becomes reduced to 200 ms after two or three presentations. Hence, in the normal mode of operation of the pursuit reflex, continuous visual feedback is enhanced by predictive estimates of eye velocity initiated under the control of the periodicity estimator and only corrected if retinal error conflict indicates an inappropriate predictive estimate.

2.1.4 Balance control

Anticipation in balance control in the presence of external perturbations is discussed in (Huxham et al., 2001).

Balance control during walking is achieved via two strategies: proactive, which reduce or counteract stresses acting on the body, and reactive, which respond to failures of proactive components or to unexpected external perturbation. Proactive balance mechanisms are visual-based. Information about environmental conditions and changes is constantly received through the eyes and interpreted in the light of experience about its impact on stability. Thus, we step around or over perceived obstacles, reduce our walking speed if the surface appears to be slippery, and maintain a higher degree of alertness in potentially hazardous situations such as rough terrain or cluttered areas.

A second form of proactive strategy termed predictive balance control, considers the forces acting on and within the body to maintain stability within the body and between the body and the support surface. It is dependent upon an accurate internal representation of the body and a learned awareness of how any movement or muscle action will alter those relationships.

Predictive control of the forces acting on the body is largely achieved by anticipatory postural adjustments, which initially are not based on sensory input but rather on what experience has taught will be the amount and direction of destabilization produced by the movement.

In summary, the balance system proactively monitors the external environment and predicts the effects of forces generated by voluntary movement on the body, making the adjustments necessary to maintain posture and equilibrium in anticipation of need. It is only when these adjustments fail or an unexpected destabilization occurs that the emergency back-up system of reactive balance responses is called in for crisis management.

2.1.5 Locomotion

Anticipatory head movements toward the direction to be walked were studied by Grasso et al. (1998). They measured head and eye movements in subjects walking along the same 90° corner trajectory both at light and with eyes closed and in forward and backward locomotion.

This study showed that coherent head and eye movements sustain a gaze orientation synergy during forward navigation tasks. Anticipation occurs relative to the direction one is about to take. In absence of visual stimuli, the orienting movements show similar behaviour. However, after inverting the locomotion direction, they are not maintained but disappear or are reversed according to the direction of steering.

These results add evidence to the hypothesis of a feed-forward navigation control system governing synergic head and eye movements aimed at anticipating future motor events.

2.2 The role of the cerebellum

Imaging and electrophysiological studies have pointed to the cerebellum as a site where internal models are learnt, allocated, and maintained, allowing predictive behaviour.

While studying grip force modulation, Kawato et al. (2003) suggested that forward models of object and arm dynamics are stored in the cerebellum predicting load force variations caused by arm/object dynamics. Functional imaging showed the activation of the right, anterior and superior cerebellum, and the biventer in the left cerebellum.

While human subjects learned to use a new tool, Imamizu et al. (2000) measured cerebellar activity by functional imaging, showing that specific voxels in the cerebellar cortex have bold signals that remain modified after a subject has learned a motor task involving the creation and storage of an internal model of the previously-unknown tool.

Cerminara et al. (2009) provided direct electrophysiological evidence for the operation of an internal model that simulates an external object's motion, expressed in simple-spike activity of Purkinje cells within the lateral cerebellum. The firing of these cells follows the velocity of the moving target even when the target has disappeared briefly.

Ghasia et al. (2008) found that putative cerebellar target neurons discharge in relation to a change in ocular torsion, suggesting that the cerebellum stores a model of ocular mechanics.

Using data from the floccular complex of the cerebellar cortex during normal smooth pursuit eye movements, and during the vestibulo-ocular reflex, Lisberger (2009) found that the simple-spike firing rates of a single group of floccular Purkinje cells may reflect the output of different internal models, such as a model of the inertia of real-world objects, and a model of the physics of the orbit, where head and eye motion sum to produce gaze motion.

Ebner and Pasalar (2008) studied monkeys performing manual pursuit tracking, and associated the simple-spike discharge of Purkinje cells in the intermediate and lateral cerebellum with a forward internal model of the arm predicting the consequences of arm movements, specifically the position, direction of movement, and speed of the limb.

Internal models are useful in sensory-motor coordination only if their predictions are generally accurate. When an accurate representation has been learnt, e.g., a forward model of how motor commands affect the motion of the arm or the eyes, motor commands can be apply to this internal model and predict the motion that will result. However, the relationship between a motor command and the movement it produces is variable, since the body and the environment can both change (e.g., bones grow and muscle mass increases during development; disease can affect the strength of muscles that act on the eyes; physical perturbations can alter the visual and proprioceptive consequences of motor commands). Hence, in order to maintain a desired level of performance, the brain needs to be "robust" to those changes by means of updating or adapting the internal models (Shadmehr et al., 2010). According to Lisberger (2009), the theory of cerebellar learning could be an important facet of the operation of internal models in the cerebellum. In this theory, errors in movement are signaled by consistently timed spikes on the climbing fiber input to the cerebellum. In turn, climbing fibers cause long-term depression of the synapses from parallel fibers onto Purkinje cells, specifically for the parallel fibers that were active at or just before the time the climbing fiber input arrived. The extension of the cerebellar learning theory to cerebellar internal models proposes that depression of the parallel fiber to Purkinje cell synapses corrects the internal model in the cerebellum, so that the next instance of a given movement is closer to perfection.

3. Robotic implementations of predictive behaviours

Anticipatory *animats* involve agent architectures based on predictive models. Underlying these predictive architectures, different computational systems may be implemented (Butz et al., 2002):

- Model-based reinforcement learning, where a model of the environment is learnt in addition to reinforcement values, and several anticipatory mechanisms can be employed such as biasing the decision maker toward the exploration of unknown/unseen regions or applying internal reinforcement updates.
- Schema mechanism, where the model is represented by rules and learnt bottom-up by generating more specialized rules where necessary, although no generalization mechanism applies and the decision maker is biased on the exploitation of the model to achieve desired items in the environment.
- The expectancy model SRS/E, which is not generalized but represented by a set of rules, and includes an additional sign list storing all states encountered so far. Reinforcement is only propagated once a desired state is generated by a behavioral module, and the propagation is accomplished using dynamic programming techniques applied to the learnt predictive model and the sign list.
- Anticipatory learning classifier systems that, similar to the schema mechanism and SRS/E, contain an explicit prediction component, and the predictive model consists of a set of rules (classifiers) which are endowed with an "effect" part to predict the next situation the agent will encounter if the action specified by the rules is executed. These systems are able to generalize over sensory input.
- Artificial neural networks (ANN), where the agent controller sends outputs to the actuators based on sensory inputs. Learning to control the agent consists in learning to associate the good set of outputs to any set of inputs that the agent may experience. The most common way to perform such learning consists in using the back-propagation

algorithm, which computes, for each set of inputs, the errors on the outputs of the controller. With respect to the computed error, the weights of the connections in the network are modified so that the error will be smaller the next time the same inputs are encountered. Back-propagation is a supervised learning method, where a supervisor indicates at each time step what the agent should have done. Nevertheless, it is difficult to build a supervisor in most control problems where the correct behavior is not known in advance. The solution to this problem relies on anticipation (Tani, 1996; Tani, 1999). If the role of an ANN is to predict what the next input will be rather than to provide an output, then the error signal is available: the difference between what the ANN predicted and what has actually happened.

Specific implementations of predictive behaviors in robots include anticipatory mechanisms in vision (Hoffmann, 2007; Datteri et al., 2003), object manipulation (Nishimoto et al., 2008; Laschi et al., 2008), and locomotion (Azevedo et al., 2004; Gross et al., 1998), as described in the following subsections.

3.1 Vision

In (Hoffmann, 2007), results are presented from experiments with a visually-guided four-wheeled mobile robot carrying out perceptual judgment based on visuo-motor anticipation to exhibit the ability to understand a spatial arrangement of obstacles in its behavioural meaning. The robot learns a forward model by moving randomly within arrangements of obstacles and observing the changing visual input. For perceptual judgment, the robot stands still, observes a single image, and internally simulates the changing images given a sequence of movement commands (wheel speeds) as specified by a certain movement plan. With this simulation, the robot judges the distance to an obstacle in front, and recognizes in an arrangement of obstacles either a dead end or a passage.

Images from the robot omni-directional camera are processed to emphasize the obstacles and reduce the number of pixels. The forward model predicts an image given the current processed image and the wheel velocities. Images are predicted using a set of multi-layer perceptrons, where each pixel is computed by one three-layer perceptron.

Datteri et al. (2003) proposed a perception-action scheme for visually-guided manipulation that includes mechanisms for visual predictions and for detecting unexpected events by comparisons between anticipated feedback and incoming feedback. Anticipated visual perceptions are based on motor commands and the associated proprioception of the robotic manipulator. If the system prediction is correct, full processing of the sensory input is not needed at this stage. Only when expected perceptions do not match incoming sensory data, full perceptual processing is activated.

Experimental results from a feeding task where the robotic arm places a spoon in its Cartesian space, showed the robot capability to monitor the spoon trajectory by vision, without full visual processing at each step in "regular" situations, and to detect unexpected events that required the activation of full perceptual processing.

3.2 Object manipulation

In the context of anticipation mechanisms while manipulating objects, Nishimoto et al. (2008) proposed a dynamic neural network model of interactions between the inferior parietal lobe (IPL), representing human behavioural skills related to object manipulation and tool usage, and cells in the ventral premotor area (PMv), allowing learning, generation and recognition of goal-directed behaviours.

Authors suggest that IPL might function as a forward sensory model by anticipating coming sensory inputs in achieving a specific goal, which is set by PMv and sent as input to IPL. The forward sensory model is built by using a continuous-time recurrent neural network that is trained with multiple sensory (visuo-proprioceptive) sequences acquired during the off-line teaching phase of a small-scale humanoid robot, where robot arm movements are guided in grasping the object to generate the desired trajectories.

During the experiments, the robot was tested to autonomously perform three types of operational grasping actions on objects with both hands: lift up, move to the right, or move to the left. Experimental conditions included placing the object at arbitrary left or right locations inside or outside the training region, and changing the object location from center to left/right abruptly at arbitrary time step after the robot movement had been initiated. Results showed the robot capability to perform and generalize each behaviour successfully considering object location variations, and adapt to sudden environmental changes in real time until 20 time steps before reaching the object, a process that takes the robot 30 time steps in the normal condition.

Laschi et al. (2008) implemented a model of human sensory-motor coordination in grasping and manipulation on a humanoid robotic system with an arm, a sensorized hand and a head with a binocular vision system. They demonstrated the robot able to reach and grasp an object detected by vision, and to predict the tactile feedback by means of internal models built by experience using neuro-fuzzy networks.

Sensory prediction is employed during the grasping phase, which is controlled by a scheme based on the approach previously proposed by Datteri et al. (2003). The scheme consists of three main modules: vision, providing information about geometric features of the object of interest based on binocular images of the scene acquired by the robot cameras; preshaping, generating a proper hand/arm configuration to grasp the object based on inputs from the vision module about the object geometric features; and tactile prediction, producing the tactile image expected when the object is contacted based on the object geometric features from the vision module and the hand/arm configuration from the preshaping module.

During training (creation of the internal models), the robot system grasps different kinds of objects in different positions in the workspace to collect correct data used to learn the correlations between visual information, hand and arm configurations, and tactile images. During the testing phase, several trials were executed where an object was located in a position in the workspace and the robot had to grasp, lift up and keep it with a stable grasp. Results showed a good system performance in terms of success rate, as well as a good system capability to predict the tactile feedback, as given by the low difference between the predicted tactile image and the actual one. In experimental conditions different from those of the training phase, the system was capable to generalize with respect to variations of object position and orientation, size and shape.

3.3 Locomotion

Azevedo et al. (2004) proposed a locomotion control scheme for two-legged robots based on the human walking principle of anticipating the consequences of motor actions by using internal models. The approach is based on the optimization technique Trajectory-Free Non-linear Model Predictive Control (TF-NMPC) that consists on optimizing the anticipated future behaviour of the system from inputs relative to contact forces employing an internal model over a finite sliding time horizon. A biped robot was successfully tested during static walking, dynamic walking, and postural control in presence of unexpected external thrusts.

Gross et al. (1998) provided a neural control architecture implemented on a mobile miniature robot performing a local navigation task, where the robot anticipates the sensory consequences of all possible motor actions in order to navigate successfully in critical environmental regions such as in front of obstacles or intersections.
The robot sensory system determines the basic 3D structure of the visual scenery using optical flow. The neural architecture learns to predict and evaluate the sensory consequences of hypothetically executed actions by simulating alternative sensory-motor sequences, selecting the best one, and executing it in reality. The subsequent flow field depends on the previous one and the executed action, thus the optical flow prediction subsystem can learn to anticipate the sensory consequences of selected actions.
Learning after executing a real action results from comparing the real and the predicted sensory situation considering reinforcement signals received from the environment. By means of internal simulation, the system can look ahead and select the action sequence that yields to the highest total reward in the future. Results from contrasting the proposed anticipatory system with a reactive one showed the robot's ability to avoid obstacles earlier.

4. Summary and conclusions

The sensory-motor coordination system in humans is able to adjust for the presence of noise and delay in sensory feedback, and for changes in the body and the environment that alter the relationship between motor commands and their sensory consequences. This adjustment is achieved by employing anticipatory mechanisms based on the concept of internal models. Specifically, forward models receive a copy of the outgoing motor commands and generate a prediction of the expected sensory consequences. This output may be used to:

i. adjust fingertip forces to object properties in anticipation of the upcoming force requirements,
ii. increase the velocity of the smooth eye movement while pursuing a moving target,
iii. make necessary adjustments to maintain body posture and equilibrium in anticipation of need,
iv. trigger corrective responses when detecting a mismatch between predicted and actual sensory input, involving the corresponding update of the relevant internal model.

Several behavioural studies have shown that the sensory-motor system acquires and maintains forward models of different systems (i.e., arm dynamics, grip force, eye velocity, external objects and tools dynamics, and postural stability within the body and between the body and the support surface), and it has been widely hypothesized that the cerebellum is the location of those internal models, and that the theory of cerebellar learning might come into play to allow the models to be adjusted. Even though the major evidence of the role of the cerebellum comes from imaging studies, recent electrophysiological research has analyzed recordings from cerebellar neurons in trying to identify patterns of neural discharge that might represent the output of diverse internal models.
As reviewed within this chapter, although not in an exhaustive manner, several independent efforts in the robotics field have been inspired on human anticipatory mechanisms based on internal models to provide efficient and adaptive robot control. Each one of those efforts addresses predictive behaviour within the context of one specific motor system; e.g, visuo-motor coordination to determine the implications of a spatial arrangement of obstacles, or to place a spoon during a feeding task, object manipulation

while performing grasping actions, postural control in presence of unexpected external thrusts, and navigation within environments having obstacles and intersections.
Nevertheless, in trying to endow a robot with the capability of exhibiting an integral predictive behaviour while performing tasks in real-world scenarios, several anticipatory mechanisms should be implemented to control the robot. Simply to follow a visual target by coordinating eye, head, and leg movements, walking smoothly and efficiently in an unstructured environment, the robot performance should be based on diverse internal models allowing anticipation in vision (saccadic and smooth pursuit systems), head orientation according to the direction to be walked, balance control adapting posture to different terrains and configurations of environment, and interpretation of the significance and permanence of obstacles within the current scene.
Assuming the cerebellum as a site involved in a wide variety of anticipatory processes by learning, allocating, and adapting different internal models in sensory-motor control, we conclude this brief review suggesting an open challenge in the biorobotics field: to design a computational model of the cerebellum as a unitary module able to operate diverse internal models necessary to support advanced perception-action coordination of robots, showing a human-like robust reactive behaviour improved by integral anticipatory and adaptive mechanisms while dynamically interacting with the real world during typical real life tasks. Anticipating the predictable part of the environment facilitates the identification of unpredictable changes, which allows the robot to improve its capability in moving in the world by exhibiting a fast reaction to those environmental changes.

5. References

Ariff, G., Donchin, O., Nanayakkara, T., and Shadmehr, R. (2002). A real-time state predictor in motor control: study of saccadic eye movements during unseen reaching movements. *Journal of Neuroscience,* Vol. 22, No. 17, pp. 7721–7729.

Azevedo, C., Poignet, P., Espiau, B. (2004). Artificial locomotion control: from human to robots. *Robotics and Autonomous Systems*, Vol. 47, pp. 203–223.

Barnes, G. R. and Asselman, P. T. (1991). The mechanism of prediction in human smooth pursuit eye movements. *Journal of Physiology,* Vol. 439, pp. 439-461.

Butz, M. V., Sigaud, O., and Gerard, P. (2002). Internal models and anticipations in adaptive learning systems, *Proceedings of 1st Workshop on Adaptive Behavior in Anticipatory Learning Systems (ABiALS).*

Cerminara, N. L., Apps, R., Marple-Horvat, D. E. (2009). An internal model of a moving visual target in the lateral cerebellum. *Journal of Physiology,* Vol. 587, No. 2, pp. 429–442.

Danion, F. and Sarlegna, F. R. (2007). Can the human brain predict the consequences of arm movement corrections when transporting an object? Hints from grip force adjustments. *Journal of Neuroscience,* Vol. 27, No. 47, pp. 12839–12843.

Datteri, E., Teti, G., Laschi, C., Tamburrini, G., Dario, P., Guglielmelli, E. (2003). Expected perception in robots: a biologically driven perception-action scheme, In: *Proceedings of 11th International Conference on Advanced Robotics (ICAR),* Vol. 3, pp. 1405-1410.

Ebner, T. J., Pasalar, S. (2008). Cerebellum predicts the future motor state. *Cerebellum,* Vol. 7, No. 4, pp. 583–588.

Ghasia, F. F., Meng, H., Angelaki, D. E. (2008). Neural correlates of forward and inverse models for eye movements: evidence from three-dimensional kinematics. *The Journal of Neuroscience*, Vol. 28, No. 19, pp. 5082–5087.

Grasso, R., Prévost, P., Ivanenko, Y. P., and Berthoz, A. (1998). Eye-head coordination for the steering of locomotion in humans: an anticipatory synergy. *Neuroscience Letters*, Vol. 253, pp. 115–118.

Gross, H-M., Stephan, V., Seiler, T. (1998). Neural architecture for sensorimotor anticipation. *Cybernetics and Systems Research*, Vol. 2, pp. 593-598.

Hoffmann, H. (2007). Perception through visuomotor anticipation in a mobile robot. *Neural Networks*, Vol. 20, pp. 22-33.

Huxham, F. E., Goldie, P. A., and Patla, A. E. (2001). Theoretical considerations in balance assessment. *Australian Journal of Physiotherapy*, Vol. 47, pp. 89-100.

Imamizu, H., Miyauchi, S., Tamada, T., Sasaki, Y., Takino, R., Pütz, B., Yoshioka, T., Kawato, M. (2000). Human cerebellar activity reflecting an acquired internal model of a new tool. *Nature*, Vol. 403, pp. 192–195.

Johansson, R. S. (1998). Sensory input and control of grip, In: *Sensory guidance of movements*, M. Glickstein (Ed.), pp. 45–59, Chichester: Wiley.

Kawato, M., Kuroda, T., Imamizu, H., Nakano, E., Miyauchi, S., and Yoshioka, T. (2003). Internal forward models in the cerebellum: fMRI study on grip force and load force coupling. *Progress in Brain Research*, Vol. 142, pp. 171–188.

Kluzik, J., Diedrichsen, J., Shadmehr, R., and Bastian, A. J. (2008). Reach adaptation: what determines whether we learn an internal model of the tool or adapt the model of our arm? *Journal of Neurophysiology*, Vol. 100, pp. 1455–1464.

Laschi, C., Asuni, G., Guglielmelli, E., Teti, G., Johansson, R., Konosu, H., Wasik, Z., Carrozza, M. C., and Dario, P. (2008). A bio-inspired predictive sensory-motor coordination scheme for robot reaching and preshaping. *Autonomous Robots*, Vol. 25, pp. 85–101.

Lisberger, S. G. (2009). Internal models of eye movement in the floccular complex of the monkey cerebellum. *Neuroscience*, Vol. 162, No. 3, pp. 763–776.

Miall, R. C., and Wolpert, D. M. (1996). Forward models for physiological motor control. *Neural Networks*, Vol. 9, No. 8, pp. 1265-1279.

Nanayakkara, T. and Shadmehr, R. (2003). Saccade adaptation in response to altered arm dynamics. *Journal of Neurophysiology*, Vol. 90, pp. 4016–4021.

Nishimoto, R., Namikawa, J., and Tani, J. (2008). Learning multiple goal-directed actions through self-organization of a dynamic neural network model: a humanoid robot experiment. Adaptive Behavior, Vol. 16, No. 2/3, pp. 166-181.

Shadmehr, R., Smith, M. A., Krakauer, J. W. (2010). Error correction, sensory prediction, and adaptation in motor control. *Annu. Rev. Neurosci.*, Vol. 33, pp. 89–108.

Stock, A. and Stock, C. (2004). A short history of ideo-motor action. *Psychological Research*, Vol. 68, pp. 176–188.

Tani, J. (1996). Model-based learning for mobile robot navigation from the dynamical system perspective. *IEEE Transactions on System, Man and Cybernetics*, Vol. 26, No. 3, pp. 421-436.

Tani, J. (1999). Learning to perceive the world as articulated: an approach for hierarchical learning in sensory-motor systems. *Neural Networks*, Vol. 12, pp. 1131-1141.

Witney, A. G., Wing, A., Thonnard, J-L., and Smith, A. M. (2004). The cutaneous contribution to adaptive precision grip. *TRENDS in Neurosciences*, Vol. 27, No. 10, pp. 637-643.

6

Reinforcement-based Robotic Memory Controller

Hassab Elgawi Osman
Tokyo
Japan

1. Introduction

Neuroscientists believe that living beings solve the daily life activities, making decisions and hence adapt to newly situations by learning from past experiences. Learning from experience implies that each event is learnt through features (i.e. sensory control inputs) analysis that aimed to specify and then recall more important features for each event or situation.

In robot learning, several works seem to suggest that the transition to the current reinforcement learning (RL) (1), as a general formalism, does correspond to observable mammal brain functionality, where 'basal ganglia' can be modeled by an *actor-critic* (AC) version of *temporal difference* (TD) learning (2; 3; 4). However, as with the most real-world intelligent learning systems, the arising of 'perceptual aliasing' (also referred to as a problem of 'incomplete perception', or 'hidden state') (5), when the system has to scale up to deal with complex nonlinear search spaces in a non-Markov settings or *Partially Observation Markov Decision Process* (POMDP) domains (6) (see Fig. 1) renders to-date RL methods impracticable, and that they must learn to estimate *value function* v^{π} instead of learning the *policy* π, limiting them mostly for solving only simple learning tasks, raising an interest in heuristic methods that directly and adaptively modifying the learning policy $\pi: S \rightarrow A$ (which maps perceptual state/observation to action) via interaction with the rest of the system (7; 8).

Inclusion of a memory to a simulated robot control system is striking because a memory learning system has the advantage to deal with perceptual aliasing in POMDP, where memoryless policies are often fail to converge (9).

In this paper, a self-optimizing memory controller is designed particularly for solving non-Markovian tasks, which correspond to a great deal of real-life stochastic predictions and control problems (10) (Fig. 2). Rather than holistic search for the whole memory contents the controller adopts associated feature analysis to successively memorize a newly experience (state-action pair) as an action of past experience. e.g., If each past experience was a chunk, the controller finds the best chunk for the current situation for policy exploration. Our aim is not to mimic the neuroanatomical structure of the brain system but to catch its properties, avoids manual 'hard coding' of behaviors. AC learning is used to adaptively tune the control parameters, while an on-line variant of decision-tree ensemble learner (11; 12) is used as memory-capable function approximator coupled with Intrinsically Motivated Reinforcement Learning (IMRL) reward function (13; 14; 15; 16) to approximate the policy of

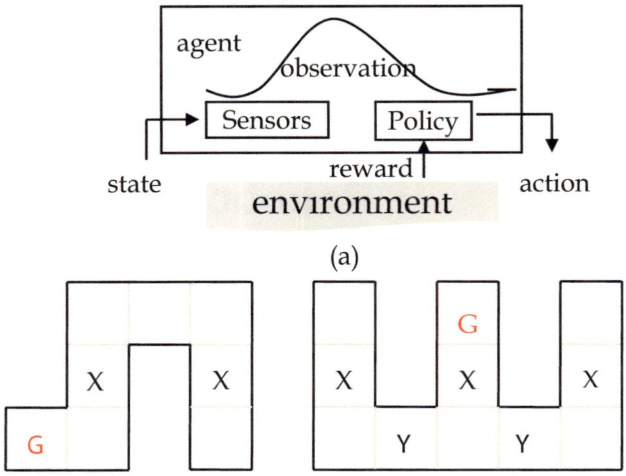

(a)

(b) (c)

Fig. 1. POMDP and Perceptual aliasing. RL agent is connected to its world via perception state S and action A. In (a) a partially observable world, in which the agent does not know which state it is in due to sensor limitations; for the value function v^{π}, the agent updates its policy parameters directly. In (b) and (c) two maze domains. States indicated with the same letter (X or Y) are perceptually aliased because the agent is sensed only wall configuration.

the *actor* and the value function of the *critic*. Section 2 briefly highlights on POMDP settings. A description with comprehensive illustration of the proposed memory controller will be given in Section 3. Then Section 4 highlights a comparison of conventional memory controller and the self-optimizing memory controller. Section 5 shows the implementation of decision-tree ensemble as memory-capable function approximator for both critic and policy. Some experimental results are presented in Section 6 as promising examples. It includes the non-Markovian cart-pole balancing tasks. The results show that our controller is able to memorize complete non-Markovian sequential tasks and develop complex behaviors such as balancing two poles simultaneously.

2. A non-Markovian and perceptual aliasing

First we present the formal setting of POMDP and then highlight on related approaches tacking perceptual aliasing.

2.1 POMDP formal setting

The formal setting of POMDP is $\mathcal{P} = \langle \mathcal{M}, \mathcal{O}, \mathcal{Z} \rangle$ consist of:

1. An MDP of a tuple $\mathcal{M}=\langle S,A,T,R \rangle$ where S is the space of possible *states* of the environment, A is a set of *actions* available to the agent (or control input), $P : S \times A \times S \rightarrow [0,1]$ defines a conditional probability distribution over *state transitions* given an action, and $R : S \times A \rightarrow R$ is a *reward function* (payoff) assigning a reward for an action,
2. A set of possible observations $\mathcal{O}$, where $\mathcal{O}$ could constitute either a set of discrete observations or a set of real-value,

3. $\mathcal{Z}$, a probability density mapping state-observation combinations $S \times \mathcal{O}$ to a probability distribution, or in the case of discrete observations combinations $S \times \mathcal{O}$ to probabilities. In other words, $Z(s, o)$ yields the probability to observing o in state s. So basically, a POMDP is like an MDP but with observations instead of direct state perception.

If a world model is available to the controller, it can easily calculate and update a *belief vector* $\vec{b_t} = \langle b_t(s_1), b_t(s_2), \cdots, b_t(s_N) \rangle$ over 'hidden states' at every time step t by taking into a account the history trace $h = o_1, o_2, \ldots, o_{t-1}, o_t$.

2.2 Perceptual aliasing

It is important to note that in several literatures, perceptual aliasing is wrongly defined as the problem of having an uncomplete instance, whereas this paper defines it as a problem related to having different states that may look similar but are related to different responses. Uncomplete instances may provoke perceptual aliasing, but they are not the same. Although the solely work in this paper is focused on POMDP, we briefly highlight on related approaches, in order to decipher the ambiguities between POMDP and perceptual aliasing:

- *Hidden Markov Models* (HMMs): are indeed applied to the more general problem of perceptual aliasing. In HMM it is accepted that we do not have control over the state transitions, whereas POMDP assume that we do. Hence, POMDP are more related to incomplete perception than to perceptual aliasing. HMMs have been thoroughly applied to robotic behavior synthesis, see, for example (18).
- *Memory-based system*: in Memory-based systems the controller is unable to take optimal transitions unless it observed the past inputs, then the controller simultaneously solve the incomplete perception while maximizing discounted long-term reward.
  For an early practice attempts with other alternative POMDP approaches, e.g., the 'model-based approach or belief-based approach', and the 'heuristic method with a world model' within TD reinforcement learning domain, see (23; 24).
- There is a large body of work on behavior learning both supervisedly and unsupervisedly using fuzzy logic, Artificial Neural Networks (ANN) and/or Case Based Reasoning (CBR). Some of them do not establish rules and, specifically, CBR uses memory as its key learning tool. This, too, has been used in robotics in loosely defined navigation problems. See, for example (19)

3. Self-optimizing controller architecture

One departing approach from manual 'hard coding' of behaviors is to let the controller build its own internal 'behavior model'–'on-the-fly' by learning from past experience. Fig. 2 illustrates the general view of our memory controller based on heuristic memory approach. We briefly explain its components. It is worth noted that in our implementation only the the capacity of the memory and reward function have be specified by a designer, the controller is self-optimized in a sense that we do not analyzing a domain *a priori*, instead we add an initially suboptimal model, which is optimized through learning[1].

[1] At this point we would like to mention that M3 Computer Architecture Group at Cornell has proposed a similar work (17) to our current interest. They implement a RL-based memory controller with a different underlying RL implementation, we inspired by them in some parts.

Past experiences. Sensory control inputs from environment would be stored at the next available empty memory location (chunk), or randomly at several empty locations.
Feature predictor. Is utilized to produce associated features for each selective experience. This predictor was designed to predict multiple experiences in different situations. When the selective experience is predicted, the associated features are converted to feature vector so the controller can handle it.
Features Map. The past experiences are mapped into multidimensional feature space using neighborhood component analysis (NCA) (20; 21), based on the Bellman error, or on the temporal difference (TD) error. In general this is done by choosing a set of features which approximate the states S of the system. A function approximator (FA) must map these features into V^{π} for each state in the system. This generalizes learning over similar states and more likely to increase learning speed, but potentially introduces generalization error as the feature will not represent the state space exactly.
Memory access. The memory access scheduling is formulated as a RL agent whose goal is to learn automatically an optimal memory scheduling policy via interaction with the rest of the system. A similar architecture that exploits heterogeneous learning modules simultaneously has been proposed (22). As can be seen in the middle of Fig. 2 two scenarios are considered. In (a) all the system parameters are *fully observable*, the agent can estimate v^{π} for each state and use its actions (e.g., past experiences). The agent's behavior, B, takes actions that tend to increase the long-run sum of values of the *reinforcement signal*, typically [0,1]. In (b) the system is *partially observable* as described in Fig. 1. Since our system is modeled as POMDP decision depends on last observation-action, and the observation transitions $s_{t+1} = \delta(s_t, a_t)$ depend on randomly past perceptual state. This transition is expressed by $Pr(s_t \mid s_{t-1}, a_{t-1}, s'_t, s''_t, \cdots)$, where s_{t-1}, a_{t-1} are the previous state and action, and t', t'' are arbitrary past time.
Learning behaviors from past experience. On each time step t, an *adaptive critic* (that is a component of the TD learning), is used to estimate future values of the *reinforcement signal* of retaining different memory locations, which represents the agent's behavior, B in choosing actions. The combinations of memory locations show to have the highest accumulated signals are more likely to be remembered. TD error–the change in expected future signal is computed based on the amount of occasional intrinsic reinforcement signal received, a long with the estimates of the adaptive critic.

4. Non-Markovian memory controller

4.1 Conventional memory controller

Conventional manually designed memory controller suffers two major limitations in regard with scheduling process and generalization capacity. First, it can not anticipate the long-term planning of its scheduling decisions. Second, it lacks learning ability, as it can not generalize and use the experience obtained through scheduling decisions made in the past to act successfully in new system states. This rigidity and lack of adaptivity can lead to severe performance degradation in many applications, raising interest in self-optimizing memory controller with generalization capacity.

4.2 Self-optimizing memory controller

The proposed self-optimizing memory controller is a fully-parallel maximum-likelihood search engine for recalling the most relevant features in the memory of past. The memory

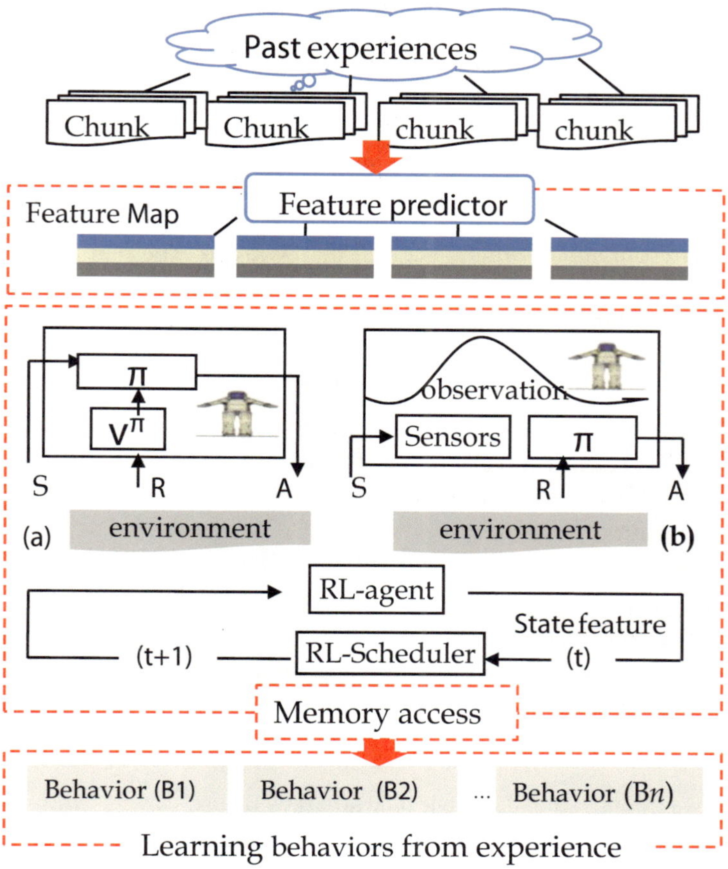

Fig. 2. Architecture of self-optimizing memory controller. The controller utilizes associated feature analysis to memorize complete non-Markovian reinforcement task as an action of past experience. The controller can acquired behaviors such as controlling objects, displays long-term planning and generalization capacity.

controller considers the long-term planning of each available action. Unlike conventional memory controllers, self-optimizing memory controller has the following capabilities: 1) Utilizes experience learnt in previous system states to make good scheduling decisions in new, previously unobserved states, 2) Adapts to the time-variant system in which the state transition function (or probability) is permitted to gradually change through time, and 3) Anticipates the long-term consequences of its scheduling decisions, and continuously optimizes its scheduling policy based on this anticipation.

No key words or pre-determined specified memory locations would be given for the stored experiences. Rather a parallel search for the memory contents would take place to recall the previously stored experience that correlates with the current newly experience. The controller handle the following tasks: (1) relate states and actions with the occasional reward for long planning, (2) take the action that is estimated to provide the highest reward value at a given state, and (3) continuously update long-term reward values associated with state-action pairs, based on IMRL.

5. Memory-capable function approximation

5.1 Actor-critic learning

Actor-critic (AC), a group of on-policy TD methods, separates the π and the v^{π} into independent memory structures. The π structure, or *actor*, is used to decide which action to pick in each state. The estimate of v^{π}, or *adaptive critic*, determines whether the actions of the *actor* are to be rewarded or punished. The algorithms use these spare measures of performance to adopt an optimal behavior over time. The adaptive critic maps its current state event onto an estimate of whether it will be rewarded. The mapping is learned from the past experience. If $s + 1$ is the situation that follows situation s in time, this expected future reward may be written as:

$$V(s) = \gamma^0 r(s) + \gamma^1 V(s+1) + \cdots + \gamma^n V(s+n) \tag{1}$$

The value of the current situation, $V(s)$, is the sum of all the rewards we will receive over the next n time steps. The rewards on each time step are "discounted" by factor, γ, in the range [0,1]. Equation (1) can be rewritten in a recursive form:

$$V(s) = \gamma^0 r(s) + \gamma^1 V(s+1) = r(s) + \gamma V(s+1) \tag{2}$$

It should be noted that the equality in Eq. 2 is valid only if n is infinite or the state at n time steps later, $s + n$, is always *a* so-called 'absorbing state.' Obviously a value function estimates that fall far from this equality in considered inaccurate, and the error is estimated based on TD error:

$$\delta(s) = (r(s) + \gamma V(s+1) - V(s)) \tag{3}$$

Adopting these methods can save much computation for selecting optimal actions, due to utilizing separate memory for value function and policy.

5.2 AC in non-Markovian domain

Due to non-Markovian characteristics, the controller infers the state of its environment from a sequence of observations it receives, learns an optimal action by detecting certain past events, that associated with its current perception. In particular, at time t, the error of the critic is given by,

$$E_c(t) = \frac{1}{2}([r(t) + \gamma J(t)] - J(t-1))^2 \tag{4}$$

while the error of the actor is

$$E_a(t) = \frac{1}{2}(J(t) - R^*)^2 \tag{5}$$

where R^* is the optimal return, which is dependent on the problem definition. The expected return is expressed as the general utility function, $J(t)$, which is to be maximized by the controller. Specifically,

$$J(t) = r(t+1) + \gamma r(t+2) + \gamma^2 r(t+3) + \cdots \tag{6}$$

where $r(t)$ is the immediate reward and γ is the time-discounting factor $0 \le \gamma \le 1$.

5.3 Decision-tree ensemble memory for optimal learning

On-line decision-tree ensemble learner has the characteristics of a simple structure, strong global approximation ability and a quick and easy training (11; 12). It has been used with TD learning for building a hybrid function approximator (26; 27). Here, in order to improve learning efficiency and to reduce the demand of storage space and to improve learning efficiency, the on-line ecision-tree ensemble approximator is structured in a way that both *actor* and *critic* can be embodied in one structure, subsequently, is used to approximate π of the *actor* and the v^{π} of the *critic* simultaneously. That is, the actor and the critic can share the input and the basis functions structure of the RF. Let DT_{Appro} represents a hybrid approximator that combines actor and critic. Given a state $s(t)$ and action $a(t)$, DT_{Appro} is defined such that $DT_{Appro}(s(t), a(t)) = (J(t), a(t+1))$, where $J(t)$ is the estimated value of the given state-action pair, and $a(t + 1)$ is the subsequent action to be taken by the controller. At the critic output the error is captured by TD error. However, at the action outputs the error is determined by the gradient of the estimated value $J(t + 1)$ w.r.t the action $a(t + 1)$ selected by the on-line RF at time t. Specifically,

$$\begin{aligned} e_a(t) &= \alpha \nabla_{a(t+1)} J(t+1) \\ &= \alpha \left(\frac{\partial J(t+1)}{\partial a_1(t+1)}, \dots, \frac{\partial J(t+1)}{\partial a_d(t+1)} \right) \end{aligned} \tag{7}$$

where α is a scaling constant and d is the choices availabilities at action a. Accumulating the error for each choice of the selected action, the overall actor error is given be:

$$E_a(t) = \frac{1}{2}\left[\sum_{i=1}^{d} e_{ai}^2(t) \right] \tag{8}$$

where $e_{ai}(t)$ is the choice of the action error gradient $e_a(t)$. In finding the gradient of the estimated value $J(t + 1)$ w.r.t the previously selected action $a(t + 1)$, the direction of change in action, which will improve the expected return at time step $t + 1$, is obtained. Thus by incrementally improving actions in this manner, an optimal policy can be achieved. $E(t) = E_c(t) + E_a(t)$ defines the reduced error for the entire on-line appriximator.

6. Experiment and results

As discussed in previous sections, the proposed controller brings a number of preferable properties for learning different behaviors. In this section, we investigate its learning capability through a task of cart-pole balancing problem, designed with non-Markovian settings.

6.1 Related work

Modeling the pole balancing algorithm for POMDP has received much interest in the field on control and artificial intelligence. Although a variation of Value and Policy Search (VAPS) algorithm (28) has been applied to this problem for the POMDP case (29), they have assumed that the position of cart on track x and the angle of pole from vertical θ are completely observable. NeuroEvolution of Augmenting Topologies (30) and evolutionary computation (31), are another promising approaches where recurrent neural networks are used to solve a harder balancing of two poles of different lengths, in both Markovian and non-Markovian settings.

6.2 Non-Markovian Cart Pole balancing

As illustrated in Fig. 3A, Cart-Pole balancing involves a vertical pole with a point-mass at its upper end installed on a cart, with the goal of balancing the pole when the cart moves by applying horizontal forces to the cart, which must not stray too far from its initial position. The state description for the controller consists of four continuous state variables, the angle θ (radial), and the speed of the pole $\dot{\theta} = \delta x / \delta t$ plus the position x and speed of the cart $\acute{x} = \delta x / \delta t$, (see Appendix A.1 for the equations of motion and Appendix A.2 for parameters used as reported by (31)). The two continuous actions set up for controller training and evaluation were RightForce (RF), (results in pushing the cart to the right), and LeftForce (LF), (results in pushing the cart left). At each time step t, the controller must only observe the θ (that is, the controller is not observing the velocities $(\dot{x}, \dot{\theta})$) and then takes appropriate action to balance the pole by learning from the past experience and the intrinsically rewards. The optimal value function is shown in Fig. 3B. A simulated sample run is shown in Fig. 4. The controller could keep the pole balanced after about 4000 steps.

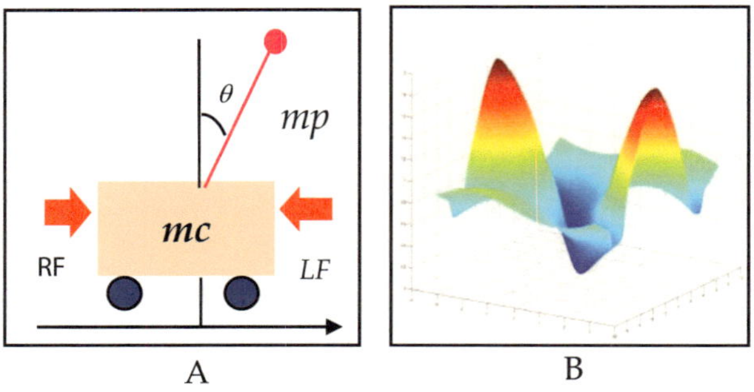

Fig. 3. (A) Illustration of the non-Markov Cart-Pole balancing problem, where the angular velocity is not observing by the controller. (B) Optimal value function.

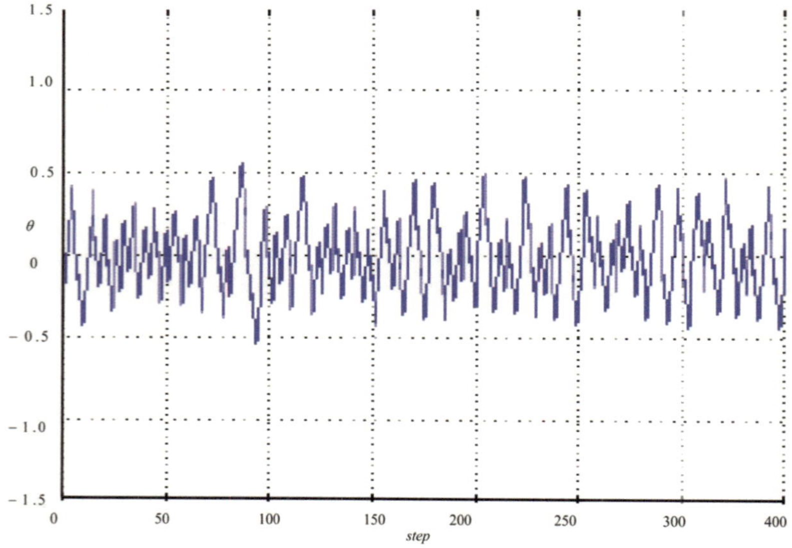

Fig. 4. A sample learning for balancing the pole. It suggests that the method could keep the pole near the top for a long time.

6.3 Non-Markovian Two-Pole balancing

Then we moved to a harder setting of this problem, balancing two poles simultaneously (see Fig. 5). Each pole has its own position and angular velocity, θ_1 and $\dot{\theta}_1$ for the first pole and θ_2 and $\dot{\theta}_2$ for the second pole respectively. See Appendix A.2 for parameters used as reported by (31).The controller must balance the two poles without velocity information. In order to assist the feasibility of our approach to balance two poles simultaneously we compared with other methods.

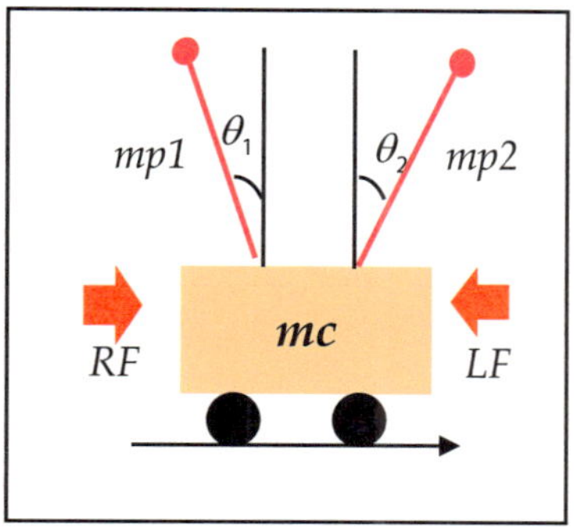

Fig. 5. Illustration of the non-Markov 2-Pole balancing problem. Parameters known are θ_1 and θ_2. The controller must balance the two poles without observing $\dot{\theta}_1$ and $\dot{\theta}_2$.

Table 1 reports the performance of our controller compared with traditional value function based methods (See Appendix B.1 for parameters used) (including SARSA-CABA (See Appendix B.2, SARSA-CMAC (See Appendix B.3, which are reported by (31), who used SARSA implementations by (32) and VAPS (See Appendix B.4) and policy search method (including Q-MLP (See Appendix B.5, as implementation of (31)). Table 1 shows that our controller takes the minimal evaluations to balance the poles. With regard to CPU time (reported in seconds) we slightly fall short to Q-MLP. However, it interesting to observe that none of the value function approaches could handle this task in within the set of steps (e.g., 100,000 time steps, which is equal to over 30 minutes in simulated time) due to the memory constraint. The result also indicates that our memory controller stand as a promising method in solving this benchmark more successful than the traditional RL techniques.

	Method	Evaluation	time (second)
V-function	SARSA-CMAC	Time Out	-
	SARSA-CABA	Time Out	-
	VAPS	Time Out	-
Policy	Q-MLP	10,582	153
Memory	Our	8,900	300

Table 1. Comparison of our result for balancing two-pole simultaneously with other value function approaches and policy based methods. 'Evaluation' indicates the total time steps for the method to be able to keep the poles near the top for a long time.

7. Conclusions

This paper proposes an architecture which avoids manual 'hard coding' of behaviors, where an RL agent uses an adaptive memory process to create its own memory and thereby perform better in partially observable domains. The algorithm uses neighborhood component analysis (NCA) to determine feature vectors for system states. Decision-trees ensemble is used to create features which are useful in predicting the state of the system (i.e. building some sort of forward model). Chunks are used with a feature predictor to get features. These features are then used as the input features to learn a policy. Results based on non-Markov Cart- Pole balancing indicate that our model can memorize complete non-Markovian sequential tasks and is able to produce behaviors that make the controlled system to behave desirably in the future. One of our future plans is to automate the capacity of memory in order to accommodate more complex tasks. In our current design the number of chunks that can be used is fixed. Another future plan will be in designing intelligent mechanism for memory updating, and to experiment with real world applications.

8. References

[1] Sutton, R., Barto, A. (1998) "Reinforcement Learning: An introduction,". *Cambring, MA: MIT Press.*

[2] Barto A. (1995) "Adaptive critics and the basal ganglia,". In *Models of Information Processing in the Basal Ganglia,* pp.215-232. Cambridge, MA: MIT Press.

[3] Suri, R.E., Schultz, W. (1999) "A neural network model with dopamine-like reinforcement signal that learns a spatial delayed response task,". *Neuroscience* 91(3):871-890.

[4] Suri, R., Schultz, W. (2001) "Temporal difference model reproduces anticipatory neural activity,". *Neural Computation* 13:841-862.

[5] Chrisman,L. (1992) "Reinforcement learning with perceptual aliasing: The perceptual distinctions approach,". *Proc. Int'l. Conf on AAAI,* pp.183-188.

[6] Cassandra, A., Kaelbling, L., Littman, M. (1994) "Acting optimally in partially observable stochastic domains,". *Proc. Int'l. Conf on AAAI,* pp.1023-1028.

[7] Sutton, R., McAllester, D., Singh, S., Mansour, Y. (2000) "Policy gradient methods for reinforcement learning with function approximation,". *Advances in Neural Information Processing Systems* 12, pp. 1057-1063. MIT Press.

[8] Aberdeen, D., Baxter, J. (2002) "Scalable Internal-State Policy-Gradient Methods for POMDPs,". In *Proc. of the 19th Int'l Conf. on Machine Learning* 12, pp.3-10. Morgan Kaufmann Publishers Inc.

[9] Tsitsiklis, J., Van Roy, B. (1996) "Featured-based methods for large scale dynamic programming,". *Machine Learning* 22:59-94.

[10] Hassab Elgawi, O. (2009) "RL-Based Memory Controller for Scalable Autonomous Systems," In Proc. of *16th Int'l. Conf on Neural Information Processing*, ICONIP, Part II, LNCS 5864, pp.83-92, 2009.

[11] Basak, J. (2004) "Online adaptive decision trees: Pattern classification and function approximation,". *Neural Comput* 18:2062-2101.

[12] Hassab Elgawi, O. (2008) "Online Random Forests based on CorrFS and CorrBE," In Proc. of *Conf on Computer Vision and Pattern Recognition Workshop*, CVPR, pp.1-7.

[13] Singh, S.; Barto, A., Chentanez, N. (2005) "Intrinsically motivated reinforcement learning," In Proc. of *Advances in Neural Information Processing Systems,* NIPS, 17, MIT Press, 2005, pp.1281-1288.

[14] Singh, S., Lewis, R., Barto, A., Chentanez, N. (2009) "Where do rewards come from?" In Proc. of the *Annual Conf. of the Cognitive Science Society*, pp.2601-2606.

[15] Oudeyer, P.-Y., Kaplan, F., Hafner, V. (2007) "Intrinsic Motivation Systems for Autonomous Mental Development," *IEEE Transactions on Evolutionary Computation*, 11 pp.265-286.

[16] Uchibe, E., Doya, K. (2008) "Finding intrinsic rewards by embodied evolution and constrained reinforcement learning," *Neural Networks*, 21, pp.1447-1455.

[17] Ipek, E., Mutlu, O., Martinez, J., Caruana, R. (2008) "Self-Optimizing Memory Controllers: A Reinforcement Learning Approach,". In *Intl. Symp. on Computer Architecture (ISCA)*, pp.39-50.

[18] Maria F., Malik G., Guillaume I., Derek L. (2006) "Robot introspection through learned hidden Markov models,". *Artificial Intelligence*, 170(2):59-113.

[19] Urdiales, C., Perez, E., V´azquez-Salceda, J., S`anchez-Marr`e. (2006) "A purely reactive navigation scheme for dynamic environments using Case-Based Reasoning,". *Auton. Robots*, 21(1):65-78.

[20] Goldberger, J., Roweis, S., Hinton, G., Salakhutdinov, R. (2005) "Neighbourhood Components Analysis,". In *Advances in Neural Information Processing Systems* 17, MIT Press, pp.513-520.

[21] Keller, P. W., Mannor, S., Precup, D. (2006) "Automatic basis function construction for approximate dynamic programming and reinforcement learning,". In *23rd International Conference on Machine Learning*, pp.449-456.

[22] Uchibe, E., Doya, K. (2006) "Competitive-Cooperative-Concurrent Reinforcement Learning with Importance Sampling,". In Proc. of the *Eighth Int'l Conf. on Simulation of Adaptive Behavior: From Animals to Animats*, 8, MIT Press,Cambridge, MA, 2004, pp.287- 296.

[23] Jaakkola, T., Singh, S., Jordan, M. (1995) "Reinforcement learning algorithms for partially observable Markov decision,". In *Advances in Neural Information Processing Systems* 7, pp.345-352, Morgan Kaufmann.

[24] Long-Ji L., Mitchell, T. (1992) "Memory approaches to reinforcement learning in non-Markovian domains,". Technical Report CMU-CS-92-138, School of Computer Science, Carnegie Mellon University.

[25] Leslie P., Michael L., Anthony R. (1995) "Planning and acting in partially observable stochastic domains,". *Artificial Intelligence*, 101:99-134.

[26] Hassab Elgawi, O. (2008) "Architecture of behavior-based Function Approximator for Adaptive Control,". In *Proc. 15th Int'l. Conf on Neural Information Processing* ICONIP, LNCS 5507, pp.104-111.

[27] Hassab Elgawi, O. (2009) "Random-TD Function Approximator," *Journal of Advanced Computational Intelligence and Intelligent Informatics* (JACIII), 13(2):155-161.

[28] Meuleau, N., Peshkin, L., Kim, K.-E., Kaelbling, L. (1999) "Learning finite-state controllers for partially observable environments,". In *Proc of the 15th Int'l Conf on Uncertainty in Artificial Intelligence*, pp.427-436.

[29] Peshkin, L., Meuleau, N., Kaelbling, L. (1999) "Learning policies with external memory,". In *Proc. of the 16th Int'l Conf on Machine Learning*, pp.307-314, I. Bratko and S. Dzeroski, (Eds.).

[30] Kenneth, O. (2004) "Efficient evolution of neural networks through complexification,". Ph.D. Thesis; Department of Computer Sciences, The University of Texas at Austin. Technical Report AI-TR-04-314.

[31] Gomez. F. (2003) "Robust non-linear control through neuroevolution,". Ph.D. Thesis; Department of Computer Sciences, The University of Texas at Austin. Technical Report AI-TR-03-303.
[32] Santamaria, J., Sutton, R., and Ram, A. (1998) "Experiments with reinforcement learning in problems with continuous state and action spaces,". *Adaptive Behavior*, 6(2):163-218.
[33] Sutton, R. (1996) "Generalization in reinforcement learning: Successful examples using sparse coarse coding,". In *Touretzky et al*, 6(2):163-218.
[34] Albus, J. (1975) "A new approach to manipulator control: The cerebellar model articulation controller (CMAC),". *Journal of Dynamic Systems, Measurement, and Control*, 97(3):220-227.
[35] Baird, L., and Moore, A. (1999) "Gradient descent reinforcement learning,". *Advances in Neural Information Processing Systems*, 12.
[36] Watkins, C., Dayan, P. (1992) "Q-learning,". *Journal of Machine Learning*, 8(3):279-292.
[37] Lin, L.-J., Mitchell, T. (1992) "Memory approaches to reinforcement learning in non-Markovian domains,". Technical Report CMU-CS-92-138, Carnegie Mellon University, School of Computer Science.
[38] Tesauro, G. (1992) "Practical issues in temporal difference learning,". *Journal of Machine Learning*, 8:257-277.

APPENDIX

A. Pole-balancing learning parameters

Below are the equations and parameters used for cart-pole balancing experiments (31)

A.1 Pole-balancing equations

The equations of motion for N unjoined poles balanced on a single cart are

$$\ddot{x} = \frac{F - \mu_c sgn(\dot{x}) + \sum_{i=1}^{N} \tilde{F}_i}{M + \sum_{i=1}^{N} \tilde{m}_i}$$

$$\ddot{\theta} = -\frac{3}{4l_i}(\ddot{x}\cos\theta_i + g\sin\theta_i + \frac{\mu_{pi}\dot{\theta}_i}{m_i l_i}),$$

where $\tilde{F}_i$ is the effective force from the ith pole on the cart,

$$\tilde{F}_i = m_i l_i \dot{\theta}_i^2 \sin\theta_i + \frac{3}{4} m_i \cos\theta_i (\frac{\mu_{pi}\dot{\theta}_i}{m_i l_i} + g\sin\theta_i),$$

and $\tilde{m}_i$ is the effective mass of the ith pole,

$$\tilde{m}_i = m_i(1 - \frac{3}{4}\cos^2\theta_i).$$

A.2 Pole-balancing learning parameters

	Parameters for the single pole	
Sym	Description	Value
x	Position of cart on track	$[-2.4, 2.4]$m
θ	Angle of pole from vertical	$[-12, 12]$deg
F	Force applied to cart	-10.10N
l	Half length of pole	0.5m
mc	Mass of cart	1.0kg
mp	Mass of pole	0.1kg
	Parameters for double pole	Value
Sym	Description	Value
x	Position of cart on track	$[-2.4, 2.4]$m
θ	Angle of pole from vertical	$[-36, 36]$deg
F	Force applied to cart	-10.10N
l_i	Half length of ith pole	$l_1 = 0.5$m $l_2 = 0.05$m
mc	Mass of cart	1.0kg
mp_i	Mass of ith pole	$mp_1 = 0.1$kg $mp_2 = 0.01$kg
μ_c	friction coef on cart on track	0.0005
μ_p	friction coef if i^{th} pole's hinge	0.0005

Table 2. Parameters for the single pole & double pole problem.

B. Parameters for comparisons in cart pole balancing

Below are the parameters used to obtain the comparison result for SARSA-CABA, SARSA-CMAC, Q-MLP (31), and VAPS (28) in Section 6.3.

B.1 Parameters for value function methods

Parameter	Description
ϵ	greediness of policy
α	learning rate
γ	discount rate
λ	eligibility

Table 3. Parameters for value function methods.

B.2 Parameters used for SARSA-CABA

Sarsa(λ) with Case-Based function approximator (SARSA-CABA (32)): Is a Sarsa method with λ that uses a case-based memory to approximate the Q-function. A newly added state-action pair is calculated by combining the values of the k-nearest neighbors.

B.3 Parameters used for SARSA-CMAC

Sarsa(λ) with CMAC function approximator (SARSA-CMAC (32)): Almost similar to SARSA-CABA except that it uses a Cerebellar Model Articulation Controller (CMAC)(34) instead of a case-based memory to approximate the Q-function. Using this method the state-action space is divided into a set of tilings, each tiling constitutes a set of discrete features. Q-value is calculated as the sum of the value in each tiling.

Parameter	Task	
	$1a$	$1b$
Γd	0.03	0.03
Γ^x_k	0.05	0.05
Γ^x_k	0.1	0.1
ϵ	0.05	0.05
α	0.4	0.1
γ	0.99	0.99
λ	0.4	0.4

Table 4. Parameters used for SARSA-CABA.

B.4 Value and policy search

(VAPS (28)): Is an extension of a method proposed by (35) to policies graph, where stochastic gradient descent is used to search the space. The graph is made of 'nodes' indicating actions and 'arcs' representing observation. Transitions between nodes are initially based on the action associated with node that the agent previously visited, while the environment continue to produce arcs labeled with observations.

Parameter	Task	
	$1a$	$1b$
ϵ	0.05	0.05
α	0.4	0.1
γ	0.9	0.9
λ	0.5	0.3
No. of tilings	45 : 10 based on $x, \dot{x}, \theta_1$ 5 based on x, θ 5 based on $x, \dot{\theta}$ 5 based on $\dot{x}, \dot{\theta}$ 5 based on x 5 based on $\dot{x}$ 5 based on θ 5 based on $\dot{\theta}$	50 : 10 based on x_t, x_{t-1}, θ_t 10 based on $x, \theta_t, \theta_{t-1}$ 5 based on x_t, θ_t 5 based on x_{t-1}, θ_{t-1} 5 based on x_t 5 based on x_{t-1} 5 based on θ_t 5 based on θ_{t-1}

Table 5. Parameters used for SARSA-CMAC.

B.5 Parameters used for Q-MLP

Q-learning with MLP (Q-MLP): This method uses a Multi-Layer Perceptron to map state-action pairs to $Q(s, a)$ that makes it different from standard Q-learning (36). Backpropagation algorithm is used to learn the network values through gradient descent, produces a single Q-value as the output layer. This approach has been thoroughly applied to pole-balancing (37), and backgammon (38).

Parameter	Task		
	$1a$	$1b$	$2a$
ϵ	0.1	0.1	0.05
α	0.4	0.4	0.2
γ	0.9	0.9	0.9
λ	0	0	0

Table 6. Parameters used for Q-LMP.

7

Towards Robotic Manipulator Grammatical Control

Aboubekeur Hamdi-Cherif[1,2]
[1]*Qassim University, Computer College, PO Box 6688 – 51452 Buraydah*
[2]*Permanent Address: Université Ferhat Abbas Setif (UFAS)*
Faculty of Engineering, 19000 Setif
[1]*Saudi Arabia*
[2]*Algeria*

1. Introduction

The present research work reports the effectiveness and appropriateness of grammatical inference (GI) as an alternative control method. Specificity is made on robotic manipulator (RM). RM control is the process whereby a physical system, namely a set of robotic linked arms, is made compliant with some prescribed task such as following an imposed trajectory or keeping in pace with a given angular velocity (Siciliano, 2009). Welding and assembly-line robots are popular examples of RM industrial applications. RM control is a much diversified field. As a result, it makes concentrated research a difficult task. While RM control has been extensively studied from the pure control side (Lewis *et al.*, 2003), for the last four decades, or so, very little attention has been made with regard to other methods such as those provided by GI. Indeed, the GI efforts as applied to control at large remain quite isolated (Martins *et al.* 2006). Our fundamental aim is to contribute to the integration of GI within RM control, considered within a larger control methodology (Hamdi-Cherif, 2009). As a subfield of machine learning, GI attempts to learn structural models, such as grammars, from diverse data patterns, such as speech, artificial and natural languages, amongst others. GI broadest aim is therefore consistent with the overall goal of machine learning defined as a computational methodology that provides automatic means of improving tasks from experience. As a general computational method, GI is the process whereby a language is automatically generated from positive and eventually negative examples of sentences. Inductive inference of formal languages, as defined by (Gold, 1967), have been studied in the case of positive data, *i.e.,* when the examples of a given formal language are successive elements of some arbitrary enumeration of the elements of the language. After Gold's negative result, a theorem due to (Angluin, 1980) characterizes when an indexed family of nonempty recursive formal languages is inferrable from positive data. In oracle-based GI, the inferred language is done with the help of a teacher who answers questions concerning the language to be inferred. Useful accounts of GI methods and algorithms can be found in (Sakakibara, 1996; Cicchello & Kremer, 2003). Grammar-based classifier system as a universal tool for grammatical inference has been studied by (Unold, 2008). For the specificity of the present work, GI is understood as the learning of the behavior of a dynamical system, namely an RM. This behavior is translated into the syntax of a language to be learned. The main issue of the present work is to answer positively our central question, *i.e.*, whether it is possible to integrate the diversified methods dealing with dynamical systems control (such as computed torque, adaptive and robust methods), exemplified by RM control, while concentrating on GI as an alternative control method. We describe the epistemological characteristics of a framework that is believed to integrate two distinct methodological fields of research (Klavins *et al.* 2006), *i.e.*, theory of formal languages and machine learning where GI is rooted, on the one hand, and control theory, from where RM control originated, on the other hand. Blending research from both fields results in the appearance of a richer community. Emphasis is now made on RM control as a prelude to other classes of robotic systems; ultimately enhancing full programmable self-assembly compounds (Klavins, 2007). The chapter is organized as follows. In Section 2, the main problem is formulated within the general area of symbolic control. Section 3 briefly describes related works with three different lines of research - conventional control, GI in control, and software systems. Section 4 summarizes RM control in standard mathematical terms. Section 5 deals with GI as an alternative control method. Results are summarized in Section 6 followed by a conclusion.

2. Problem formulation

2.1 From machine learning to GI

The objective of machine learning is to produce general hypotheses by induction, which will make predictions about future instances. The externally supplied instances are usually referred to as training set. Generally speaking, machine learning explores algorithms that reason from externally supplied instances, also called inputs, examples, data, observations, or patterns, according to the community where these appear (Mitchell, 1997). To induce a hypothesis from a given training set, a learning system needs to make assumptions, or biases, about the hypothesis to be learned. A learning system without any assumption cannot generate a useful hypothesis since the number of hypotheses that are consistent with the training set is practically infinite and many of these are totally irrelevant. Because GI is considered as a sub-field of machine learning, it therefore inherits this fundamental characteristic (de la Higuera, 2005).

2.2 GI formalism

2.2.1 Formal grammar

A *formal string grammar* or simply *grammar* G has four components (Cohen, 1991):

- A set of symbols N called non-terminals.
- A set of symbols T, called terminals with the restriction that T and N are disjoint.
- A special non-terminal symbol S, called a start symbol.
- A set of production rules P.

In other words, a formal grammar is a set of rules that tells whether a string of characters (*e.g.* a sentence in a natural language), constructed from the starting symbol, can be expressed in the form of terminals (words), *i.e.*, in the general accepted structure of a sentence.

2.2.2 Inference

Inference or inductive learning is a generalization process which attempts to identify a hidden function, given a set of its values. As mentioned above, in formal languages settings, learning the syntax of a language is usually referred to as *grammatical induction* or *grammar inference* (GI); an important domain for both cognitive and psycholinguistic domain as well as science and engineering. We are concerned with the problem of constructing a grammar from some given data. These latter, whether sequential or structured, are composed from a finite alphabet, and may have unbounded string-lengths. In relatively simple situations, induction considers a deterministic finite-state automaton, or DFA, that takes strings of symbols as input, and produces a binary output, indicating whether that string, or sentence, is a part of the DFA's encoded language. In this particular example, GI builds a model of the hidden DFA internal structure, based only on pairs of input sentences and classifications, or outputs. From a control theory point of view, this is a classical input-output *identification* problem. The most successful GI algorithms produced so far are heuristic in nature. For our implementation example, we will concentrate only on one of these algorithms, namely *ILSGInf* (Hamdi-Cherif, 2007). An overview of some out of many other algorithms can be found in (de la Higuera, 2005).

2.3 Motivation for grammatical control approach

Any grammar codes for the class of all possible syntactical patterns that belong to the language produced by the grammar. The basic idea is to design a parser (or classifier) that recognizes strings accepted by the grammar. There is a mapping signals-to-strings. Each signal is quantized and each value is given a terminal symbol. Under normal operations, signals are compatible with the grammar. Once the grammar is learnt, it is used as a reference by the nominal system. If at a later time, there is some faulty output from the dynamical system then the faulty generated signals are translated as "odd" strings, reporting anomaly detection. The basic procedure is described in Figure 1. An input of non-terminals is used for both the nominal and actual dynamical systems. An error is evaluated between the strings generated by both systems. Two modes are possible. In the open-loop mode, the grammar generates the working patterns imposed by the external input command. If this error exceeds some threshold, a fault is reported. A closed-loop control is used when the control U is generated for an output y to be within some prescribed values.

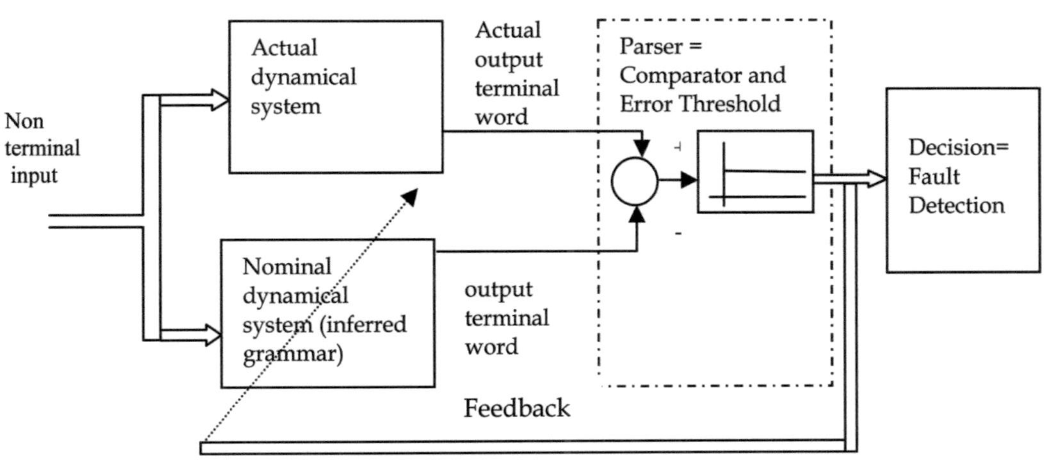

Fig. 1. Grammatical control used in open-loop/closed-loop modes

2.4 From hybrid control to grammatical control

The closest application field of GI-oriented control is the area of symbolic control, developed within the larger area of hybrid control. In the early sixties, the discipline of hybrid control referred to controlled systems using both discrete and continuous components. This discipline spanned a substantial area of research from basic switched linear systems to full-scale hybrid automata. In short, symbolic control methods include abstracting continuous dynamics to symbolic descriptions, instruction selection and coding in finite-bandwidth control applications, and applying formal language theory to the continuous systems domain. A number of results have emerged in this area with a conventional control-theoretic orientation, including optimal control, stability, system identification, observers, and well-posedness of solutions. However, a new line of research in hybrid systems has also been initiated that studies issues not quite standard to the controls community, including formal verification, abstractions, model expressiveness, computational tools, and specification languages. These issues were usually addressed in other areas, such as software engineering and formal languages. For our concern, we will consider symbolic control as an integration of pure control and formal language theory. As a result, symbolic control addresses questions at the highest level, *i.e.*, at the level of symbols, and as such is as close to computer science and discrete mathematics as much as to classic control theory. At the same time, symbolic control provides faithful descriptions of the continuous level performance of the actual system, and as such, provides a formal bridge between its continuous and the discrete characteristics (Egerstedt *et al.*, 2006).

2.5 GI in self-assembly of robotic systems

The second motivation for using GI as a robot control method is its applicability to self-assembly. It is easy to see that assembling shapes into a given pattern can be seen as a "language" where the elementary shapes are the "words" and the obtained pattern correspond to a "sentence" or "string" obeying some specific rules or "grammar" for generating grammatically correct sentences. The process of self-assembly can therefore be seen as the automatic generation of a language. Since assembling geometrical shapes into some desired shape can be viewed as a set of sentences of a language, it is therefore not surprising to address this issue from the standpoint of grammars. Specifically, graph grammars are used as an emerging field that is believed to be promising in self-assembly (Klavins, 2007). One of the strigent questions in robotic self-organized systems is to know whether it is possible to synthesize a set of local controllers that produce a prescribed global behavior that is sufficiently robust to uncertainties about the environmental conditions (Hamdi-Cherif, 2009).

3. Related works

Related works are described under three different lines of research, namely pure control, GI approach to control, and software applications.

3.1 Conventional RM control

On the control side, we concentrate on some classes of control methods such as adaptive control and passivity-based control. From the vast literature on adaptive control, only a small portion is applicable to RM control. One of the first approaches to adaptive control, based on the assumption of decoupled joint dynamics, is presented in (Craig, 1988). In general, multi-input multi-output (MIMO) adaptive control provides the means of solving problems of coupled motion, though nonlinear robot dynamics with rapidly changing operating conditions complicate the adaptive control problem involved, even if there are also advantages when compared with the adaptive control of linear systems. Specialized literature has appeared in the field, *e.g.*, the interesting tutorial reported in (Ortega & Spong, 1989). As far as adaptive control is concerned, some methods assume that acceleration is available for measurement and that the inertia matrix inverse is bounded (*e.g.* Craig *et al.*, 1986). Others avoid at least the boundedness constraint (*e.g.* Amestegui *et al.*, 1987) while passivity-based control avoids both limitations. We propose to classify the specialized contributions in the field as follows:

a. *Parameter estimation:* such as the linear estimation models suitable for identification of the payload of a partially known robot, going back to (Vukabratovic *et al.*, 1984).
b. *Direct adaptive control* of robot motion as studied by:
    1. (Craig *et al.*, 1987) in conjunction with model reference adaptive control (MRAC). Here stability is studied using strictly positive real transfer functions (SPR-TF).
    2. (Slotine & Li, 1987) in conjunction with the so-called "MIT rule". Here the regulator is independent of the acceleration measurement and linear in the parameters.
    3. Johansson has still improved the work of (Craig *et al.*, 1987) in terms of stability. This method avoids matrix inversion and SPR-TF requirements (Johansson, 1990).
c. *Decentralized control* for adaptive independent joint control as proposed by (Seraji, 1989).
d. *Control and stability analysis* such as passivity-based control developed by (Landau and Horowitz, 1989).

3.2 Grammatical control

GI as applied to robot control at large is relatively a new area of research. As an indication, a rapid search in *IEEE* site (http://www.ieee.org) using *ieeexplore* search engines and keywords (formal language control + dynamical systems + grammatical inference) hits one journal paper and two conferences papers, all by the same team of authors (Martins, 2006). Moreover, the majority of other results deals with control systems in general and none with RM control. The closest works relied on graph grammars. For instance, in (Hasemann, 1994), new concepts for robot control architectures are presented. The key techniques used to model decision making and plan modification are fuzzy logic and graph grammars. Fuzzy logic is used to guide planning and graph grammars provide the framework for expanding plan components. Special emphasis is put on planning and monitoring for task level control. New features introduced are behavior switching, complete monitoring of plan execution and plan validity and rigorous explicit representation of activities and mutual dependencies within plans. Moreover, a behavior switching mechanism is proposed, which allows critical behaviors to interrupt or abandon a current less critical behavior. Graphs grammars have alternatively been used in self-assembly (*e.g.* Klavins, 2007). In (Burbidge *et al.*, 2009), an autonomous mobile robot requires an onboard controller that allows it to perform its tasks for long periods in isolation. Grammatical evolution is a recent evolutionary algorithm that has been applied to various problems, particularly those for which genetic programming has been successful. Indeed, evolutionary techniques such as genetic programming offer the possibility of automatically programming the controller based on the robot's experience of its environment. A method for applying grammatical evolution to autonomous robot control has been presented and evaluated in simulation for the Khepera robot.

3.3 Robot control: numeric and symbolic software

Few authors have addressed the issue of designing and developing software systems that cater for general-purpose RM control. For example (Yae *et al.* 1994) have extended the EASY5 - the Boeing Engineering and Analysis SYstem - incorporating constrained dynamics. (Polyakov *et al.* (1994) have developed, in MATHEMATICA™, a symbolic computer algebra system toolbox for nonlinear and adaptive control synthesis and simulation which provides flexible simulation *via* C and MATLAB™ code generation. MATHEMATICA™ has also been used in a simulation program that generates animated graphics representing the motion of a simple planar mechanical manipulator with three revolute joints for teaching purposes (Etxebarria, 1994). A toolbox is available for RM control running on MATLAB™ (Corke, 1996). For supplementary and more general applications of computer algebra to CACSD (computer-aided control system design), we refer to (Eldeib and Tsai, 1989). Other environments tackled the general control problem from a CASCD standpoint (Hamdi-Cherif, 1994). Recent research directions aim at the development of operating systems for robots, not necessarily RM. An overview of ROS, an open source robot operating system has been recently reported. ROS is not an operating system in the traditional sense of process handling and scheduling. It provides a structured communications layer above the host operating systems of a heterogenous cluster. ROS was designed to meet a specific set of challenges encountered when developing large-scale service robots as part of the so-called STAIR project [http://stair.stanford.edu/papers.php]. The way how ROS relates to existing robot software frameworks, and a brief overview of some of the available application software which uses ROS are reported in (Quigley, *et al.* 2009). However, none of these works addressed the issue of using the grammatical control approach to solve the RM control problem to enhance it.

4. RM classic control problem

4.1 Brief history

The development of RM control algorithms has gone through at least three historical phases.

4.1.1 Model reference adaptive control and self-tuning control

The first phase (1978-1985) concentrated its efforts on the approximation approach. The methods developed during this period are well-documented in the literature and some review papers have been written for that period (*e.g.* Hsia, 1986). Researches were concentrated on issues expanded below.

a. *Model reference adaptive control approach* (MRAC) guided by the minimization of the error between the actual system and some conveniently chosen model of it. At the methodological level, this represents a traditional example of supervised learning based on comparison between the actual and desired outputs while trying to minimize the error between desired and actual values.
b. *Self-tuning control* based on performance criteria minimization.

4.1.2 Parametrization approach

The methods developed during the second period that followed with some time overlaps with the previous period, concentrated on the parameterization approach. The methods developed within this period can be further separated in two broad classes, namely inverse dynamics and passivity-based control.

a. *Inverse dynamics*
The first set of methods treats the inverse dynamics-based control or computed torque method. It relies on the exact cancellation of all the nonlinearities in the system. In the ideal case, the closed-loop system is decoupled and linear. Stability in this case is based on the Lyapunov direct method. A dynamical system is said to be stable in the sense of Lyapunov if it has the characteristics that when it loses an un-restored energy over time, then it will stabilize at some final state, called the attractor. In Lord Kelvin's terms this means that conservative systems in the presence of dissipative forcing elements will decay to a local minimum of their potential energy. However, finding a function that gives the precise energy of a given physical system can be extremely difficult. On the other hand, for some systems (*e.g.* econometric and biological systems), the Lyapunov function has no physical meaning.

b. *Passivity-based control*
The second set of methods deals with passivity-based control. The aim is to find a control law that preserves the passivity of the rigid RM in closed-loop. Stability here is based on the Popov hyperstability method (Popov, 1973). One of the main motivations for using these control laws, as far as stability is concerned, is that they avoid looking for complex Lyapunov functions - a bottleneck of the Lyapunov-based design. These laws also lead, in the adaptive case, to error equations where the regressor is independent of the joint acceleration. The difficult issue of inertia matrix inversion is also avoided. At the opposite of inverse dynamics methods, passivity-based methods do not look for linearization but rather for the passivity of the closed-loop system. Stability is granted if the energy of the closed-loop system is dissipated. The resulting control laws are therefore different for the two previous classes.

4.1.3 Soft computing approach

Later methods, in the third period, concentrated on soft computing methods such as:

a. *Neural networks (NNs).*
In (Kwan *et al.*, 2001), a desired compensation adaptive law-based neural network controller is proposed for the robust position control of rigid-link robots where the NN is used to approximate a highly nonlinear function. Global asymptotic stability is obtained with tracking errors and boundedness of NN weights. No offline learning phase is required as learning is done on-line. Compared with classic adaptive RM controllers, parameters linearity and determination of a regression matrix are not needed. However, time for converging to a solution might be prohibitive.

b. *Fuzzy-Genetic.*
In (Merchán-Cruz and Morris, 2006), a simple genetic algorithm planner is used to produce an initial estimation of the movements of two RMs' articulations and collision free motion is obtained by the corrective action of the collision-avoidance fuzzy units.

4.2 RM dynamics

A standard mathematical model is needed for any RM control problem. The RM dynamics are modeled as a set of n linked rigid bodies (Craig, 2005). The model is given by the following standard ordinary differential equation in matrix form.

$$\tau(t) = M(q)\ddot{q} + C(q,\dot{q})\dot{q} + G(q) + V(\dot{q}) \quad (1)$$

Time arguments are omitted for simplicity. The notations used have the following meaning:
q : joint angular position, *nx1* real vector.

$\dot{q}$: joint angular velocity, *nx1* real vector.

$\ddot{q}$: joint angular acceleration, *nx1* real vector.

$\tau(t)$: joint torque, *nx1* real vector.

$M(q)$: matrix of moment of inertia or inertia matrix, *nxn* real matrix.

$C(q,\dot{q})\dot{q}$: Coriolis, centrifugal and frictional forces. C is *nxn* real matrix.

$G(q)$: gravitational forces. G is an *nx1* real vector describing gravity.

$V(\dot{q})$: *nx1* real vector for viscous friction. It is neglected in our forthcoming treatment.

4.3 RM PID control

Proportional integral and derivative (PID) control is one of the simplest control schemes. It has been successfully used for the last six decades, or so, in many diversified applications of control. Despite its simplicity, PID is still active as an applied research field. In February 2006, a special issue of *IEEE Control Systems Magazine* has been devoted to the subject to account for its importance and actuality. Insofar as automatically-tuned PID's (or autotuners) are concerned, commercial products became available around the early eighties. Since the Ziegler-Nichols rules of thumb developed in the 1940's, many attempts have been made in the "intelligent" choice of the three gains (*e.g.* Åström *et al.* 1992). The intelligent approach also helps in explanation of control actions usage. Indeed, in many real-life applications, explanation of control actions is desirable, *e.g.*, why derivative action is necessary. In expert-systems approach, the knowledge elicited from human operators is codified and embodied within the knowledge base in the form of IF-THEN rules.
The PID control $u(t)$ is given by:

$$u(t) = K_p e(t) + K_v \dot{e}(t) + K_i \int_0^t e(n)dn \quad (2)$$

$$e(t) = q(t) - q_d(t) \quad (3)$$

$$\dot{e}(t) = \dot{q}(t) - \dot{q}_d(t) \quad (4)$$

Equation (1) describes the control *u(t)*. *Kp, Ki, Kv* are the gains for the proportional (P), integral (I) and derivative (D) actions, respectively.
Equation (3) defines the position error *e(t)*, *i.e.*, the difference between the actual system position *q(t)* and the desired position $q_d(t)$.
Equation (4) defines the velocity error and is simply the time-derivative of the error given in Equation (3) above. Equation (4) describes the difference between the actual system velocity and the desired velocity. The PID scheme block-diagram is given in Figure 2.

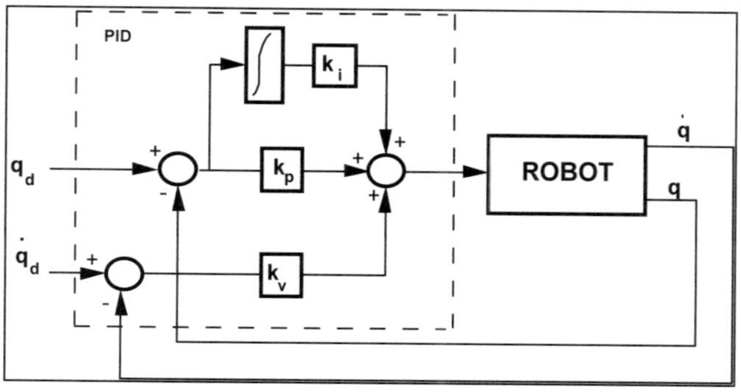

Fig. 2. RM PID Control

4.4 RM adaptive control

4.4.1 Purpose of adaptive control

The general adaptive controller design problem is as follows : given the desired trajectory $q_d(t)$, with some (perhaps all) manipulator parameters being unknown, derive a control law for the actuator torques and an estimation law for the unknown parameters such that the manipulator output $q(t)$ tracks the desired trajectories after an initial adaptation process. Adaptive control laws may be classified on the basis of their control objective and the signal that drives the parameter update law. This latter can either be driven by the error signal between the estimated parameters and the true parameters (prediction or parametric error) or by the error signal between the desired and actual outputs (tracking error). Stability investigations are at the basis of acceptability of the proposed scheme.

4.4.2 Example of adaptive control scheme

As an example, the method due to (Amestegui *et al.*, 1987) compensates the modeling errors by a supplementary control $\boldsymbol{\delta\tau}$. First, the computed torque approach is used whereby the linearizing control is obtained by a suitable choice of the torque. This amounts to simply replacing the acceleration $\ddot{q}$ by the control u in (1) above resulting in:

$$\tau(t) = M(q)u + C(q,\dot{q})\dot{q} + G(q) + V(\dot{q}) \tag{5}$$

Combining (1) and (5) yields:

$$M(q)(\ddot{q} - u) = 0 \tag{6}$$

Which amounts to n decoupled integrators $(\ddot{q} = u)$. In this case, the control u can be expressed in terms of the desired acceleration as a PD compensator.

Now compensate the modeling errors by a supplementary control $\boldsymbol{\delta\tau}$ and neglect viscous friction.

$$\tau(t) = M_0(q)(u) + C_0(q,\dot{q})\dot{q} + G(q) + \delta\tau \tag{7}$$

Using the linear parametrization property, we obtain:

$$M_0(q)(u-\ddot{q})+\delta\tau=\psi(q,\dot{q},\ddot{q})\Delta\theta \tag{8}$$

The compensating control is then given by:

$$\delta\tau=\psi(q,\dot{q},\ddot{q})\Delta\hat{\theta} \tag{9}$$

and the estimated parametric error vector is solution of:

$$\Delta\dot{\hat{\theta}}=-\Gamma\psi^T(q,\dot{q},\ddot{q})\hat{M}_0(q)(u-\ddot{q}) \tag{10}$$

In the previous equations, the following notations are used:

$\psi(q,\dot{q},\ddot{q})$ represents the regressor matrix, of appropriate dimensions.

The parametric error vector:

$$\Delta\theta=\theta_0-\theta \tag{11}$$

where θ is the actual parameter vector and

θ_0 a constant and linear vector with respect to the nominal robot model.

$\Delta\hat{\theta}$ is the estimate of $\Delta\theta$ and

$$\Gamma=diag(\gamma_1,\gamma_2 ...,\gamma_n) \tag{12}$$

is a positive-definite diagonal matrix with $\gamma_i>0$, representing the adaptation gain for the gradient parametric estimation method. Note that this last scheme avoids the inversion of the inertia matrix. It reduces the calculations complexity. However the measurement of the acceleration is always required. The block-diagram is given in Figure 3.

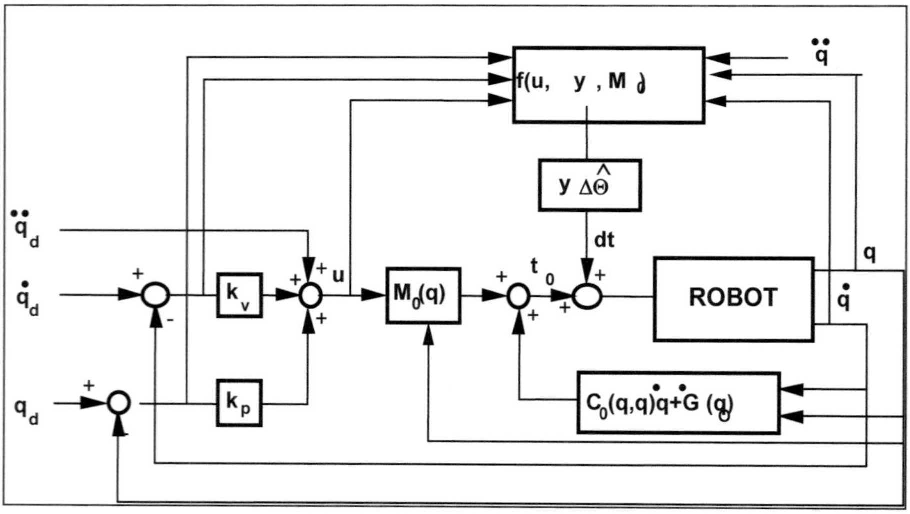

Fig. 3. Amestegui's adaptive compensation scheme

NB: In Figure 3, the following notations are used: $y=\psi$; $t=\tau$ $t_0=\tau_0$

4.5 RM robust control

Robust control approach considers adding a correcting term to the control signal. This compensates the parametric error. This supplementary signal gives better tracking and makes the system more robust with respect to parametric error. We can classify the robust methods as Lyapunov-based methods, variable structure methods and non-chattering high gains methods.

4.5.1 Lyapunov-Based methods

This class of methods is based on the Lyapunov direct method and is based on (Spong and Vidyasagar, 2006). The main problem encountered by Lyapunov-based class of RM control algorithms is the so-called *chattering effect* which results from commutation of the supplementary signal. This behavior creates control discontinuities. Research efforts have been accomplished that cater for this undesirable chattering effect. The algorithm proposed by (Cai and Goldenberg 1988) is a tentative answer to the problem of chattering. The issue of chattering represents a predilection area for the applicability of GI methods, since chattering can be modeled as an "odd" language departing from a nominal language, learned under normal operations.

4.5.2 Variable structure methods

Variable structure methods, such as the one proposed by (Slotine, 1985) are based on high-speed switching feedback control where the control law switches to different values according to some rule. This class of methods drives the nonlinear plant's trajectory onto an adequately designed sliding surface in the phase space independently of modeling errors. In (Chen and Papavassilopoulos, 1991) four position control laws have been analyzed and compared for a single-arm RM dynamics with bounded disturbances, unknown parameter, and unmodeled actuator dynamics. Although very robust to system's disturbance and simplifying the complexity of control laws implementation, these methods suffer from undesirable control chattering at high frequencies.

4.5.3 Non-Chattering high gains methods

The non-chattering high gains class of methods is based on the singular perturbation theory and considers two time scales. This class avoids the chattering effect (Samson, 1987). However, robustness in this case is guaranteed by the choice of a nonlinear gain which is calculated from the *a priori* knowledge of the parametric uncertainties and from the model chosen for control calculation. The resulting control can be considered as a regulator which automatically adapts the gains in accordance with the displacement errors (Seraji, 1989) and uses high gains only when these are needed, for instance when displacement error is large.

4.5.4 Example of robust control scheme

In this case, the parameters are not known but their range of variations is known. The basic idea of this method is to add a compensating term to the control which is obtained from an *a priori* estimated model. This compensation term takes into account the parameters bounds and tries to compensate the difference between the estimated and the real parameters of the robot. This makes possible an improved trajectory tracking and provides robustness with respect to the parametric errors. Several schemes of RM robust control have been studied and compared (Abdallah *et al.*, 1991). As an example, only one robust algorithm is described here, whose control law is given by:

$$\tau(t) = M_0(q)(u+\delta u) + C_0(q,\dot{q})\dot{q} + G_0(q) \tag{13}$$

where

* M_0, C_0 and G_0 are the *a priori* estimates of M, C and G, respectively.
* δu is the compensating control supplement.
* u is given by a PD compensator of the form:

$$u(t) = \ddot{q}_d(t) - K_p e(t) - K_v \dot{e}(t) \tag{14}$$

The additional control δu is chosen so as to ensure robustness of the control by compensating the parametric errors. Stability must be guaranteed. A reformulation of this control gives:

$$\dot{x} = Ax + B(\delta u + \eta(u,q,\dot{q})) \tag{15}$$

$$E_1 = Cx \tag{16}$$

where A, B, C and x are given by

$$A = \begin{bmatrix} 0 & I \\ -K_p & -K_v \end{bmatrix} \quad B = \begin{bmatrix} 0 \\ I \end{bmatrix} \quad C = \begin{bmatrix} \alpha & I \end{bmatrix} \quad x = \begin{bmatrix} e \\ \dot{e} \end{bmatrix} \tag{17}$$

with α is a diagonal constant positive-definite matrix of rank n, and

$$\eta(u,q,\dot{q}) = E(q)\delta u + E_1 u + M^{-1}(q)\Delta H(q,\dot{q}) \tag{18}$$

$$E(q) = M^{-1}(q)M_0(q) - I \tag{19}$$

$$\Delta H(q,\dot{q}) = [C_0(q,\dot{q}) - C(q,\dot{q})]\dot{q} + [G_0(q) - G] \tag{20}$$

Stability is granted only if the vector $\eta(u,q,\dot{q})$ is bounded. These bounds are estimated on the worst-case basis. Furthermore, under the assumption that there exists a function ρ such that:

$$\|\delta u\| < \rho(e,\dot{e},t) \tag{21}$$

$$\|\eta\| \le \rho(e,\dot{e},t) \tag{22}$$

the compensating control δu can be obtained from:

$$\delta u = \begin{cases} -\rho(e,\dot{e},t)\dfrac{E_1}{\|E_1\|} & if \quad \|E_1\| \neq 0 \\ 0 \quad if & \|E_1\| = 0 \end{cases} \tag{23}$$

This last control δu presents a chattering effect due to the discontinuities in (23). This phenomenon can cause unwanted sustained oscillations. Another control has been proposed which reduces these unwanted control jumps, (Cai & Goldenberg, 1988) as given in equation (24).

$$\delta u = \begin{cases} -\rho(e,\dot{e},t)\dfrac{E_1}{\|E\|} & if \quad \|E_1\| > \varepsilon \\ \dfrac{-\rho(e,\dot{e},t)}{\varepsilon}E_1 & if \quad \|E_1\| \leq \varepsilon \end{cases} \tag{24}$$

The robust control scheme is represented in Figure 4.

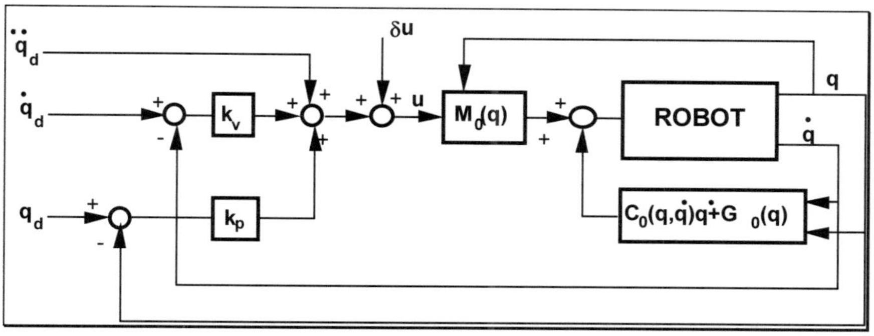

Fig. 4. Spong and Vidyasagar's robust control algorithm

4.6 Example of Implementation with Matlab/Simulink™

These implementations show two different classes of algorithms; one with adaptation and the other without.

5. GI for dynamical systems

5.1 Dynamical systems

A model for a controlled dynamical system has the general form

$$\dot{x}(t) = f(x(t), U(t)) \tag{25}$$

$$y(t) = h(x(y(t))) \tag{26}$$

or, considering it in a discrete-time form

$$x_{k+1} = f(x_k, U_k) \tag{27}$$

$$y_k = h(x_k) \tag{28}$$

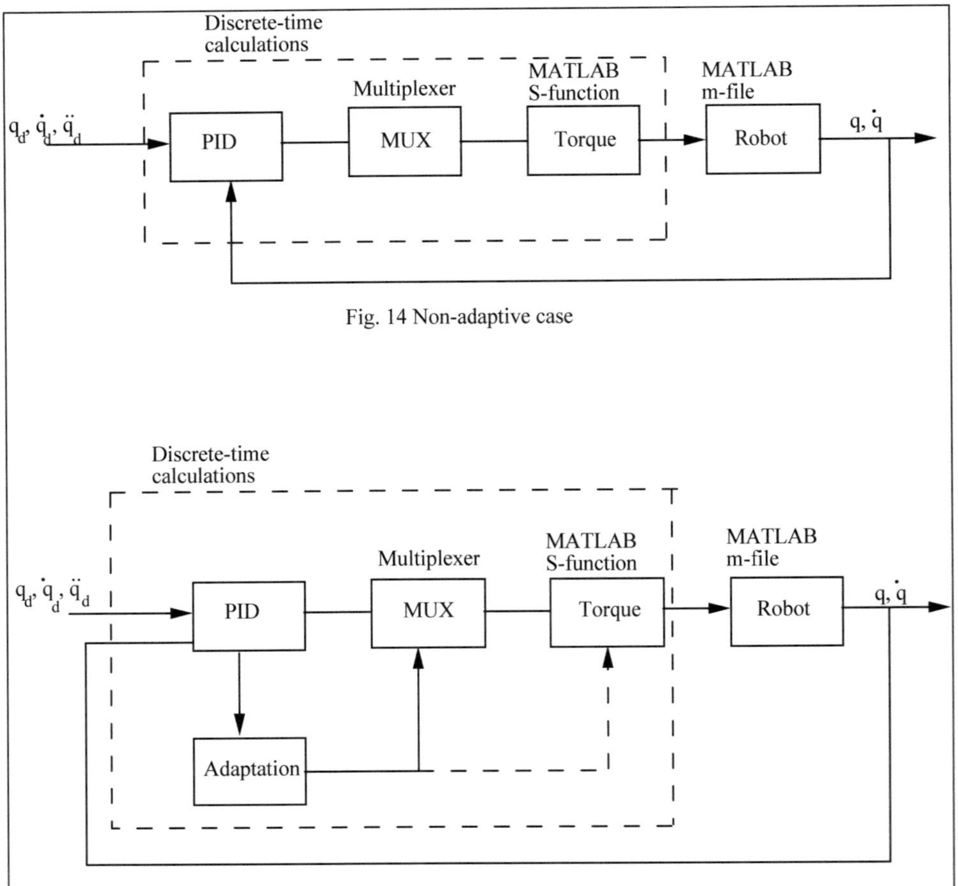

Fig. 14 Non-adaptive case

Fig. 15 Adaptive case

Fig. 5. RM classic control implementation with and without adaptation

where x is the state variable; y the output or observed variable; U the input or control variable; k denotes time in discrete case. Equations (25)-(28) also establish a functional relationship between the output variables at different times

$$y_{k+1} = g(x_k, U_k) \tag{29}$$

However, in most systems used in technology, including RM control, not all state variables are observable. Therefore, (29) does not provide a complete specification of the system. In general, specification of the dynamics in terms of the output variables requires a set of functional relationships involving many time steps in the past, namely:

$$\begin{aligned} y_{k+1} &= g_o(U_k) \\ y_{k+1} &= g_1(y_k, U_k) \\ y_{k+1} &= g_2(y_k, y_{k-1}, U_k) \\ y_{k+1} &= g_3(y_k, y_{k-1}, y_{k-2}, U_k) \\ y_{k+1} &= g_4(y_k, y_{k-1}, y_{k-2}, y_{k-3}, U_k) \end{aligned} \tag{30}$$

It is this structure which is required by dynamical considerations on actual controlled systems that leads in a natural way to the use of π-type productions, explained in the sequel.

5.2 Steps for using GI in control systems

To develop a grammatical description and a GI algorithm for controlled dynamical systems three steps are required (Martins *et al.*, 2006). First, the quantification of the variables are obtained, then the specification of the nature of the productions and finally a learning algorithm to extract the productions from the experimental data.

5.2.1 Quantification of the variables

Quantification refers to the choice of alphabets for the output (controlled) variable y and the control variable U. The objective is to generate the control U in order to maintain the output y within some prescribed values. A terminal alphabet T is associated to the output variable y and the nonterminal alphabet N to the control variable U. The feedback control law generates the required value of the input U so as to keep the controlled output y within a specified range. For so doing, a quantification of the variables is made, in a discrete way, dividing the variables range into equal intervals and associating each interval to a terminal symbol in the alphabet.

5.2.2 Production rules

π-type productions are defined by the human expert as some substitution rules of a given form. This human-supplied codification is necessary. A π-type production codes the evolution of the output variable, depending on its π past values and on the value of the control variable U. Therefore, there is a functional relationship between the dynamics of the system and the π-type productions. Note that a π-type production is usually written p-type. We prefer to represent it as π-type to avoid confusion with Proportional-control or P-type control action. An interesting line of research would be the use of knowledge-based systems approach to codify the human expertise and incorporate it with the final control system.

5.2.3 Learning

A learning algorithm is necessary to extract the productions from the experimental data. To obtain a sample of the language, a sequence of control signals is applied to the system in such a way that the output variable y takes values in a sufficiently wide region. The signal evolution is then quantified as described above, and a learning procedure is followed.

6. Results

For simplicity, we use a 2-symbol alphabet and show how the language is system generated by generalization, step by step.

6.1 Use of *ILSGINf*

ILSGINF is a heuristics-based inductive learning algorithm that induces grammars from positive examples. The main idea behind the algorithm is to take full advantage of the syntactic structure of available sentences. It divides the sentence into sub-sentences using partial derivatives PaDe's. Given a recognized sentence as reference, the parser is able to recognize part of the sentence (or sub-sentence(s)) while rejecting the other unrecognized part. Moreover the algorithm contributes to the resolution of a difficult problem in inductive learning and allows additional search reduction in the partial derivatives (PaDe's) space which is equal to the length of the sentence, in the worst case (Hamdi-Cherif, 2007). In the example, we suppose that all data are pre-processed from previous steps.

6.2 Example

6.2.1 ILSGInf results

We suppose that are given the following grammar for induction: G = (N, T P, S), where:

N = {S, A, B}, T ={b, *}, P = {S → AB, A → b, B→* A}

Let F= (b*b)*(b*b) be a global sentence to be parsed.
ILSGInf generates the following sub-sentences:

C_1 = (, C_2 = b * b, C_3 =), C_4 = *, C_5 = (, C_6 = b * b, C_7=)

Using the dotted (•) representation as in (Earley, 1970), *ILSGInf* gives the following results of sub-lists and sub-sentences:

	sub-list 0	*sub-list 1*	*sub-list 2*	*sub-list 3*
sub-sentence 1	I_{01} S → •AB, 0 A → • b, 0	I_{11} empty	I_{21} empty	I_{31} empty
sub-sentence 2	I_{02} S →• AB, 0 A → • b, 0	I_{12} A → b • , 0 S →A•B , 0 B →• +A, 1	I_{22} B →+•A, 1 A → • b , 2	I_{32} A → b • , 2 B →+A•, 1 S →AB•, 0
sub-sentence 3	I_{03} S →•AB, 0 A → • b , 0	I_{13} empty	I_{23} empty	I_{33} empty
sub-sentence 4	I_{04} S →•AB, 0 A → • b , 0	I_{14} empty	I_{24} empty	I_{34} empty
sub-sentence 5	I_{05} S →•AB, 0 A → • b , 0	I_{15} empty	I_{25} empty	I_{35} empty
sub-sentence 6	I_{06} S →• AB, 0 A → • b, 0	I_{16} A → b • , 0 S →A•B , 0 B→•+A,1	I_{26} B→ +•A, 1 A→ • b , 2	I_{36} A → b • , 2 B →+A•, 1 S →AB•, 0
sub-sentence 7	I_{07} S →•AB, 0 A→ • b , 0	I_{17} empty	I_{27} empty	I_{37} empty

Table 1. Progressive construction of sub-lists

6.1.2 Discussions

For the sub-sentences 1, 3, 4, 5 and 7, we note that:

i. I_{1x} (x=1,3,4,5,7) is empty. In this case, while no classical algorithm (*e.g.* Earley-like) proceeds further, the algorithm looks for other partial derivatives. Because sub-sentences are refused, then no transformation is needed.

ii. In sub-sentences 2, 6 all I_{3x} (x=2,6) are accepted. In each of these, we find an item of the form $S \rightarrow \alpha \bullet ,0$ which is $S \rightarrow AB \bullet ,0$. Then respective sub-sentences are totally accepted and transformed as S.

iii. Partial derivatives (PaDe's) of the global sentence (b*b)*(b*b) have the form: D = (S)*(S). Other partial derivatives of b*b are :
    b*A from item $A \rightarrow b \bullet ,2$ in I_{3x}, (x=2,6)
    bB from item $B \rightarrow *A \bullet ,1$ in I_{3x}, (x=2,6)
    A*b from item $A \rightarrow b \bullet ,0$ in I_{1x} (x = 2,6)
    AB from item $A \rightarrow b \bullet ,0$ in I_{1x} and I_{3x}, (x=2,6)

iv. Local sorting is done as follows: S, AB, bB, b*A, A*b.

7. Conclusion

We have described the foundational steps integrating robotic manipulator control and formal languages. More specifically, this research work reports some features of grammatical inference approach as applied to robotic manipulator control. As such, this research represents an early contribution towards an objective evaluation and a basic study of the effectiveness and usefulness of grammatical inference as applied to robotic manipulator control. Grammars and languages are used as supervising entities within control of robotic manipulators. A unification of the diversified works dealing with robotic manipulators, while concentrating on formal grammars as an alternative control method, is therefore made possible. The fundamental constraints of the proposed method is that it requires a choice of an appropriate quantification for the feature space. This choice has a direct impact on the size of the alphabets and the dimension and complexity of the grammars to be inferred. Like any machine learning method, the proposed procedure also requires a diversified coverage of the working domain during the learning stage to obtain rich generalization properties. As a consequence, the results report only some aspects of the overall issue, since these describe only the case of a small class of learnable languages. Much work is still required on both sides, *i.e.*, robotics and formal languages, for the development of fully-integrated systems that meet the challenges of efficient real-life applications.

8. References

Abdallah, C.; Dawson, D.; Dorato, P. & Jamshidi, M. (1991). Survey of robust control for rigid robots, *IEEE Control Systems Magazine*, Vol. 11, No. 2 (February 1991) page 24–30, ISSN: 0272-1708.

Amestegui, M.; Ortega, R. & Ibarra, J.M. (1987). Adaptive linearizing and decoupling robot control : a comparative study of different parametrizations, *Proceedings of 5th Yale Workshop on Applications of Adaptive Systems Theory*, 1987, New Haven, CN, USA.

Angluin, D. (1980). Inductive inference of formal languages from positive data. *Information and Control*, Vol. 45, No. 2 (May 1980) page 117–135, ISSN: 0019-9958.

Åström, K.J.; Hang, C.C.; Persson P. & Ho W.K. (1992). Towards intelligent PID control, *Automatica*, Vol. 28, No. 1 (January 1992) page 1-9, ISSN 0005-1098.

Burbidge, R.; Walker, J.H. & Wilson, M.S. (2009). Grammatical evolution of a robot controller, *International Conference on Intelligent Robots and Systems, IROS 2009. IEEE/RSJ* pp. 357–362, ISBN: 978-1-4244-3803-7, St. Louis, MO, USA, 10-15 Oct. 2009, IEEE, New Jersey, USA.

Cai, L. & Goldenberg, A.A. (1988). Robust control of unconstrained maneuvers and collision for a robot manipulator with bounded parameter uncertainty. *Proceedings IEEE Conference on Robotics and Automation,* pp. 1010–1015, Vo. 2, 1988, Philadelphia, IEEE, NJ, USA.

Chen, L.W. & Papavassilopoulos, G.P. (1991). Robust variable structure and adaptive control of single-arm dynamics. *Proceedings 30th Conference on Decision and Control,* pp. 367-372, Brighton, UK, 11–13 December 1991, IEEE, NJ, USA.

Cicchello, O. & Kremer, S. C. (2003). Inducing grammars from sparse data sets: A survey of algorithms and results, *Journal of Machine Learning Research,* Vol. 4 (October 2003) page 603–632, ISSN: 1938-7228

Cohen, D.I.A. (1991). *Introduction to Computer Theory*. John Wiley & Sons, Inc., ISBN: 0-471-51010-6, New York, USA.

Corke, P.I. (1996). A robotics toolbox for MATLAB, *IEEE Robotics and Automation Magazine,* Vol. 3, No. (March 1996) page 24-32, ISSN: 1070-9932.

Craig, J.J. (2005). *Introduction to Robotics: Mechanics and Control* , 3rd Ed., Pearson Prentice Hall, ISBN: 0201-54361-3, Upper Saddle River, NJ, USA.

Craig, J.J. (1988). *Adaptive Control of Mechanical Manipulators,* Addison-Wesley, ISBN: -201-10490-3, Reading, MA, USA.

Craig, J.J., Hsu, P. & Sastry, S. (1987). Adaptive control of mechanical manipulators. *International Journal of Robotics Research,* Vol. 6, No. 2 (June 1987) page 16-28, ISSN: 0278-3649.

de La Higuera, C. (2005). A bibliographical study of grammatical inference. *Pattern Recognition*, Vol. 38 No. 9 (September 2005) page 1332-1348, ISSN: 0031-3203.

Earley, J., (1970). An efficient context-free parsing algorithm *Communications of the ACM,* Vol. 13, No. 2 (February 1970) pp. 94-102, ISSN: 0001-0782.

Egerstedt, M.; Frazzoli, E. & Pappas, G. (2006). Special section on symbolic methods for complex control systems, *IEEE Transactions On Automatic Control.* Vol. 51, No. 6 (June 2006) page 921-923, ISSN: 0018-9286.

Eldeib, H.K. & Tsai S. (1989). Applications of symbolic manipulation in control system analysis and design. *Proceedings of the IEEE Symposium on Intelligent Control* page 269-274, 1989, Albany, NY, USA.

Etxebarria, V. (1994). Animation of a simple planar robotic arm. *Proceedings of the European Simulation Multiconference (ESM'94),* pp. 809-813, Barcelona, Spain, 1-3 June 1994.

Gold, E.M. (1967). Language identification in the limit, *Information and Control*, Vol. 10, No. 5 (1967) page 447–474, ISSN: 0019-9958.

Hamdi-Cherif, A. & Kara-Mohammed (*alias* Hamdi-Cherif), C. (2009). Grammatical inference methodology for control systems. *WSEAS Transactions on Computers,* Vol. 8, No. 4 (April 2009) page 610-619, ISSN: 1109-2750.

Hamdi-Cherif, A. (1994). The CASCIDA project - A computer-aided system control for interactive design and analysis. *Proceedings of IEEE / IFAC Joint Symposium On CACSD (CASCD'94)*, pp. 247-251, Tucson, AZ, 7-9 March 1994, IEEE, NJ, USA.

Hamdi-Cherif, C. & Hamdi-Cherif, A. (2007). ILSGInf : Inductive learning system for grammatical inference. *WSEAS Transactions on Computers*, Vol. 6, No. 7 (July 2007) page 991-996. ISSN: 1109-2750.

Hasemann, J.M. (1994). A robot control architecture based on graph grammars and fuzzy logic. *Proceedings of the IEEE/RSJ/GI International Conference on Intelligent Robots and Systems '94. 'Advanced Robotic Systems and the Real World', IROS '94*, Vol.3, pp. 2123-2130, ISBN: 0-7803-1933-8, 12-16 Sep 1994, Munich, Germany.

Hsia, T.C. (1986). Adaptive control of robot manipulators: a review. *IEEE International Conference on Robotics and Automation*, San Fransisco, CA, USA, 1986, IEEE, NJ, USA.

Johansson, R. (1990). Adaptive control of robot manipulator motion. *IEEE Transactions on Robotics and Automation*, Vol. 6 No. 4 (August 1990) pp. 483-490, ISSN: 1042-296X.

Klavins, E., Ghrist, R. & Lipsky, D. (2006). A grammatical approach to self-organizing robotic systems, *IEEE Transactions on Automatic Control.* Vol. 51, No. 6, (June 2006) page 949–962, ISSN: 0018-9286.

Klavins, E. (2007). Programmable self-assembly. *IEEE Control Systems Magazine*. Vol. 27, No. 4 (August 2007) page 43-56. ISSN: 0272-1708.

Kwan, C.; Dawson, D.M. & Lewis F.L. (2001). Robust adaptive control of robots using neural network: global stability. *Asian Journal of Control*, Vol. 3, No. 2 (June 2001) page 111-121, ISSN: 1561-8625.

Landau, I.D. & Horowitz R. (1989). Applications of the passive systems approach to the stability analysis of the adaptive controllers for robot manipulators. *International Journal of Adaptive Control and Signal Processing*, Vol. 3, No. 1 (January 1989) pp. 23-38, ISSN: 0890-6327.

Lewis, F.L.; Dawson, D.M. & Abdallah, C.T. (2003). *Robot Manipulator Control: Theory and Practice, Control Engineering Series*, 2nd Ed., CRC Press, Taylor & Francis Group, ISBN: 978-0824740726, New York, USA.

Ortega, R. & Spong, M.W. (1989). Adaptive motion control of rigid robots: A tutorial, *Automatica*, Vol. 25, No. 6 (November 1989) page 877–888, ISSN: 0005-1098.

Polyakov, V.; Ghanadan R. & Blackenship G.L. (1994). Symbolic numerical computation tools for nonlinear and adaptive control. *Proceedings of IEEE-IFAC Joint Symposium on CACSD*, pp. 117-122, Tucson, AZ, USA, 7-9 March 1994, IEEE, NJ, USA.

Quigley, M.; Gerkey B.; Conley, K.; Faust, J.; Foote, T., Leibs, J.; Berger, E.; Wheeler, R. & Ng, A. (2009). ROS: an open-source Robot Operating System. http://www.cs.stanford.edu/people/ang/papers/icraoss09-ROS.pdf

Martins, J. F.; Dente, J.A.; Pires, A.J. & Vilela Mendes, R. (2001). Language identification of controlled systems: modeling, control, and anomaly detection. *IEEE Transactions On Systems Man and Cybernetics– Part C: Applications And Reviews* Vol. 31, No. 2 (April 2001) page 234-242, ISSN: 1094-6977.

Mitchell, T.M. (1997). *Machine Learning*. McGraw-Hill, ISBN: 0070428077, New York, USA.

Merchán-Cruz, E.A. & Morris, A.S. (2006). Fuzzy-GA-based trajectory planner for robot manipulators sharing a common workspace, *IEEE Transactions on Robotics*, Vol. 22, No. 4 (August 2006) page 613-624, ISSN: 1042-296X.

Popov, V.M. (1973). *Hyperstability of Control Systems.* Springer Verlag, ISBN: 0387063730, Berlin, Germany.

Sakakibara, Y. (1997). Recent advances in grammatical inference. *Theoretical Computer Science.* Vol. 185, No. 1 (October 1997) pp. 15–45, ISSN: 0304-3975.

Siciliano, B.; Sciavicco, L.; Villani, L. & Oriolo, G. (2009). *Robotics Modeling, Planning and Control.* Springer, ISBN 978-1-84628-641-4, e-ISBN 978-1-84628-642-1, Series published under ISSN 1439-2232, London, UK.

Samson, C. (1987). Robust control of a class of nonlinear systems and applications to robotics. *International Journal of Adaptive Control and Signal Processing,* Vol. 1, No. 1 (January 1987) page 49-68, ISSN: 0890-6327.

Seraji, H. (1989). Decentralized adaptive control of manipulators: theory, simulation and experimentation. *IEEE Transactions on Robotics and Automation,* Vol. 5 No. 2 (April 1989) Page 183-201, ISSN: 1042-296X.

Slotine, J.J.E. (1985). The robust control of robot manipulators. *International Journal of Robotics Research.* Vol. 4, No. 2 (June 1985) page 465-492, ISSN: 0278-3649.

Slotine, J.J.E. & W. Li (1987). On the adaptive control of robot manipulators. *International Journal of Robotics Research,* Vol. 6, No. 3 (September 1987) page 49-59, ISSN: 0278-3649.

Spong, M.W.; Hutchinson, S. & Vidyasagar M. (2006). *Robot Modeling and Control,* Wiley, ISBN: 0471649902, New York, USA.

Unold, O., (2008). Grammar-based classifier system: a universal tool for grammatical inference. *WSEAS Transactions on Computers* Vol. 7, No. 10 (October 2008) page 1584-1593. ISSN: 1109-2750.

Vukabratovic, M.; Stoic D. & Kirchanski, N. (1984). Towards non-adaptive and adaptive control of manipulation robots. *IEEE Transactions on Automatic Control.* Vol. 29, No.9 (September 1984) page 841-844, ISSN: 0018-9286.

Yae, K.H.l; Lin, T.C. & Lin S.T. (1994). Constrained multibody library within EASY5. *Simulation,* Vol. 62, No. 5 (May 1994) page 329-336, ISSN (Online): 1741-3133, ISSN (Print): 0037-5497.

8

Multi-Robot Systems Control Implementation

José Manuel López-Guede, Ekaitz Zulueta,
Borja Fernández and Manuel Graña
Computational Intelligence Group, University of the Basque Country (UPV/EHU)
Spain

1. Introduction

Nowadays it is clear that multi-robot systems offer several advantages that are very difficult to reach with single systems. However, to leave the simulators and the academic environment it is a mandatory condition that they must fill: these systems must be economically attractive to increment their implantation in realistic scenarios. Due to multi-robots systems are composed of several robots that generally are similar, if an economic optimisation is done in one of them, such optimisation can be replicated in each member of the team.

In this paper we show a work to implement low level controllers with small computational needs that can be used in each of the subsystems that must be controlled in each of the robots that belongs to a multi-robot system. If a robot is in a multi-robot system that robot needs bigger computational capacity, because it has to do some tasks derived from being in the team, for example, coordination and communication with the remaining members of the team. Besides, occasionally, it has to deduce cooperatively the global strategy of the team. One of the theoretical advantage of multi-robot systems is that the cost of the team must be lower than the cost of a single robot with the same capabilities. To become this idea true it is mandatory that the cost of each member was under a certain value, and we can get this if each of them is equipped with very cheap computational systems. One of the cheapest and more flexible devices for control systems implementation are Field Programmable Gate Arrays (FPGAs). If we could implement a control loop using a very simple FPGA structure, the economic cost of each of them could be about 10 dollars.

On the other hand, and under a pessimistic vision, the subsystems to control could have problems to be controlled using classic and well known control schemas as PID controllers. In this situation we can use other advanced control systems which try to emulate the human brain, as Predictive Control. This kind of control works using a world model and calculating some predictions about the response that it will show under some stimulus, and it obtains the better way of control the subsystem knowing which is the desired behavior from this moment until a certain instant later. The predictive controller tuning is a process that is done using analytical and manual methods. Such tuning process is expensive in computational terms, but it is done one time and in this paper we don't deal with this problem.

However, in spite of the great advantage of predictive control, which contributes to control systems that the classic control is unable to do, it has a great drawback: it is very computationally expensive while it is working. In section 4 we will revise the cause of this problem. A way of avoiding this drawback is to model the predictive controller using neural networks, because once these devices are trained they perform the calculus at great speed and with very small computational requirements, and at the same time, we can implement them using very cheap FPGA devices. In this paper we propose a learning model to be used with Time Delayed Neural Networks, so once the neural network is trained, the neuronal predictive controller is ready and it responds properly showing its generalization capabilities in environments that it hasn't seen in the training phase. This way we could get a very cheap implementation of each of the control loops that each robot of the multi-robot team needs, avoiding the rise of the total cost of the team.

In the literature there are several sources indicating that each robot of a multi-robot system must be as cheap as possible. There is a quantitative support for the argument that larger teams of less-reliable and cheaper robots can perform certain missions more reliably than smaller teams of more-reliable robots (Stancliff et al., 2006). There are examples of using very cheap discrete components. In (O'Hara & Balch, 2007) very cheap sensorless nodes are used to support a complex multi-robot foraging task. On the other hand, in (Wu et al., 2008) a kind of sensors is used because they became cheaper that others. In (Kornienko et al., 2005), the components of the developed system consume energy provided by microcontroller's I/O ports, are cheap and available on micro-component market. Besides the use of individual components, (Andrews et al., 2007) integrate economic and technical issues into an unified engineering design framework for the manufacturers of robots. There are examples that have been done as previous works in the same direction that this paper (López-Guede et al., 2008).

Section 2 gives a summary of the objective of the work of this paper. Section 3 gives background information about Predictive Control and a technique called Dynamic Matrix Control, and about a kind of neural nets called Time Delayed Neural Networks. Section 4 discusses a concrete case study and the results that we obtain. Finally, conclusions are covered in section 5.

2. Objective

The main objective of this paper is to get cheap implementation of low level control loops that could be used by each member of a multi-robot system. To get this objective Time Delayed Neural Networks are used to model predictive controllers, because these can control subsystems that classics controllers can't.

3. Background

This section gives a brief introduction about a general technique called Model Predictive Control, and about a concrete technique called Dynamic Matrix Control. We also present a brief introduction about Time Delayed Neural Networks.

We consider that it is necessary to understand the advantages of this kind of control, that make it very useful in some circumstances, and their drawbacks, and then understand how a neural network based implementation can eliminate these drawbacks.

3.1 Model Predictive Control (MPC)

Model Predictive Control (MPC) is an advanced control technique used to deal with systems that are not controllable using classic control schemas as PID. This kind of controllers works like the human brain in the sense that instead of using the past error between the output of the system and the desired value, it controls the system predicting the value of the output in a short time, so the system output is as closer as possible to its desired value for these moments. Predictive Control isn't a concrete technique. It's a set of techniques that have several common characteristics: there is a world model that is used to predict the system output from the actual moment until p samples, an objective function that must be minimized and a control law that minimizes the objective function. The predictive controllers follow these steeps:

- Each sampling time, through the system model, the controller calculates the system output from now until p sampling times (prediction horizon), which depends on the future control signals that the controller will generate.
- A set of m control signals is calculated optimizing the objective function to be used along m sampling times (control horizon).
- In each sampling time only the first of the set of m control signals is used, and in the next sampling time, all the process is repeated again.

The concept of Predictive Control is a set of techniques that share certain characteristics, and the engineer has liberty to choose in each of them. So, there are several types of predictive controllers. These characteristics are the following:

- There is a plant model, and there can be used a step response model, an impulse step response model, a transfer funcion, etc.
- There is an objective funcion that the controller has to optimize.
- There is a control law to minimize the objective function.

To learn more about Predictive Control in general and about diverse predictive control algorithms, see (Camacho & Bordons, 2004), (Camacho & Bordons, 1995), (Maciejowski, 2002), (Sunan et al., 2002), (Rawlings, 1999) and (Soeterboek, 1992).

3.1.1 Model predictive control advantages

From a theoretical point of view, model predictive based controllers have some advantages:

- It is an open methodology, with possibility of new algorithms.
- They can include constraints on manipulated variables as well as on controlled variables. This is important to save energy and to get the working point as near as possible from the optimum.
- They can deal with multivariable systems in a simplest way than other algorithms.

From a practical point of view, model predictive based controllers have the advantage that they can deal with systems that show stability problems with classical control schemes. To show this property we will use one of these systems in Section 4.

3.1.2 Model predictive control drawbacks

The main drawback of predictive controllers isn't that it was very expensive in computationally terms in the tuning phase, because it is carried out only one time. The main drawback is that the computational requirements of the shown controller are great when it's in its working phase. Each sample time the controller must calculate the control law of the equation (1), and there are involved several matrix operations, as several multiplication, an addition and a subtraction. Performing these operations we obtain a set of m control signals, but only the first of them is used in this sample time, the rest are ignored. The algorithm woks in this way, but it is computationally inefficient.

3.2 Dynamic Matrix Control (DMC)

The technique called Dynamic Matrix Control (DMC) is a concrete MPC algorithm that fixes each of the three characteristics that we have seen inf the following way.
To learn more about Dynamic Matrix Control in particular, see (Camacho & Bordons, 2004), (Camacho & Bordons, 1995), (Maciejowski, 2002) and (Sunan et al., 2002).

3.2.1 Subsystem model

The plant model used by DMC algorithm is the step response model. This model obtains the g_i coefficients that are the output of the lineal subsystem when it is excited using a step. To reduce the number of coefficients we assume that the subsystem is stable and the output doesn't change after a certain sampling time *k*.

$$y(t)=\sum_{i=1}^{k} g_i \Delta u(t-i) \tag{1}$$

3.2.2 Prediction model

Using the step response model to model the subsystem and maintaining the hypothesis that perturbations over the subsystem are constants, it is possible to calculate a prediction in the instant *t* of the output until the instant $(t + p)$ under the effect of *m* control actions:

$$\hat{y} = G\Delta u + f \tag{2}$$

being $\hat{y}$ the prediction of the output, *G* a matrix that contains the subsystem's dynamics and *f* the free response of the subsystem. Following we show the dimension of this matrix and these vectors:

$$\hat{y}=\begin{bmatrix} \hat{y}(t+1|t) \\ \hat{y}(t+2|t) \\ \vdots \\ \hat{y}(t+p|t) \end{bmatrix}_p \quad G=\begin{bmatrix} g_1 & 0 & \cdots & 0 \\ g_2 & g_1 & \cdots & 0 \\ \vdots & \vdots & \ddots & \vdots \\ g_m & g_{m-1} & \cdots & g_1 \\ \vdots & \vdots & \ddots & \vdots \\ g_p & g_{p-1} & \cdots & g_{p-m+1} \end{bmatrix}_{pxm}$$
$$\Delta u=\begin{bmatrix} \Delta u(t) \\ \Delta u(t+1) \\ \vdots \\ \Delta u(t+m-1) \end{bmatrix}_m \quad f=\begin{bmatrix} f(t,1) \\ f(t,2) \\ \vdots \\ f(t,p) \end{bmatrix}_p \tag{3}$$

In the equation (5) we show how the free response of the subsystem *f(t,k)* is calculated:

$$f(t,k)=y_m(t)+\sum_{i=1}^{N}(g_{k+i}-g_i)\Delta u(t-i) \tag{4}$$

3.2.3 Control law

The obtention of the control law is based on the existence of an objective function, which uses the future outputs prediction model that we have described before. As objective function we used the described by this equation:

$$J=\sum_{j=1}^{p}\left[\hat{y}(t+j\mid t)-w(t+j)\right]^{2}+\sum_{j=1}^{m}\lambda\left[\Delta u(t+j-1)\right]^{2} \tag{5}$$

We have to minimize the difference between the reference and the output prediction along a prediction horizon p with the m control actions generated in the control horizon, ponderating the rougness in the variation of the manipulated variables using λ. Minimizing the objective funcition J described in the equation (5) we obtain the folowing expression, that produces m control actions, although in t only one of the is used:

$$\Delta u=\left[\left(G^{t}G+\lambda I\right)^{-1}G^{t}\left(w-f\right)\right]_{m} \tag{6}$$

3.3 Neuronal implementation

Following with the discussion about the computationally inefficiency of the analytical predictive control shown in the previous section, we think that it would be convenient to have a mechanism that could implement such controller requiring less computational power. An alternative to get this is to use neural networks, and more precisely, Time Delayed Neural Networks, because as the rest of neural networks, they are very fast, computationally inexpensive and they have the ability of generalizing their responses.

This section gives a brief introduction about a kind of neural networks called Time Delayed Neural Networks, that we have used to model the previous model predictive controller to eliminate the shown drawbacks. To learn more about neural networks in general see (Braspenning et al., 1995), (Chester, 1993) and (Widrow & Lehr, 1990). To learn more about identification and control of dynamical systems, see (Narendra & Parthasarathy, 1990) and (Norgaard et al., 2003), and about neural identification applied to predictive control see (Arahal et al., 1998) and (Huang, 2000). There are interesting approximations to the prediction capacity of neuronal models when predictive control is present, (McKinstry et al., 2006), (Aleksic et al., 2008) and (Kang, 1991). Stability of these neural networks is an important issue, (Wilson, 1995).

3.3.1 Time Delayed Neural Networks

Time Delayed Neural Networks (TDNN) are a kind of multi-layer perceptron neural networks. They have an input layer, where are the neurons that accept the exterior inputs; one or more hidden layers, that generate intermediate values; and a final layer, that puts outside the data generated by the net. The TDNN special feature is that they are a kind of dynamic neural networks, because delayed versions of the input signals are introduced to the input layer. Due to this, the outputs don't depend only on the actual values of the signals, they depend on the past value of the signals too. This is one of the main parameters of a TDNN: the size of the delay line. The TDNNs that are going to be used in this work only have forward conections, so they aren't neither recurrent nor partially recurrent. This kind of neural network can be trained using the Backpropagation algorithm or the Generalized Delta Rule. In the experiments that we show in this paper the Levenberg-

Marquardt method has been used. To learn more about Time Delayed Neural Networks, see (Huang et al., 2000), (Huang et al., 2006), (Waibel et al., 1989), (Wang et al., 2005) and (Taskaya-Temizel & Casey, 2005).

3.3.2 Structural parameters

As we are worried about the computational cost of our implementation of the predictive controller, we have limited the number of hidden layers to one, so we assume that we are working with a time delayed neural network that has the simplest structure. Once we have established this constraint, the main parameters that configure the structure of this TDNN are the number of neurons of the hidden layer and the size of the time delay line, in other words, the number of delayed versions of the input signals are introduced to the input layer. We will try to get these parameters as small as possible to minimize the computational cost of the resultant implementation. The last main parameter to establish is the kind of the function that will be executed in each neuron, and we will take into account that the linear function is the least expensive from the computational point of view. In Fig. 1 we show the structure of the Time Delayed Neural Network that we have used to get our purpose, in which we have fitted the size of time delay line *d* and the size of hidden layer *h* parameters.

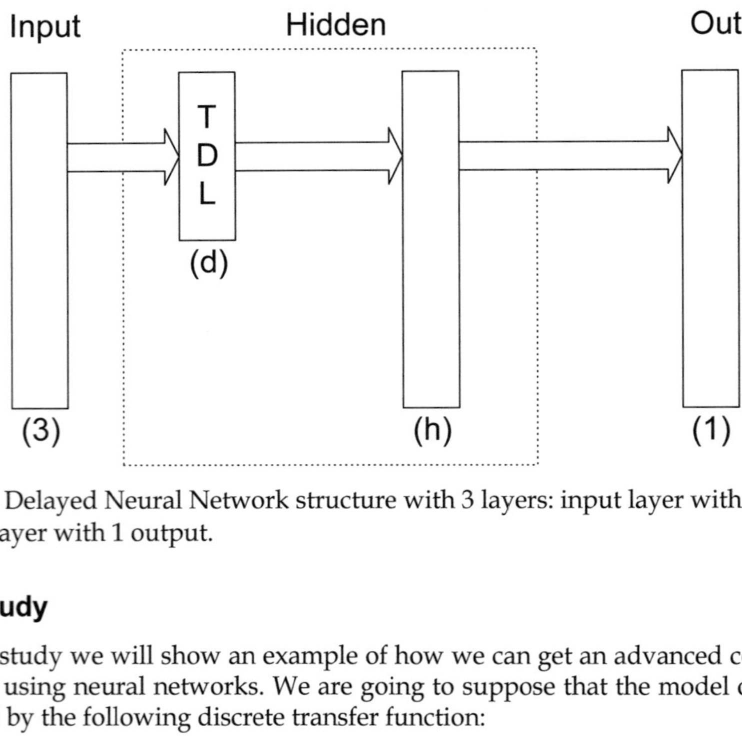

Fig. 1. Time Delayed Neural Network structure with 3 layers: input layer with 3 inputs, and the output layer with 1 output.

4. Case study

In this case study we will show an example of how we can get an advanced control of robot subsystems using neural networks. We are going to suppose that the model of a subsystem is described by the following discrete transfer function:

$$H(z) = \frac{1}{z - 0.5} \tag{7}$$

As we can see analyzing the poles, this subsystem is stable. Although it is a stable subsystem, its response is unstable if we try to control it using a discrete PID controller tuned through classic and well-known method as Ziegler-Nichols, as we can see in Fig. 2.

Once we have seen that the respone is unstable, we decide to use Model Predictive Control. To work with this kind of control we have to stablish the working point. To do this, we examine the Bode diagram of the Fig. 3 and we choose the frecuency of the marked point of this figure.

Once we have determined the working point in Fig. 3, we design the reference signal. As it is shown in Fig. 4, using a properly tuned DMC predictive controller, for example, with the values for its parameters $p = 5$, $m = 3$ y $\lambda = 1$, a right control is obtained.

To get this control it has been mandatory to tune the DMC controller. This phase is very expensive in computationally terms, but it's carried out only one time. However, the computational requirements of DMC controller are great when it's in its working phase, due to the operations that it must perform to get the control law, and although it obtains set of m control signals, only first of them is used in this sample time, the rest are ignored. Because of this, it would be convenient to have a mechanism that could implement such controller requiring less computational power. Besides, it may be necessary to control several subsystems of this kind in each robot of the multi-robot team. An alternative to get this is to use neural networks, and more precisely, Time Delayed Neural Networks, because, as the rest of neural networks, they are very fast and they have the ability of generalizing their responses.

In the literature there are works comparing PID and MPC controllers (Voicu et al., 1995).

Now we deal with the concrete problem of getting a neuronal predictive controller that could control the system described by the discrete transfer function of the equation (7) using Time Delayed Neural Networks.

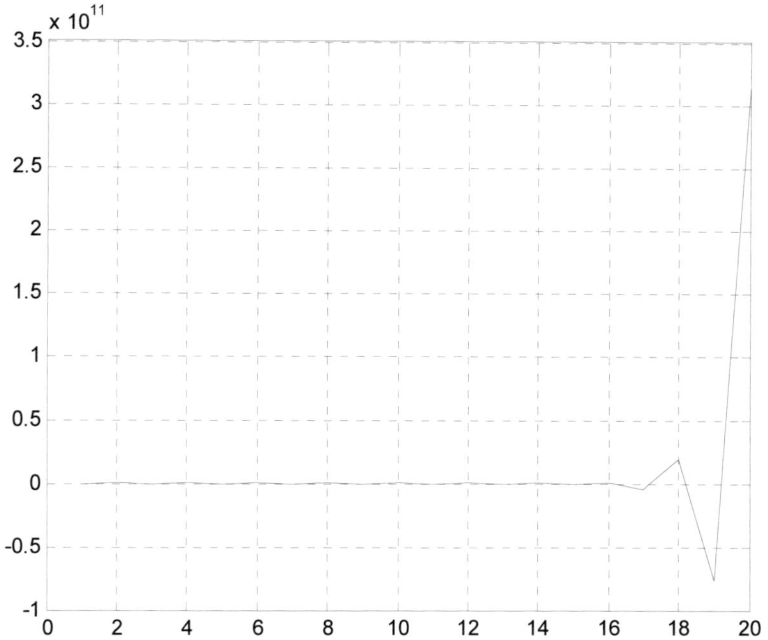

Fig. 2. Unstable response of the subsystem under the control of a discrete PID controller.

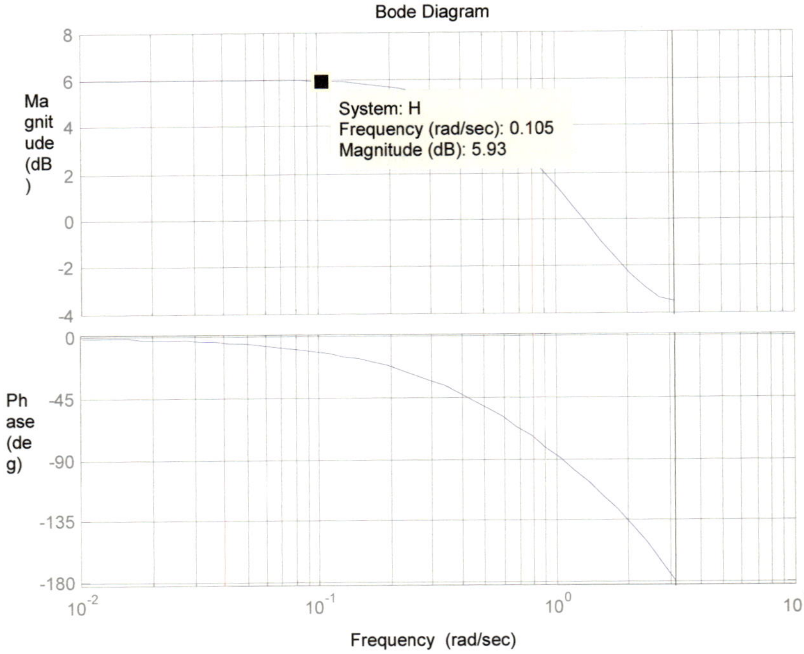

Fig. 3. Bode diagram of the subsystem, showing the chosen point.

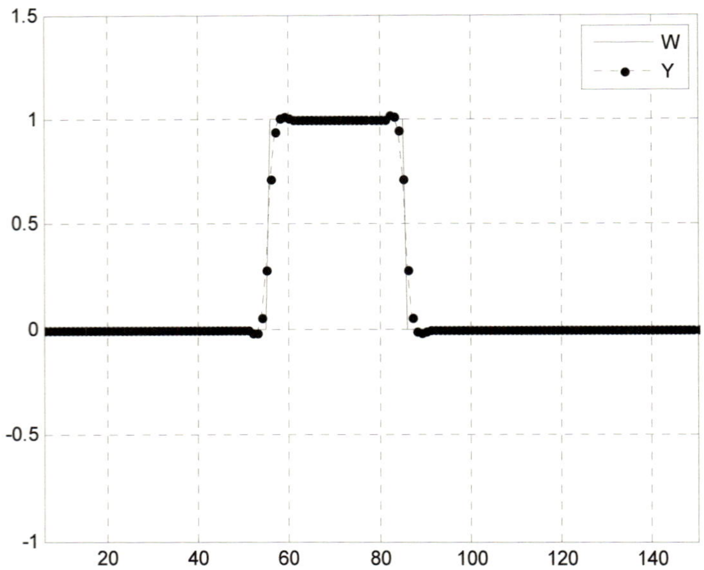

Fig. 4. Control of a robot subsystem using Predictive Control when the reference is a pure step, with the values of the parameters $p = 5$, $m = 3$ y $\lambda = 1$.

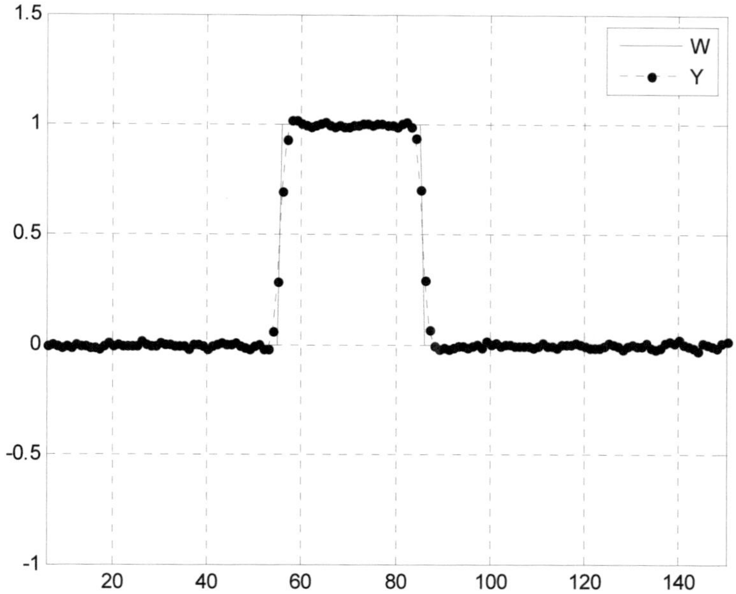

Fig. 5. Control of a robot subsystem using Predictive Control when the reference is a noisy step, with the values of the parameters $p = 5$, $m = 3$ y $\lambda = 1$.

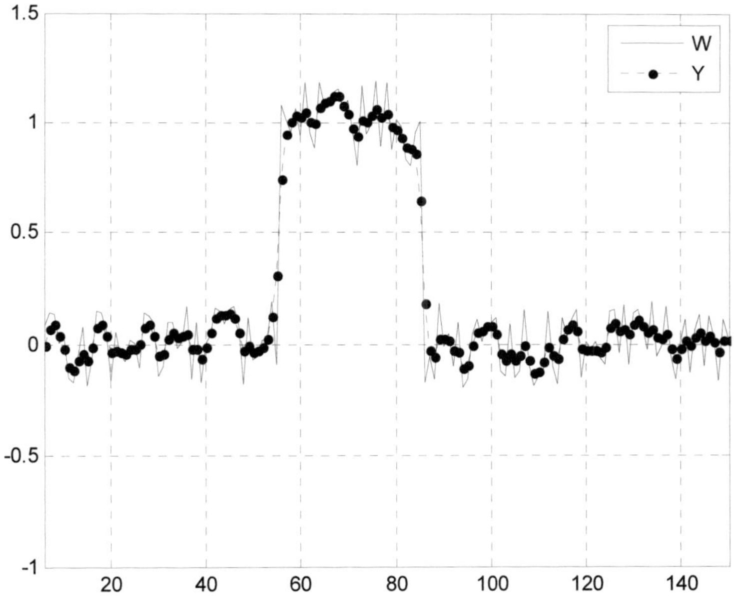

Fig. 6. Control of a robot subsystem using Predictive Control when the reference is a noisy step, with the values of the parameters $p = 5$, $m = 3$ y $\lambda = 1$.

To implement a predictive controller using a neural network we have done training experiments with multiple structures, varying two structural parameters: the number of the hidden layer neurons *h* and the number of delays of the time delay line *d*, having in mind that linear function is computationally efficient.

We have used the Levenberg-Marquardt method to carry out the training of each structure, and the training model has consisted of a target vector $P=\left[w(k), y(k), \Delta u(k-1)\right]'$ and an output $\Delta u(k)$ to get the same control that equation (6).

As it has be shown in Fig. 7, there is a perfect control when we use references that we have used in the training phase of the time delayed neural network. In Fig. 8 and Fig. 9, we can see that the control of the neuronal controller is right even with noisy references that hadn't been used in the training phase.

To implement these predictive controllers using neural networks we have chosen FPGA devices. We have used a device commercialized by Altera Corporation, the EPF10K70 device, in a 240-pin power quad flat pack (RQFP) package.

The way that we have used to implement the neural network in this device is to describe the behavior of that neural network using VHDL languaje, including in the entity that is in this description the same inputs and outputs that the neural network has. VHDL is a description language used to describe the desired behavior of circuits and to automatically synthesize them through specific tools.

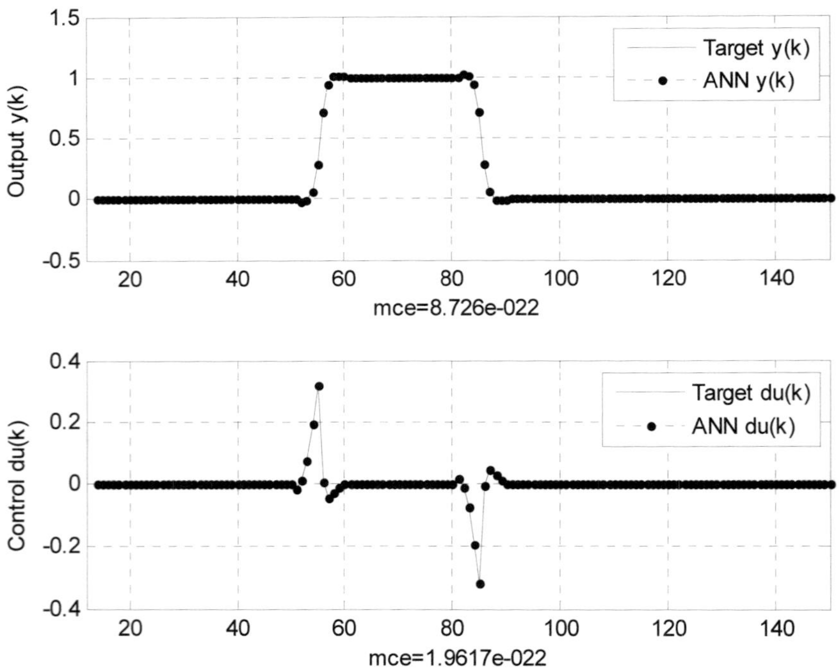

Fig. 7. Control of a system with a Time Delayed Neural Network with a time delay line of $d = 7$ delays in the input, and $h = 5$ neurons in the hidden layer. The reference to follow is a signal that the neural network has been used in the training phase.

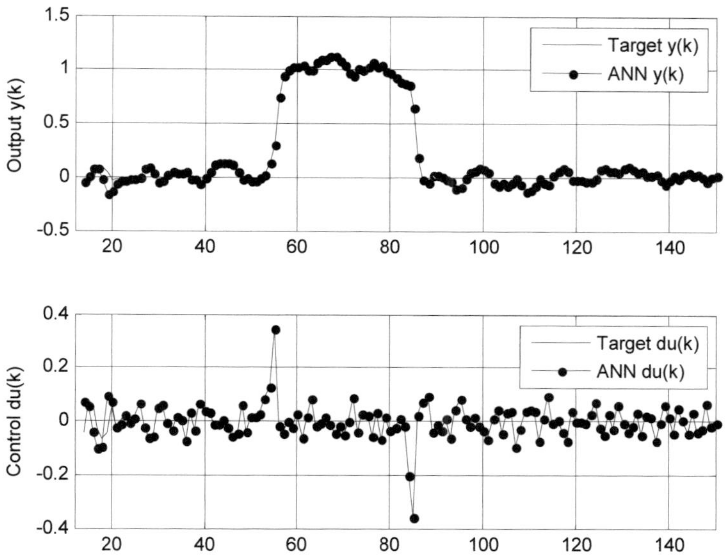

Fig. 8. Control of a robot subsystem with a Time Delayed Neural Network with a time delay line of $d = 7$ delays in the input, and $h = 5$ neurons in the hidden layer. The reference to follow is a signal that the neural network hasn't seen in the training phase.

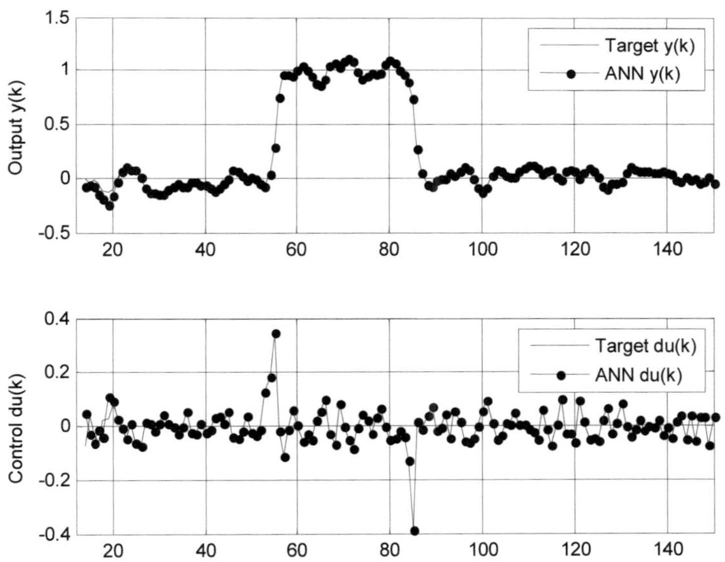

Fig. 9. Control of a robot subsystem with a Time Delayed Neural Network with a time delay line of $d = 7$ delays in the input, and $h = 5$ neurons in the hidden layer. The reference to follow is a signal that the neural network hasn't seen in the training phase.

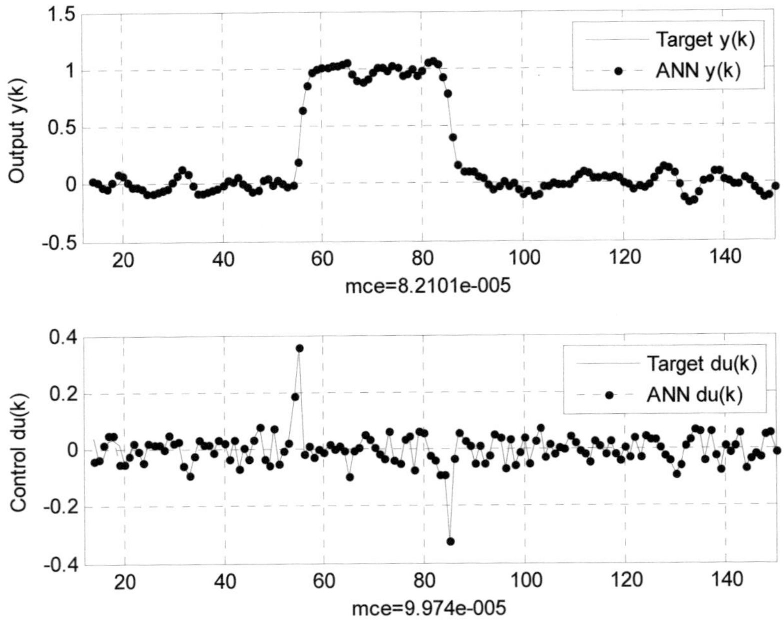

Fig. 10. Control of a robot system with a Time Delayed Neural Network with a time delay line of $d = 7$ delays in the input, and $h = 5$ neurons in the hidden layer. The reference to follow is a signal that the neural network hasn't been used in the training phase.

5. Conclusions

This paper has started thinking about the convenience that the computational capacity of robots that belong to multi-robot systems was devoted exclusively to high level functions they have to perform due to being a member of such system. However, each robot must have so many internal control loops as subsystems, and in some cases they aren't controllable through classic techniques. In these cases, predictive control is a good option because it can deal with subsystems that classical PID controllers can't, but it's computationally expensive. In this paper it has been shown how the predictive controllers can be modeled using Time Delayed Neural Networks, which implementation is very cheap using very low cost FPGAs. This way we can reduce de price of each member of multi-robot system, because the investment in computational capacity must cover only the high level functions, ignoring the subsystems that it had, which are solved with very low cost FPGAs.

6. References

Aleksic, M., Luebke, T., Heckenkamp, J., Gawenda, M., et al. (2008). Implementation of an Artificial Neural Network to Predict Shunt Necessity in Carotid Surgery. *Annals if Vascular Surgery*, 22, 5, 635--642.

Andrews, B. W., Passino K. M., Waite, T. A. (2007). Social Foraging Theory for Robust Multiagent System Desing. *IEEE Transactions on Automation Science and Engineering*, 4, 1, 79--86

Arahal, M.R., Berenguel, M., Camacho, E.F. (1998). Neural identification applied to predictive control of a solar plant. *Control Engineering Practice*, 6, 333--344

Braspenning, P. J., Thuijsman, F., Weijters, A. (1995). *Artificial neuronal networks. An introduction to ANN theory an practice*. Springer-Verlag, Berlin.

Camacho, E.F., Bordons, C. (2004). *Model Predictive Control*. Springer-Verlag, London.

Camacho, E. F., Bordons, C. (1995). *Model Predictive Control in the Process Industry*. Springer-Verlag, London.

Chester, M. (1993). *Neural Networks*. Prentice Hall, New Jersey.

Huang, J. Q., Lewis, F. L., Liu, K. (2000). A Neural Net Predictive Control for Telerobots with Time Delay. *Journal of Intelligent and Robotic Systems*, 29, 1--25

Huang, B.Q., Rashid, T., Kechadi, M.T. (2006). Multi-Context Recurrent Neural Network for Time Series Applications. *International Journal of Computational Intelligence*. Vol. 3 Number 1, ISSN pp 45--54.

Kang, H. (1991). A neural network based identification-control paradigm via adaptative prediction. *Proceedings of the 30th IEEE Conference on Decision and Control*, 3, 2939-2941.

Kornienko, S., Kornienko, O., Levi, P. (2005). Minimalistic approach towards communication and perception in microrobotic swarms. *IEEE/RSJ International Conference on Intelligent Robots and Systems*, 2228--2234

López-Guede, J.M., Graña, M., Zulueta, E., Barambones, O. (2008). Economical Implementation of Control Loops for Multi-robot Systems. *15th International Conference, ICONIP 2008*, Auckland, New Zealand. ISBN: 978-3-642-02489-4

Maciejowski, J. M. (2002). *Predictive Control with Constraints*. Prentice Hall, London.

McKinstry, J.L., Edelman, G.M., Krichmar, J.L. (2006). A cerebellar model for predictive motor control tested in a brain-based device. *Proceedings of the National Academy of Sciences of The United States of America*, 103, 9, 3387--3392

Narendra, K. S., Parthasarathy, K. (1990). Identification and Control of Dynamical Systems Using Neural Networks. *IEEE Trans. Neural Networks*, Vol. 1, NO.1, pp 4--27

Norgaard M., Ravn, O., Poulsen, N.K., Hansen, L.K. (2003). *Neural Networks for Modelling and Control of Dynamic Systems*. Springer-Verlag, London.

O'Hara, K.J., Balch, T.R. (2007). Pervasive Sensor-less networks for cooperative multi-robot tasks. *7th International Symposium on Distributed Autonomous Robotic Systems* (DARS 2004), 305--314

Rawlings, J.B. (1999). Tutorial: Model Predictive Control Technology. *Proceedings of the American Control Conference* San Diego, California. pp 662--676.

Soeterboek, R. (1992). *Predictive control. A unified approach*. Prentice Hall.

Stancliff, S.B., Dolan, J.M., Trebi-Ollennu, A. (2006). Mission Reliability Estimation for Multirobot Team Design. *IEEE International Conference on Intelligent Robots and Systems*, 2206--2211

Sunan, H., Kok T., Tong L. (2002). *Applied Predictive Control*. Springer-Verlag. London.

Taskaya-Temizel, T., Casey, M.C. (2005). *Configuration of Neural Networks for the Analysis of Seasonal Time Series*. LNCS, vol. 3686, pp. 297--304. Springer, Heidelberg

Voicu , M., Lazăr, C., Schönberger, F., Păstravanu, O., Ifrim, S. (1995). Predictive Control vs. PID Control of Thermal Treatment Processes. *Control Engineering Solution: a Practical Approach.* 163--174.

Waibel, A., Hanazawa, T., Hinton, G., Shikano, K., Lang, K. (1989). Phoneme Recognition Using Time Delay Neural Networks. *IEEE Transactions on Accoustics, Speech and Signal Processing*, 37:328—339.

Wang, Y., Kim, S.-P., Principe, J. C. (2005). Comparison of TDNN training algorithms in brain machine interfaces. *Proceedings of the IEEE International Joint Conference on Neural Networks (IJCNN '05)*, vol. 4, pp. 2459--2462

Widrow, B., Lehr, M.A. (1990). 30 Years of Adaptive Neural Networks: Perceptron, Madaline, and Backpropagation. *Proceedings of the IEEE*, Vol. 78, No.9. pp 1415 -- 1442.

Wilson, W.H. (1995). Stability of Learning in Classes of Recurrent and Feedforward Networks. *Proceedings of the Sixth Australian Conference on Neuronal Networks, (ACNN´95)* 142--145.

Wu, H., Tian, G., Huang, B. (2008). Multi-robot collaborative localization methods based on Wireless Sensor Network. *IEEE International Conference on Automation and Logistics*, 2053--2058